NEVER LEAVING LARAMIE

T0164363

NEVER LEAVING LARAMIE

Travels in a Restless World

■
■
■

John W. Haines

Oregon State University Press   Corvallis

Library of Congress Cataloging-in-Publication Data

Names: Haines, John W., author.
Title: Never leaving Laramie : travels in a restless world / John W. Haines.
Description: Corvallis : Oregon State University Press, 2020.
Identifiers: LCCN 2020029156 (print) | LCCN 2020029157 (ebook) | ISBN 9780870710315 (trade paperback) | ISBN 9780870710322 (ebook)
Subjects: LCSH: Haines, John W.—Travel. | Voyages and travels. | Travelers' writings, American. | Bankers—United States—Biography. | Paralytics—United States—Biography. | Laramie (Wyo.)—Description and travel.
Classification: LCC G465 .H3345 2020 (print) | LCC G465 (ebook) | DDC 910.4092 [B]—dc23
LC record available at https://lccn.loc.gov/2020029156
LC ebook record available at https://lccn.loc.gov/2020029157

♾ This paper meets the requirements of ANSI/NISO Z39.48-1992 (Permanence of Paper).

First published in 2020 by Oregon State University Press
Printed in the United States of America

Naomi Shihab Nye, "Famous" from *Words Under the Words: Selected Poems by Naomi Shihab Nye*, copyright © 1995. Used with permission of Far Corner Books.

William Stafford, "Ask Me" and "Assurance" from *Ask Me: 100 Essential Poems*. Copyright © 1977, 1978, 2014 by William Stafford and the Estate of William Stafford. Reprinted with the permission of The Permissions Company, LLC on behalf of Graywolf Press, Minneapolis, Minnesota, graywolfpress.org.

Oregon State University Press
121 The Valley Library
Corvallis OR 97331-4501
541-737-3166 • fax 541-737-3170
www.osupress.oregonstate.edu

Contents

Acknowledgments

THIS BOOK WAS CONSTRUCTED from travel for over two decades in many places. The writing of it spanned many years of attention and inattention, restarts on a new chapter or tale thread to make a book out of stories. Over time, writing about my travels in the world blended with my hometown of Laramie, Wyoming. This book is the result of that juxtaposition.

I asked people who feature in this book to fact-check stories in which they appear. I adjusted accordingly because truth matters to me. This book is not, therefore, constructed to tell tall tales but is rooted in authentic experiences, as much as our memories allow. I asked others from Laramie and some who have never set foot in Laramie for their impressions. I thank these readers for assuring me that this book, a collection of essayistic memoirs, rang true and felt right. Some of these people pushed me to include more of myself in these stories, which initially I did not want to do. I hope they were right.

I thank two poets whom I regularly read and admire, and whose poems I was inspired to include in three chapters: Naomi Shihab Nye for the use of "Famous," and her publisher Far Corner Books; and the family of William Stafford and Graywolf Press for his poems "Ask Me" and "Assurance."

I am grateful to have met Jane Cavolina, a cat-loving Catholic, editor, writer, and inveterate knitter based in the borough of Queens, who told me not to make it hard to understand my stories. "Chronology matters," she guided me.

The novelist and writer David James Duncan took time from his writing and fishing in Montana to share his own writing, thoughts, and support, which helped me keep pushing my pen with an eye on the river.

I am thankful to many friends who read chapters to authenticate their own place in the book and to examine the aspects I write of Laramie, including Rick Smith, Jennifer Slater, Jeff Alford, Janet Lawrence-Garland, Stacy Bradley-Fox, Garth Massey, Sheila Nyhus, Doug Haines, Emerson Steinberg, Jill Ory-Cissna, Arthur Combs, Tripp Somerville, Mignon Mazique, and Lisa Hoashi. Others who have never set foot in Laramie but whose impressions matter to me also graciously read earlier drafts or chapters, including Bija Gutoff, Denna Prichep, Courtney Dillard, Karen Campbell, Karen Gunderson, and Jennie Kramer.

Ted Wolf, a writer and unwavering conservationist, deserves more than a nod. I gave him a copy of this book, a stack of paper that had sat in a drawer for two years, when he and his wife, Karen, moved from Portland to Bellingham, Washington, after sending their girls into the world. The manuscript was a going-away gesture. A few months later he emailed me with contacts to two publishers. To my surprise, both were interested in this book, which would have sat under my socks but for Ted.

I thank David Oates, a thoughtful writer who leads a small press, Kelson Books, in Portland, Oregon. Over a coffee and a beer in a neighborhood coffeeshop, he provided sage guidance on the need for a transitional chapter from Nigeria to Bosnia.

I have respect for Oregon State University Press and its director, Tom Booth. Kim Hogeland, acquisitions editor, accepted my book and guided the thoughtful process of peer and faculty review, which I appreciated. To be published by the long-standing substance of Oregon State University Press is an honor.

Finally, I thank my love, Molly Baer Kramer. Over six years, you listened and applauded, like no other, my continual deviations between work and side projects, such as this book. You add more to my mind and spirit than is imaginable.

Prologue

TO BE FROM LARAMIE IS TO LEAVE IT. Only then does Laramie become clearer, which inevitably brings you back home for exactly the reasons you left: Such as the isolation of living under the unchanging enormity of the sky and bright sun, summer or winter, that is never more than a storm day away. Such as horrendous and regular snowstorms that hit in September and extend into May, and the willingness of people to help anyone stranded on a road at any hour during the worst of those storms. Or the wind that ceases but always returns, bringing purple storm clouds of rain, snow, and hail, pushing out smoke from forest fires, a wind that takes anything not nailed down away, as if cleansing the town.

I couldn't be nailed down, and left Laramie for many places in the world where I was drawn, some dangerous and most in transition, as I was. As I remain. This book covers travel for two decades through a lens of my home and its people, my friends from Laramie with whom I shared a tent, a beer, a story, and a life.

It is unlikely I would have written this book had I not broken my neck. I would not have taken the time when the next place in the world was available to experience and a new project or job loomed on the horizon. But my physical life turned more interior, and I had more time to think and write. I am grateful for having written detailed journals when I traveled, a source I dusted off to inform details in the book.

On November 10, 1999, the tenth anniversary of the fall of the Berlin Wall, I moved by train from Prague to Berlin to witness the celebration, after last being in East and West Berlin in 1985. At a stop in the northern Czech Republic, I jumped from the train to get a cup of coffee, something I had done hundreds of times in a dozen countries from India to China to the former Soviet Union and most of Europe. I loved trains, still do, but that one nearly killed me.

Friends told me in early 2000, after I had been in three hospitals in three countries, paralyzed with a broken neck, fractured skull, and broken leg, that my accident could not have happened to a worse person. They meant, I believe, that I was done with the pursuits I lived for—skiing, kayaking, climbing, and bicycling. I felt the same fear but had acquiesced to the value of small physical advancements, such as more movement in my fingers and the slow gathering of strength in my shoulders. I was thrilled beyond skiing a steep chute when I got on a toilet with my own strength, two nurses and an occupational therapist applauding as if I had emerged upright out of a cloud of snow. A physical therapist in Denver's Craig Hospital, who had worked with me twice a day for two months, looked me in my eyes, holding my weak hands, and said that my accident could not have happened to a better person. She swiftly clarified that she believed I had something it takes to be in a wheelchair. I was inspired by her words, her touch, her everything. I prayed she was right.

A yearning for the next place, another experience, had pushed me onward for as long as I could remember. In a wheelchair, the next place became less widely geographic than interior and lonely. I eventually accepted that a broken neck and paralysis was part of my long-held passion for experiences. My exploratory life had led to decisions that might have put me in a wheelchair earlier. Risk-taking verging on recklessness is a common trait of people from Laramie. But I also came from people who took risks to get to Wyoming four generations ago.

If one person offered a clue to a genetic predisposition to travel beyond prescribed boundaries or predictable paths, it may have been my grandmother's grandmother Elizabeth Pierce Jennings Pugh, who was born in 1837 and lived for ninety years.

Elizabeth took a leap of faith or inspiration at age twenty and emigrated from London to St. Louis in 1857 with her husband and three young children on a ship chartered by a new church, the Church of Jesus Christ of Latter-day Saints. One child died on the journey, and the rest of the family settled in St. Louis. They later set off for Utah by prairie schooner on the Oregon Trail and then the Mormon Trail, only to find conditions in Utah under Mormon control not to their liking. They returned to St. Louis, where they created a lean farming life along the Mississippi River. In 1862 Elizabeth's husband drowned in that river. His horses and knife were found on the riverbank, but his body was never located.

Not long afterward, Elizabeth married an immigrant from Wales named John Pugh, an older man from Llandudno. Unfortunately, John died when a few of his own horses pinned him against a fence in 1868. Their child together, William John Pugh, my grandmother's father, was five years old.

Elizabeth set out again from St. Louis, this time with her three children from two deceased husbands, in search of a better life in the American West. She traveled the second time by the transcontinental railroad as far as it had been constructed, retracing her previous route to an area near the changing territorial borders of what would eventually become the states of Wyoming and Utah.

My grandmother Elizabeth Pugh was named for her grandmother. But she never talked of this pioneering, exploring woman. I learned of her from my grandmother's sister, Wilma Pugh, a history professor at Mount Holyoke College in South Hadley, Massachusetts. She thought I lived in a "searching fashion" that reminded her of her grandmother.

"Searching fashion" sounded old-fashioned to me, perhaps a polite way to say uncommitted or inconsistent. There was a consistency in my mind to the pursuit of experiencing as much as I could in as many places as I could. There was little I could not imagine myself doing, and no place was too far away. I had told her about the far-flung scattershot jobs I had had after graduating from college, from teaching skiing to kids from international schools in Saas-Fee, Switzerland, to reconstructing a historic lodge in the mountains of Wyoming. I baked bread in Laramie and painted houses in Oregon. Eventually, I settled into a conventional job as a banker in Oregon and then started a nonprofit loan fund in New Jersey. I did not disclose a brief stint of smuggling gold for men of the remote Manang region of Nepal from Hong Kong and Bangkok into Kathmandu, which was not a job but a practical financial pursuit to keep traveling, like my other short-term quasi jobs such as international mail courier and an entrepreneurial effort to sell inexpensive jewelry from Nepal to women in sorority houses in Eugene, Oregon. I always kept my eyes peeled for black-market opportunities involving currency dysfunctions between adjoining nations; this was easy money in Eastern Europe and much of Southeast Asia, where economic policies were based more on xenophobia than on global markets.

My grandmother's father, William Pugh, was most prominent in my Aunt Wilma's and my family's stories. Pugh worked first as a train dispatcher, then as a postmaster, before founding two stockgrower banks, one in Evanston and another in Mountain View, a settlement near Fort Bridger. His banks supported the seasonal needs of sheep and cattle ranchers after Fort Bridger had become an inconsequential historical landmark surrounded by remote ranchland. He had a third-grade education and sent his five children from Evanston, a small railroad and ranch town, to colleges in Michigan, Pennsylvania, Utah, New Hampshire, and Wyoming. My grandmother, his eldest, was the only one to stay in Wyoming.

This book chronicles my travels through places in transition—from war to peace, from peace to war, from isolation to tourist destination, from Communism to a market economy—from 1984 through 2004, when I made my first trip overseas alone in a wheelchair, back to China. The sixteen chapters are, by intention, essays with a memoir thread, spanning much of the world from Laramie to Japan, and from Tibet and China to the former USSR and East Berlin. Six chapters recount—as a miniature book in the center of this one—a long journey down the length of the Niger River in West Africa, following the route of an eighteenth-century Scottish explorer, Mungo Park, by sea kayak and wooden pirogue in 1991–1992. The book leaps, as I did back then, to work in Central Europe, including supervising elections in postwar Bosnia in 1997 and 1998, followed by my brutal accident in the Czech Republic in 1999.

My travel companions were almost always from Laramie, a percolating university town at 7,220 feet, isolated in all directions by a hundred miles of wide-open prairie and mountains. The town maintains the continuous energy of a university whose students comprise one-third of the population, which, including the students, has never touched more than fifty thousand people. Laramie is a place that paradoxically inspires a deep loyalty in its inhabitants but also an inclination to leave it.

Laramie is a launchpad for university students into a wider world. It is also a refueling oasis for highway travelers, and a remote island. It is strangely like Hawaii in that respect—out there, self-contained and confined, with its natives stubbornly proud of that hard reality. People have come to call it "cowboy tough," the brand of our college football team, which makes most of us smile and shrug. But we don't argue. It is true: Laramie toughens people. It can be constraining but not restraining, especially when we buckle down and when we venture out.

A village chief in the roadless, dense, and many-hued green bush in Guinea along the bank of the Niger River once said to me, "Ee barabo ee bara, ee barase ibara" (You left your home, you found your home). I understood it as a welcoming "make yourself at home," as we say to visitors in Laramie. After other village chiefs said the same thing to me, in Malinke in Guinea and in Bambara in Mali, I began to hear something more in the warm welcome from a foreign tongue, spoken always within a circle of villagers. I heard a challenge to see something of my home there, and by extension to view my home in Laramie as I saw the remote, busy village. A Guinean village and Laramie could not be further apart in development, culture, topography, and weather. Yet they are so nearly the same in their isolation, generosity, and curiosity about the outside world.

1

The Cost of Freedom

I DIDN'T KNOW WHAT INDEPENDENCE MEANT, but I had it in Laramie as a boy. I was let loose to roam past our front door to our yard and to neighbors' yards, all fenceless borders between families. I had a younger brother and sister, twins, who received more attention, direction, and boundaries than I did.

I was never neglected but was lucky to be given the chance to leave home alone. I didn't think of the freedom to wander as luck or anything but simply the way it was, though it shaped my life to be able to move alone as a boy. My mom gave me directions: "Look both ways and don't cross Grand," she repeated. "I trust you, John," she said. That meant I had a boundary of Laramie's main street, Grand Avenue, but could go to Washington Park across Sheridan, our street, past the park to Rainbow, Custer, and Garfield Streets. The university was on the other side of Grand Avenue, which was a long way away.

I always took the long route through the park to get to and from grade school, and I went there to build snow forts in winter and climb trees in summer, gradually scaling each of the spruce trees in a small grove in one corner of the park. I slept in a bedroom I shared with my brother Doug, feeling secure and happy. But I dreamed about the park and climbing trees. I would start climbing higher into the spruce trees, each of which had its own route, some easy at first and harder higher up, others with a leap to start but a way up as easy as a ladder. Tree climbing became a test for me that was more important than completing school-work. Yet once I had reached the top of the spruce trees, they were not high enough or as far away as I had first imagined. Soon, Washington Park's boundaries cinched, and a determination to find new places dominated my daydreams and distracted me further from schoolwork.

I had parents who loved each other and cared for me and my siblings. We had predictably timed and plentiful meals, a house filled with laughter, cats, and a dog. Mom made pizza or a casserole or roast beef, Dad came home, and then we all watched television. As comfortable as my life was, and perhaps because of that comfort, I needed to have something to explore ahead of me. I cannot pinpoint why this happened, but even books, movies, or sports never amounted to as much as the next place I could explore—first the park, then the slippery alkaline hills at the edge of town, creeks wherever I found them, walking into the prairie, followed by bicycling farther into the prairie on paths made by pronghorn antelope and coyotes. In 1976, when I got a driver's license, the edge of Laramie instantly blew wide open with a paved route out of town.

Fence line leading along the highway into Laramie.

Every sixteen-year-old in Laramie starts driving on their birthday, usually a handed-down family car or a used one bought at any one of the auto dealers, named after families we knew—Burman, Ockers, or Lueras—on Grand Avenue or Third Street, the two main roads leading out of town. I never considered driving my truck, which I purchased with my own savings, a privilege. It was the way it was, a stage in life the same as moving from one grade in school to the next. I had earned it by turning sixteen.

Just a short distance up a steep grade on Interstate 80 was an area named Vedauwoo, where my friends and I climbed the rocks in daylight and went to drink beer at night. Vedauwoo is an Arapaho name meaning "earthborn spirit." The area is the remnant of 1.4-billion-year-old volcanic activity, with igneous rock now rounded off by centuries of wind and weather, but firm and loaded with quartz crystals. Near Vedauwoo, the one line of pavement that crosses southern Wyoming rises to the summit of Sherman Hill, where a bronze bust of Abraham Lincoln marks the highest point on the nation's first transcontinental highway, the Lincoln Highway, now known as Interstate 80. The statue was made by a local sculptor, Robert Russin, an artist who wore a beret and walked from his home to his studio at the university.

Leaving Laramie and going up the twelve miles to Lincoln Summit and on to Vedauwoo was a test of patience and an engine. But coming home from Vedauwoo was even harder. Some never made it. Below Lincoln's steady stare, we drove with little restraint. Friends died one after another in the easing of each spring into summer, their deaths somehow a surprise each time, year after year.

No one thought much about who had car keys, or the risk of the road home. An open door was an open door. We rolled with the taste of freedom we were given, every chance we had. We sped out of Laramie to climb rocks, to drink, dance, kiss, or fight, and jump over a bonfire casting its bright light against the hard rock of Vedauwoo.

I never felt the danger of that road until a friend since grade school, Tom Pikl, died there one May, coming home late at night in his Ford pickup after drinking beer with most of the rest of our high school. The skid marks showed he had swerved his way down Sherman Hill from Lincoln Summit as if he were skiing slalom for miles before his truck caught the road's edge at a bend and catapulted into the prairie. Tom's truck got towed behind the Chevron station on Third Street, sagebrush stuck between its roof and seat. The bed was pounded as flat as creek willows after a heavy snow.

The *Laramie Boomerang* reported that Tom had died instantly. The truck behind the Chevron station was proof of that. We saw it every day for two weeks before Rinker's Scrap Yard took it behind their fence. I started driving on an alternate route because I could not avert my eyes from Tom's truck. My dad also saw it every day on his way to work. "What in the hell was he thinking," he said one evening at dinner. Everyone wondered.

Tom had driven up and down the steep grade twice that night. The first was with Janet, a seventeen-year-old beauty. She had her own car, an Audi Fox with a cartoon fox her father had painted for her on the front driver's-side panel. Janet could have driven herself or talked her way into any truck, but she went with Tom that night. He had driven Janet home and kissed her good-night—a first kiss, she later told me—before heading back up the hill to Vedauwoo to finish a fight. After that gentle kiss and the drama of yet another kegger fight, Tom swerved at a bend of the highway on his second trip down from the summit that night, rolling his pickup onto the hard prairie that broke his neck.

Graduation was a week later. June arrived and summer started. Tom was gone and Janet and Laramie moved on in the same way we had after my cousin Donny died, four years earlier, on the night of the summer solstice. Driving "too fast for conditions," the *Boomerang* reported, on Ninth Street Canyon Road, he crashed a borrowed MG convertible. His friend Calvin Gonzales also died in the accident.

And then, on the same bend of the same road, Janet's best friend, Datha, and her boyfriend, Greg, the principal's son, died a year later. They had been shooting bottles off a fence on a warm March afternoon, a glimpse of summer that is a gift to us in Laramie. Greg drove "too fast for conditions," the *Boomerang* again reported, and killed himself and the sweet Datha, whose family had moved to Laramie from Coos Bay, Oregon. All five died young and instantly in three unthinkable accidents. Tom, Donny, Calvin, Greg, and Datha—their lives ended far too early.

"What in the hell was he thinking," my dad said, this time about Greg. We all asked.

They were all drinking, driving, and in love, but we didn't linger on the question of why our friends and family came to die on the roads. My dad's question was all of Laramie's—a statement, not a question, and left at that. Young and old, we always moved on, or thought we did.

We might have done something practical, like pushing someone we knew at Albany County to put up guardrails or signs at the most dangerous places on our roads, but to this day no such signs exist in those places. They wouldn't have made a difference anyway. Road signs cannot protect people from themselves.

We drove without seatbelts. We shot guns and drank straight from the bottle. And even if some of us didn't live this hard, bad luck was around the corner in a blur of love and life in Laramie, our high prairie island, isolated from everything but ourselves. Had we thought then of implications as large as death, we might have warned ourselves about drinking while driving or driving while crying. We had few rules or restrictions in Laramie, despite having caring parents, good schools, a conservative bent to our town, and an overly exertive police department looking to find and stop trouble. "Live and let live" was something I heard over and over. I interpreted this then as: don't mess with other people's business and do as you want so long as it doesn't mess with other people's business.

After moving from Laramie some years later, I asked my mother whether she had ever considered keeping the keys to our vehicles—my sister's Dodge, my brother's Datsun, or my Chevrolet truck. (We each had our own vehicle and drove it individually to school and to Vedauwoo, as did most everyone.)

"No," Mom said after a long pause. "We trusted you and . . ." She stopped. "John, we couldn't stop any of you kids. You'd go anyway, especially if we told you not to."

But the cost of freedom is steep. The young dead take a big piece of their families to the grave with them. In Laramie, we never stopped to notice that they took a piece of us all.

▪ ▪ ▪

My boundaries grew wider during and after college. Few of my friends had oriented themselves toward a career, even though many of us had a degree from the University of Wyoming. Most of my friends would work for a plane ticket somewhere—to Europe, Central America, or Southeast Asia, maybe with someone, but often alone for months. One year of doing almost any kind of work in Laramie in the early 1980s—baking bread, bartending, or carpentry—could earn a person enough in savings to live and move on the cheap for a year outside the country.

After a few years of such traveling, I was relaxing outside Laramie at our cabin near Centennial with friends at a barbecue, like so many other similar gatherings before it, a time and place to pause before moving again. In August, the stream next to us had slimmed over summer from a torrent to a trickle. Then the thunderbolt hit. The one question I had never asked myself became obvious in an instant, as if I had been jolted from wherever in clear-sky hell lightning arrives before the purple clouds and rain—the flash before a downpour that turns streams into rivers in seconds. Between beer and steak, the storm no one saw coming whispered in my ear over the laughter around me: "Look around," it told me. "Who is next?" I immediately turned away from my friends, as if seeing someone at that moment would single them out for death.

"The road went left and my bike went right," Sean Bradley had started. Everyone was laughing and Sean was on to one of his tales. "My feet tight in the toe clips and I went over the fence. My bike landed on me, brand new, bent and ruined. Seven hundred bucks down the drain just like that!"

I kept my eyes on the ground, pushing dirt around with my boots. My mind flashed to friends who were not at the barbecue with us, boys who'd be men today, men we never got to know and now rarely talked about. Which person around me today would be gone tomorrow?

When I finally raised my head, I saw that no one was looking at me. Grateful not to be noticed, I grabbed another beer and joined my friends at the grill.

It turned out that the next person would be Sean. He died soon after the barbecue when he put a gun to his head and fired it. I gasped at the news but then walked away from friends telling me what had happened. I needed time alone before coming together with others. I think we all need that time alone. I would go instead to another time, when we talked while huddled together in the mountains, beneath lightning.

Sean chronicled a night he had spent walking around the climbing walls of Vedauwoo with a bottle of Jack Daniel's, working out in his head just exactly how he would end a relationship with a woman he said he loved, but couldn't stay with. He told me how he put the bottle away in one long walk, confirming for himself along the way that he wasn't ready to stop living by his own rules alone. I understood his self-ishness, but that word did not emerge in the conversation. Freedom did. I accepted his need and lust for freedom over stability as if I had walked in his boots. Sean was a compatriot, who moved into and out of love with little restraint, just as he went into the mountains alone.

I thought of another time I had spent with Sean, when he yelled to me from his Jeep as he came out of the alley between First and Second Streets near his shop, Bradley Mountainwear. "Whoa, a bear almost got us up on Rock Creek," he howled, followed with a long laugh. He climbed out of his Jeep to tell me what had happened.

Sean was alone with his dog trying to get to a section of Rock Creek to kayak, but he encountered a bear that he and his dog had surprised. Although it was summer, the snowpack was still deep in the high elevations, and the creeks and rivers were running full and fast, well into July. He stepped in his snowshoes between the angry bear and his dog, tethered in towropes hooked to a kayak. Sean prodded the bear with his paddle but was unable to lunge out of the way when the bear took a swipe deep into his calf. He continued to fight the bear with his kayak paddle, finally getting it to back off, likely saving his dog and maybe himself. He managed to hike out, his leg bound with a tourniquet he'd made from the dog's harness.

"Look here," Sean said, pulling back bandages. His leg had been stitched in the emergency room at Laramie's Ivinson Memorial Hospital. He laughed. Sean always laughed when he told a story.

Then one night, Sean grabbed a gun and, though the man we had known forever would try anything, he did the one unimaginable thing.

I was dismayed and angry. Did the son of a bitch know I loved him, that we all loved him?

Everyone in Laramie knew Sean in specific personal ways, having been given a piece of a story or a piece of clothing he had sewn. Sean had made a living designing and sewing backpacks and outdoor clothing that many of us in Laramie relied on to protect us from the cold wind. He had made me the first backpack he charged money for and replaced its straps and zippers with care for years. He would drop everything to perform a repair for a friend, sometimes working into the night. Sean didn't need to tell us that he guaranteed his work for life.

I doubted Sean considered—in that moment with himself, a bottle, and his gun, wandering alone again—that all of us in Laramie trusted him. The way he moved in the world—large and with modesty—is what we admired about Sean. Until the instant when it wasn't, life was lucky for him. Sean performed life without a camera or notebook, usually alone with a kayak, climbing shoes, or a bicycle, and often with the dog he had come to nickname Bear.

Eventually I'd commune with friends to share the facts that would become our common story: how it had happened—which never became a deeper discussion of how it all happened—the events in a life that led to death. He would be another man from Laramie who would live in us, and through us, for life. After a brief public reflection but a deeper thunder in our memories, we moved on.

And then another friend would die in his own way.

Chris lived alone on the prairie outside Laramie in a one-bedroom home with his two hunting dogs and a falcon housed in a shed, constructed from leftover lumber and scrap wire.

One late autumn day, I dropped in at his home from town just after a storm had passed. Chris had his falcon indoors with him, hooded after a hunt for sage grouse that had been cut short by the hailstorm. The bird was perched on a lodgepole pine stump on the concrete floor of his living room. Chris's dogs sat beside the bird, touching the sides of the falcon's beak, which was still bloody from the hunt, with their long tongues. The cool room smelled of wet dogs and grouse blood.

"These grouse are my favorite prairie bird," Chris told me. "They are most exuberant in mating and true to their habitat."

He held up a grouse tail to show me a wide fan of feathers, spiked bronze, burnt hues, and pillow patches like snow. "Look at the way they display plumage," he exclaimed. "These birds puff their chest like red balloons and strut. They are nature's Elvis but they put even him to shame. I don't hunt them often, but there are plenty of sage grouse this year north of Laramie. I had to walk quite a ways to get to them."

"You carry your falcon?" I asked.

"That is the only way," Chris said. "My dogs follow close, then split off to flush birds. Everything fits together if all of us do our jobs." The four of them had been working together for three years.

"Today was especially good for the falcon to go high," Chris explained to me. "She maneuvered into a stoop—a dive," he added. "Maybe close to ninety miles an hour," Chris said, finally getting excited. "You don't see that with my bird hunting waterfowl, but the grouse stay in close range and low. This one here," he bragged about the bird on the stump, "is a beautiful predator."

"She lives to fly and flies to hunt and hunts to kill and she kills quickly, efficiently. This falcon," he said, waving his arm to the hooded bird perched on a stump in the middle of the room, "is like no other except the peregrine and definitely the kestrel."

Chris was cooking a portion of the grouse breast for himself and began cooking a portion for me, too, without asking whether I was hungry.

"One or two potatoes?" he asked. I indicated one, and he put another potato in boiling water and turned back to the conversation we had started the night before at my cabin. We were formulating a journey together to kayak the coast of Baffin Island. "Maybe we could get some money to document the raptors there," Chris suggested.

Raptors roost in great numbers on Baffin Island's cliffs, and Chris, a naturalist who had documented the birds on nearby Ellesmere Island, had dreamed of doing a sea kayak journey along Baffin's coast, where enormous walls of granite tower a thousand feet over the ice-cold sea.

"Maybe you can," I said. "I don't know the difference between your falcon and a hawk."

"Easy. I'll teach you and, besides, you can take the notes," he offered.

Our challenge was finding the money, but also timing a thin window of access, not always available in the ice floes of the Arctic, the following August. I knew Chris through backcountry skiing, not kayaking, but it was enough to start us planning a trip together, discussions centering on the risks of polar bears, cold water, and extreme tidal fluctuations.

I put another log in the wood stove and watched Chris work. The house warmed and began to smell of woodsmoke. The dogs dried. Chris pulled feathers and carved out the breast meat of the grouse. He handed me the grouse's tail to take home.

Later that winter, Chris was caught in an avalanche while skiing in the Snowy Range nearby. Another friend descended ahead of Chris without incident. But when Chris skied, the slope slid in a flash into the trees at the base of the hill, capturing him with no warning, suffocating him in wet, compacted snow. Our friend, a French woman named Emmanuelle, watched it happen. She saw Chris "once and quickly, a glimpse of him surfacing in the white."

"The snow," she told me, "fell away from the hill down to dried grass and dead flowers. The whole place and everything left bare." The snow had stopped with Chris trapped in a mound, she explained. It was so quiet and so peaceful after the violence of it, in that time when all time stops, she believed nothing had happened. She imagined that Chris might not be under the snow under her boots. But she dug with her hands until she found him, his open mouth stuffed with snow.

I shouldn't have been surprised by Chris and other friends dying after taking chances that no one considered risky. Early and repeated experiences of death by freezing, falling, or snow never sunk in, because no one I knew slowed down or reevaluated their approach to the world.

When I was a child, the mother of the Freytags, a big family with two boys in my grade school, drowned in Libby Creek below our cabin, when her horse slipped while fording the creek during a flood after a storm had taken the bridge out. The family ran the old Snowy Range Lodge, a relic in disrepair, with one-room cabins in the woods around it. After their mother died, we never saw the Freytags again. "They moved on," people said.

Snowy Range Lodge on Libby Creek in the Snowy Range above Centennial, Wyoming, near Laramie.

The Forest Service rebuilt the washed-out bridge with two metal culverts and stacked river rocks that have funneled the creek safely ever since. "That'll do it," Dad said time and time again when we crossed the bridge. I have looked back at that place on Libby Creek a thousand times since then and can never imagine how the creek could be so powerful it could take a road out and a horse down.

"You stay away from the creek," my parents warned my brother and me. It could be dangerous; we knew that before the Freytags' mother drowned. But Doug and I didn't take to the warning and kept climbing along the creek, on boulders and logs, up and up until we could go no farther.

Libby Creek falls fast out of the mountains. Ice and snow in winter cover much of the creek downstream and upstream. But in front of our cabin it runs year round, even in the dead of winter, because it falls over rocks and does not freeze.

"Why doesn't it freeze?" I asked my dad over and over.

"Just doesn't," he told me.

"Springs," Mom explained. "Spring water comes from under the ground all year," she said.

Just like that, I had to find these springs.

"We'll find them in summer," my mother told me.

Dad pulled out maps, road maps mostly, and laid them in front of the fireplace.

"Now here we are," he said, pointing to a place on the map without a name, a blank space with a blue line that was our Libby Creek. "And there is the road to Laramie." He lined the black route on the map with his finger.

It was hard to understand creeks and rivers using road maps, but he showed us where the rivers went as they meandered away from the highways. He had us repeat the route our ice-cold Libby Creek took after passing our cabin. My brother, sister, and I memorized it: Libby Creek, North Fork, Little Laramie, Laramie, North Platte, Missouri, and Mississippi. It was like memorizing prayers at catechism or the Scout's Motto at Troop 134 meetings in the church basement, except that I wanted most to remember where the water went. Remembering mottoes or commandments was memorizing for its own sake, but memorizing Libby Creek's route was fun. It was an adventure to think about and follow the water's changing name, moving always to the ocean.

The roads near Laramie don't follow the paths of rivers, as they do most everywhere else. The contours of the land around town do not accommodate roads along the rivers. The land in all directions is either flat or steep, with little middle ground. Creeks find their way down canyons too narrow for roads, and they join other streams in rivers that meander over the flat prairie. Early settlers made their trails as straight as possible through passes with the least elevation gain. The rivers intersect now and then with trails and roads, the routes that accommodated horses, carriages, and steam engines.

Laramie was settled for the transcontinental railroad. Dad showed us that straight route across the state on maps, too. Our main highway follows the rail route, expedient for drivers crossing the state and unquestionably logical to those who designed and built the interstate highway. But for Wyoming people, the side roads are the main roads. They connect ranches, hunting areas, and the beautiful places. Dirt roads lead to fishing, too, and they lead to where you can get away.

Near the Union Pacific Depot in town, the highway and railroad meet the Laramie River, which comes through quietly and slow moving, having run through ranchland in persistent arcs after crashing out of the mountains. By the time the river meets Laramie, it sweeps by in silence, flooding its banks now and then but not touching homes. No one in town pays much attention to the river, because the fishing is better upstream and downstream than it is in the docile flow around Laramie.

But we pay attention to our Libby Creek that feeds the Laramie River. In summer throughout my adolescence and teenage years, I would watch the creek water and imagine it going to Laramie and beyond. I threw sticks, pinecones, and eventually logs into the creek and wondered how long it would take for the object in front of me just now to get to the sea. I watched water move out of sight and repeated to myself the creek's route we had memorized from the maps.

One summer, Dad took us to Libby Lake, the source of our creek, up the road some six miles. I could not see the spring Mom had told me about.

"Where is the spring?" I asked.

"Below us, along the creek, there are many springs. Think of them like your own blood in the veins in your body, moving around," Mom said.

In that instant, the creek became a living thing. It was not like a person or an animal, but alive nevertheless. Alive in its own way. That our living creek had also killed a classmate's mother a year earlier was not a contradiction to me.

The creek became an entity to me, not exactly like a friend but like an entire school, with its familiar faces, many classrooms, predictable alarms, and unpredictable fights on the playground. And the distance between Libby Lake and Libby Creek at our cabin became a six-mile question mark I could not shake. I knew by the map what was below our cabin, the route of the creek to the sea. What mattered most to me was the space I did not know between where we looked at Libby Lake, in alpine rock and snowfields in July, and the creek that went past our cabin. It became a dream, a journey in my mind, and eventually an obsession to walk the creek's length.

Rummaging through Dad's maps, I discovered tributaries of Libby Creek. One named Silver Run was near our cabin. A whole new dream took hold of me. Where did it start?

One summer, Doug and I found where Silver Run joined Libby Creek just below our cabin. We hiked partway up Silver Run and found waterfalls, and downed trees we could use as a bridge. We discovered an old silver or gold mine, a dump full of rusted cans and bottles. We took artifacts—a root beer can, pieces of broken plates, a fork and two spoons—to the cabin and put them on a shelf like museum pieces.

By the following year, Doug grew uninterested in finding a hiking route up the creek to its source. And I, too, soon got distracted by everything that would come to distract us at that age—skiing, friends, and saving money to buy a pickup truck.

But one summer day a few years later, the urge to get to the top of Silver Run resurrected itself. It came when I was at the cabin alone cutting firewood, and I set the chainsaw down in the shed and started walking up the creek before noon. I pushed into evening on a night when, to my surprise and benefit, the moon was rising early. I didn't have a watch and had not been paying attention to the time. The day had gone long, though, as if the sun would not set. Then the moon took hold of the sky where the sun left off. The night was bright and the sky clear. I had no food or tent but it was a warm night and I kept moving, not because I was obsessed with getting to the source of the creek, but because I did not consider why I should stop.

I came to a lake hours after the moon had risen. I guessed that it had taken me half a day to walk the entire length of the creek. I sat down on a rock along the bank of the lake and watched it for some time in the moonlight. I drank from the lake with my hands and fell asleep in dirt and pine needles below a stand of lodgepole pine.

Pine needles in the corner of my mouth woke me. I drank more water out of the lake and took off back down the stream. It was just getting light and the forest was so quiet, no birds singing yet. The creek gathered strength as I walked, and soon all I could hear was the sound of the creek over the thump of my footsteps.

Nobody would have judged me as having taken a risk to hike alone with no gear, but I didn't tell anyone. It wasn't a story to tell, but a hike I had to do. People in Laramie never thought of how we approached life as taking chances. But in retrospect, none of it should have happened—the slip of a horse in the creek, the loaded gun available in Sean's closet, or the temperature of snow loosening its hold on a hill—but it did and we adjusted to yet another unthinkable surprise.

I drank Jack Daniel's for Sean and walked alone at night at Vedauwoo, as I imagined him doing. For Chris, I took a feather of the grouse tail he had given me after our meal together, put it in the current of the Laramie River, and watched it move out of sight. My curiosity about a single creek because of the death of a classmate's mother grew into a love of rivers.

Life in Laramie was surrounded by death. Because we could not have lived any other way, death became part of us. Friends and families carried onward, adjusting to loss but seldom changing the way they lived. Every death began to make the next death seem inevitable, a part of surviving, a part of living in Laramie.

2

Saved in Tokyo

FOR YEARS BEFORE SEAN AND CHRIS DIED, in accidents two years apart, I could not envision slowing down. Their passing didn't help calm me, either. But before both of my friends were gone, I had had a chance to consider an alternative to the continuous movement around the world I had grown accustomed to and thrived on. The chance happened in Japan, where I landed after traveling in Nepal and Thailand with my girlfriend, Jennifer. She had returned home to finish her college degree. But I was yearning to go to Tibet and was more committed to getting there than I was to our relationship.

Japan might have helped me think about the long-term value of commitment, had I been in the right state of mind to slow down and learn. But I was anxious to keep traveling, and to make the money I needed to keep moving. It was a different kind of commitment to not commit. I was avoiding a career choice, for sure, and also the pursuit of a single passion, like music, skiing, cooking, or kayaking. It wasn't that I was indecisive; I was curious, and I could not take my eyes off maps.

Tokyo had a reputation in 1985, when I arrived. For one, it was said that money could practically be taken from the streets: if someone lost a 10,000-yen note—something like fifty dollars—it would remain on the ground until the person who lost it returned for it. Also, there was a neighborhood with real estate so expensive that a 10,000-yen note would not pay a day's rent for the space it took up. I calculated the value of the floor of my apartment back home. In Japan, it would be worth $1,000 a day, as much rent as I paid with a roommate in two months. The tales of honesty and wealth in Japan were unfathomable to me.

I had also heard on the circuit of world wanderers in Hong Kong, Bangkok, and Kathmandu that teaching English in Japan was easy work to get and paid real money, more than my benchmark of good pay, which was roughneck work in Wyoming's oil fields at twenty dollars an hour, plus overtime. My chest felt swollen with longing for Jennifer, but I needed money. I had to get money to keep traveling, and I needed to keep moving more than I needed love.

I had known Jennifer's family since I was a boy, when I saw her and her sisters every Sunday at St. Laurence O'Toole Church. From the front pew where my family always sat, I watched a line of sisters getting Communion with their hair so tightly braided by their mother that I thought they were from another country. Our parents were friends, but I had not once talked to Jennifer through grade school, junior high school, or high school until, one night outside the Buckhorn Bar, she grabbed me by the arm, pulled me close, and kissed me long and with a conviction no one would fight. She had come home for a visit from the University of Oregon. A month later, we left for Nepal without telling anyone, calling home from Hong Kong to inform our parents we had gone together.

Jennifer Slater and Haines, Muktinath, 1984.

That was four months ago. Now, three days without her had already been too long, a lifetime. Her tears and departure, my restart and now: moving again alone. She had returned home to her oil painting and art history studies. The splatters of yellow and blue paint that I loved in her long brown hair had grown out gradually, to be replaced by streaks of sun-bleached blond during the time we traveled together in sun and love. But she was broke and ready to paint again, and she craved the structure of the same university in Oregon that she had needed to escape only a few months earlier.

A day after arriving in Tokyo from Bangkok, where we had left each other, I secured a job teaching conversational English. It was easy work. The dialogue I was given to teach was provided by the school and all the students had the same job, which I was told meant that they had the same language needs.

"What is your favorite pastime?" I asked.

"Shopping" is what I heard from every woman, all flight attendants for Japanese Airlines. I tried to convince myself that it could not be true that they all loved shopping. But each woman repeated the words of the woman before, hour after hour, day after day, for three weeks. Repetition and pronunciation consistency were my aims as a teacher.

"Have you been to America?"

"Yes, beautiful, big. I love America, California, Los Angeles, San Francisco" (all JAL destinations).

"What do you shop for?"

"Bags, jewelry, golf. Shopping, any shopping."

"Do you play golf?"

"Japanese love golf, golf in America."

I started detouring from the script in an attempt to discover a personality behind the uniform beauty of these women.

"Do you love Wyoming? It is in America, too. Yellowstone? Cowboys?"

There was no answer to my question. They were not learning to have a real conversation but were being taught to repeat phrases casually based on word prompts and common phrases they would encounter with Americans on flights. They didn't know of Wyoming, national parks, or men on horses. I smiled, amused but not surprised. They smiled back demurely, each of them like the one before, the same smile, the same legs crossed in physical perfection. The women were beautiful as a group and individually. Work was easy. I wanted to scream.

The Japanese firm that hired me planned to retain my pay for two months, a scheme that would give me cash on their books but would leave me close to broke between checks and dependent, I feared, on my next check in perpetuity. The language school had closed my teaching contract with sincerity but ultimately to its advantage. It was smart, and necessary because I could, and probably would, leave with my first month's paycheck, which was more than I needed for three months in China and Tibet. Money was the only reason I had come to Japan, where it was expensive to live, even holed up at a business hotel in a room the size of an American bathroom, eating at the same place every night. My daily indulgence was a cup of strong coffee in the morning, and one beer at night from a vending machine on the street behind my hotel.

After three weeks, January moved into February and the cold and cloudy city had not captured my heart. My first day off, a Sunday, I went to Shinjuku, feeling as alone as I had ever been, walking among thousands of strangers shopping in the most expensive land in the world, a cold fact on that sunless Sunday. I was walking the central square, circling the area without direction when a man approached.

"Hello, American?"

"Yes," I responded.

"You look lost," he said, and I was, but I did not need or want directions. "Do you want to be saved?" he asked.

"Yes," I said, stunned with the directness of the question.

"Come nearby," he said. "Please, come with me."

As unlikely as it was for me to follow anyone I had just met, I followed this small man, who was completely unthreatening. I wasn't bored, but I was lonely and felt as if I were not in my own skin, not completely part of my own life, as if I were watching someone else go through the motions of acquiescence. I was curious and not worried. Where he took me was not nearby, but to the Yamanote train line, where he bought my ticket, round trip I noted, to just outside the city.

On the train, we sat next to each other on a busy car filled with quiet people. I judged that the man was incapable of taking advantage of me physically. My time with flight attendants had predisposed me to trust the Japanese based solely on their physical demeanor and style, however strategically derived.

We got off the train and walked without talking in a neighborhood of houses behind short walls. Behind the walls were trees, none of which were leafy or blooming but all of which were beautifully sculpted. The man smiled at me, and I felt a warmth and intrigue for Japan for the first time in nearly a month. After about fifteen minutes, we came to a small compound that was spotless and white—from the walls outside to the interior, which had no art, photos, or adornments. The floor was tiled but the interior felt warm, with wooden benches and a simple wooden table. Two older men joined us, and my companion left the room. I would not see him again. I was led to a room and guided by one of the men, who communicated with simple gestures and no words, to put on a white cotton robe. I was in a religious facility of some sort but not a church. I saw that these men were Christian, as they all wore a crucifix around their neck. I undressed in private and was then directed to an outdoor pool that, based on my experience with the warm indoor bath-house near my hotel, looked inviting in the rainy January air. It dawned on me, finally, that they were preparing to baptize me.

I told one of the men that I had already been baptized a Catholic. This was not an issue, he assured me. I was to be baptized again today and "saved," he said. After weeks of work that had blended into an indecipherable blob of boredom and money making, I was unconcerned about religion. I was here less out of inspiration than as a drone. That might have made me question my new baptism, but it didn't, because if this was what I needed and deserved, or had walked into by choice or in negligence, I'd accept it. It was my first adventure in Tokyo, which I had experienced as a city where people worked hard but played in private or not at all.

Two men, also dressed in white, told me to walk down the steps and into the water up to my chest. It was cold, a surprise that I did not fight. A man with white hair in a white robe joined me in the water to per-form the ceremony. I started shivering as the elegant old Japanese man placed his hands on my head and gently began pushing me underwater twelve times, once for each of the dozen names of deceased relatives I had written down on a piece of paper he had provided me. I had made a complete list of my grandparents, uncles, aunts, and cousins. As I wrote each name, a relief came over me because I had not lost anyone in my immediate family. The act of reflection felt peaceful and took my mind back to my family. I felt them with me there.

The dunking began to move in slow motion, just as a branch bends in and out of the pulsing water on the edge of a stream. The cold deepened until I felt it to the bones in my legs. I was losing control of myself physically but my brain was as alert as I had ever recalled it being. I was feeling everything at once—the warmth of family history and the freezing water, the silence in the air and the sense of drowning. In a moment of surprise and panic underwater, I had the urge to grab the old man by the throat to stop him. But when he raised his hand from my head, I realized I was safe. And then the dunking was over, and I breathed deeply.

I climbed up the steps out of the water, feeling weak. I could barely walk and had little sensation or strength in my legs, and my heart raced in a reflexive effort to pump blood to my extremities. Without speaking a word, two other men held me up, took off my wet cotton robe, wrapped me gently in white towels and a blanket, poured me hot tea, and took me into a clean white room. I sipped the tea, gradually warming up, dressed myself, and walked around the quiet compound. I eventually found my way back to the foyer where I had arrived an hour or so earlier, looking for a way out. Instead, I was greeted by the two men and the old man who had baptized me. They told me that I had a place there to stay that night, tomorrow, or anytime I needed or wished. But I left, thanking them and assuring them that I needed no help to find my way back into the city.

I retraced my route and went to my tiny hotel room. I felt liberated by the baptism rather than constrained or pinned down, so I could not face the confining space of my hotel room. I went instead to a hidden garden that I had found days earlier but had not explored. The garden was easy to miss behind its whitewashed walls, which were just high enough that I couldn't see over them. In a narrow opening in the wall was this garden that, despite being only a few hundred or so square feet, held real space, a design illusion the Japanese have perfected. In afternoon light creating a long shadow off a bench, I sat down, free from the suffocation of Tokyo.

Rounded rocks, dark and wet in the winter light, had been placed into contours that caused my eyes to trace and retrace their pattern. Two small pine trees and a tall bamboo had been planted in a way that invited observation and led me in a path of circular thought as I looked back and forth at the slight sway of the bamboo stalks and firm pines. I was relieved to be alone. I sat for a long time, lost in the distraction of a book on the Zen mind and how one could seek to forever be in a state of beginning. The beginner's mind, the writer called it. I interpreted this as a commitment to starting, exploring, and not settling. It sounded selfish, but right for me because I had too much I wanted to see, so much to learn.

"Where from?" I heard a man ask.

I looked up, surprised to see him in the garden. "United States," I said.

"You enjoy my garden?" he said in clear English.

"Yes," I said, "very much. This is yours?"

"I care for it," he said. "Why do you come to Tokyo?" he asked.

"I came to make money. Teaching," I said.

"Teaching," he repeated. "Why?" he asked.

"I want to go to Tibet. I need money," I explained.

He nodded, started picking up leaves, and walked a few steps away. Some time passed before he turned to me again. "You see these stones? When I place one, I choose its position carefully because it must be where it belongs. It will be there for at least five years, but most times it is never moved."

"But what if it is in the wrong place?" I asked.

"This is possible, but it is not my experience here." He told me he had taught himself the placement of stones and plants. "I am too old to make mistakes," he said.

The following day I walked from work back to my hotel room along a different route, passing the office of Alitalia. I went in on a whim, checked flight times, and booked a flight to Hong Kong, where I could get into China easily and cheaply. I had not been paid but could not wait another five weeks while my travel funds dwindled to nothing. Without calling to quit my job, I decided that night that I would leave Tokyo.

Before I left for the airport, I called home to talk with Jennifer. She had reenrolled in college and was painting again. She sounded pleased about being home but asked me to take a deep breath.

"I may not be here for you when you return," she said.

"I can come home tomorrow," I told her.

"I'll never forgive you if you do," she responded quickly. I waited.

Jennifer was a woman not to be argued with, but I said, "I want to be there," which was true, but I wanted to be in Tibet more. She was prepared for my response and was persuading me to believe that whatever happened between us would be fine for her and should be for me, too.

"Keep going, please, for me. John, listen to me. I am concerned for myself, and for us. I will see you when you come home," she said.

I took Jennifer at her word, left Tokyo that night for Hong Kong, and then went to China and Tibet in the dead of winter. I felt irresponsible toward my work, selfish toward everyone including Jennifer, disconnected and alone in the world. But I had my moving garden, in which I could not yet place a stone.

3
Buried in the Sky

FIVE MONTHS EARLIER, I was traveling from Laramie to Nepal. A spark of romance with Jennifer in Laramie led me through Eugene, Oregon, to visit her. In a week, she would drop out of the university and use her student loan money to purchase a plane ticket to travel with me to Nepal. I never suggested she go to Asia with me. But she was spectacularly impulsive, which I loved, and smart in subjects such as art and literature, which I admired. We were in love and on a path together we could not avoid. The sky was the limit for us.

I went to a pawnshop in Eugene to sell camera gear to pay help pay for my own ticket to Nepal. A man there, Pema, wore a name tag, which was the only formality in the stacked and spilled mess of musical instruments, power tools, kitchen gadgets, cameras, and jewelry. I trusted Pema from the moment he looked at me. Pema. A first name or last? I wondered but did not ask him. I was concerned only with the price I could get for the lens.

"Interested?" I asked, holding the lens toward him. He was a big man with a large sun-browned face.

"Nikon. Okay, yes," he said. "Where is the camera?" he asked.

"I'm keeping it for a trip to Nepal," I answered.

He wrote a price on a piece of paper and handed it to me. "You look at my camera shelf," he said, "and tell me yes." He laughed and sat down to work on a chainsaw he had dismantled on the floor.

I did as he said and began to eye prices, gauging the value of my lenses. But my feet were on their way to the airport, in a state of mind choreographed for practical matters alone, like the money for a plane ticket. It was a not a mind-set suited for bargaining.

I failed to discover at that time that this strong man in the pawnshop was Tibetan. Or that he had fled his country a quarter century earlier, as a boy, crossing the greatest and coldest mountain pass in the world from Tibet into Nepal, and then to India, where most of the exiled Tibetans fled. He had moved through the brittle-cold high altitude wearing maroon robes covered by a yak-hide coat, walking in boots made also of yak leather. He traveled with the Dalai Lama, the twenty-five-year-old reincarnate god-king, who walked ahead of him. Along with elder monks and other boys from the monasteries of Sera, Drepung, and Ganden, Pema was walking Tibetan Buddhism out of its home.

"Two hundred," I said in response to his written offer of $125. Pema laughed at my counteroffer without saying a word. I took his $125, a fair price for a traveler desperate for money. My need for cash and inability to barter was evident in my eyes, I reasoned—like most people in a pawnshop.

Once the transaction was settled, Pema sat me down and began to brew tea. I was anxious to leave, but I waited for the tea. Pema suggested where I could sleep in Kathmandu, and the routes I might trek around the Annapurna mountain range, where he told me he had once worked. He explained that he had guided treks in Nepal before coming to the United States to study, but that his intention had been transformed into work at the pawnshop, where he fit in perfectly with the worn handles on hammers and handsaws. His face radiated a calm needed in this disheveled shop, and he laughed at small things, like the parts of the chainsaw he had encircled himself with. He did not mention Tibet, a place I didn't know of at the time anyway. But in a single stroke of luck, I left Pema's pawnshop with guidance for Kathmandu and just enough money to get there.

In Nepal, Jennifer and I heard about Tibet almost immediately. The people of the high plateau of Tibet, just beyond the Himalayas on the northern border of Nepal, had been kept isolated by geography for centuries, and then by the Chinese for decades. For the first time in many years, China had opened the opportunity for independent travelers to enter Tibet in 1984, while we were in Nepal, but it could be accessed only from China. The idea of getting to Tibet was on our minds the entire time we spent in Nepal.

■ ■ ■

Alone in China after leaving Japan, I moved around to cities to find the cheapest route to Lhasa. I finally arrived in Lhasa by a long route through China, where I had met no other travelers like me except for a man from Hong Kong named Franklin. He helped me buy a one-way ticket from Xian to Lhasa. Foreigners were not allowed to take that route to Lhasa, but he was from Hong Kong and passed as a man from China, and he purchased my ticket. I was allowed onto the plane and landed in Lhasa without difficulties, but also without Jennifer, who shared my passion for Tibet.

I carried Jennifer's desire to see Tibet with me and harbored increasing guilt for my inability to commit to a life that I knew I would want eventually with her—one with children, steady work, a house in a neighborhood. But getting to Tibet had become as much a mystery to pursue as a pilgrimage.

The sky in Lhasa was clear that first day. At an altitude of 11,450 feet, the city was crisp cold and nearly empty of other foreign travelers. The streets were used mostly by Tibetan traders on foot. Groups of men and women bundled in wool camped along the road after pilgrimage walks from the far reaches of Tibet. Towering above the Tibetan travelers was the Potala Palace, once the home of the Dalai Lama. The white-rock palace built on and into a hill is capped in golden spires and draped in deep gold- and mahogany-colored walls.

The Chinese ran the official hotel where I was required to stay. While the old, central part of Lhasa was filled mostly with Tibetans, the Chinese worked in shops along the main roads on the edges of the city.

On a map I purchased at a truck depot in the Chinese area of Lhasa, there was a line called the "Friendship Highway" that led from Lhasa to Kathmandu. Men at the truck depot staged their trade of cigarettes from China to India and, on the return trip, matches from India to China. A trucker told me the dirt road was good, but cold and windy. Mountain bike, I thought. That might be the way to travel the Friendship Highway to Nepal someday. But for now, I was intent on experiencing Tibet's sky burials.

Jennifer and I had heard of sky burials in Nepal from an Englishman, a bird watcher we had met north of Annapurna IV. He told us that people perform traditional Tibetan Buddhist sky burials somewhere deep in the mountains near the Mustang region, but he had not found them there.

"Griffons. You know, vultures," he told us, "they are scavengers who live off carrion. The men who prepare the bodies work as an independent caste of people, like the untouchables in India, but in a Buddhist land," he explained. "In Tibet, bodies are taken north of Lhasa before dawn by these men whose sole role in the world is to prepare bodies to be eaten by these incredible birds. The men leave Lhasa in the night, their work acknowledged and respected by all Tibetans but seen by almost no one."

Now I am in Tibet, walking north of Lhasa in the predawn darkness to find these men, the dead, and what they and the vultures do together. I walk out of Lhasa through the quiet dark toward hills I see outlined in moonlight. It is cold. I am alone, walking first on pavement, then on a dirt road, and finally on the dried grasses and packed earth of Tibet in March. I am a bird watcher, and walking in the early morning is part of seeing birds, but at this high altitude my head is throbbing. I had come from an altitude over ten thousand feet lower in Xian. I'll make it, I say to myself. But I do not know where I am going or what I might find.

I aim for dark shadows that appear to be the rocky hills north of the city, my direction based on my recollection of the Brit's story. "Hills on the north edge of Lhasa" is what I remember him saying.

The tops of rocky hills come into view in the emerging sun. I steer northeast toward an area where large angled rocks on the hills—like the Flatirons outside Boulder, Colorado, though less dramatic and much less dominant—start shining in the new day's light. Two hours into my pursuit, my head is pounding. I am also thirsty but have no water. I am dressed adequately with a coat, and the temperature is above freezing, not as cold as China had been, but I am frustrated at myself for not bringing water or a snack.

Keep moving.

Eventually, a kilometer or so later, I see men in the distance with a human body up on an angled slab of stone the size of a swimming pool. They are tying it by its limbs to a rope at the top of the rock. I move closer and sit low, some thirty or so yards away, trying to stay hidden. The men do not look toward me, but I sense they know I am there in the treeless area. I do not move as several corpses are cut into pieces, one body after another, men and women, all thin and wrinkled. Four men move quickly with the bodies, working with precision in a dismembering process that appears immune to distraction or alteration. Blood seems to have been drained from the bodies, but I see some trickling down the stone in long meandering streaks to dry soil at the base of the rock, where it absorbs into a dark patch of earth. After the dissection, men pulverize the bones—mostly large bones like femurs, ribs, and backbones—with wooden mallets after the flesh is cut from them and set aside. From a distance, the bones do not appear to shatter but are flattened into stringy pieces that look like the white bark of an aspen tree. The bones and flesh are then placed aside on the long, sloping rock.

With the light of a new day now upon us, the men continue to move without changing their pace or adjusting their clothing or hats to the sun's bright and beautiful arrival. Nor do they speak with each other. I witness a ritual, but the men do not pause or pray.

I hear the vultures behind me on the rocks. The birds begin to rumble, unseen in the high cliffs. They do not sound like a convergence of crows with their high-pitched craws but like the building of a deeper thunder of bigger birds, like an approaching train coming down the canyon. Then they are above me, a circling dozen at first, then more, then fifty, and then I lose count. Other men join those who performed the dissections to throw the human flesh and bones into the air. The huge birds start swooping down over the big rock slab. Many of the griffons take the flesh from the air. Others pick at body parts on the ground. Then the birds circle away into the sky and their collective roar turns to individual sounds, long songs screaming into the swirling sky.

The funerals I had attended were in churches, with burials at cemeteries. Priests presented a calming perspective, eulogies from family and friends stirred comfort but also created regret. I always left less reflective than wanting. Not for more words, though. I needed action, any action, a dance or a walk outdoors. But as much as I appreciated the simplicity and metaphorical thoughtfulness of the sky burials, I could not imagine watching a friend go to the sky that way, though it was comforting to consider my own body going to the sky as sustenance for lives in flight.

I sneak away after the griffon vultures settle in the high rocks and become quiet. I remember only a hazy struggle to retrace my route back to Lhasa, each step a trudge against my growing fatigue and headache. When I wake up the next morning in my hotel room, my head is still hammering. I am reaching for each breath and know I am in danger from altitude sickness. The woman assigned to clean my room brings a corked thermos of hot water. I drink it. A Swedish traveler I meet in the bathroom at the end of the hall brings me mandarin oranges in cans. I eat them. I vomit and cannot move. I drink more hot water. I pee in the empty orange cans. I eat more oranges. I see vultures in my dreams. I see the vultures when I wake. Without definition between day and night, one day moves into many days. My energy is gone. I imagine being dead in Lhasa with no one except the woman with hot water and the Swede knowing I have died.

I get to the airport by taxi with help from the Swede and descend to Chengdu in China, where I find a room at a large hotel, one of the few places the Chinese allow foreigners to stay. I am weak but revived by the lower elevation. My headache stops as if a switch has been turned off. It is St. Patrick's Day, which I do not realize until my friend from Laramie, Jeff Alford, unexpectedly comes into the cavernous and empty dining hall. Jeff and I baked bread together in a Laramie restaurant; we had seen each other months earlier in Kathmandu, and now we are here. He tells me he is on his way to Lhasa. He uncorks a bottle of Irish whiskey he's carried for months, and we talk.

My advice: be careful of altitude. Find the sky burials. I want to explain more, but that would be like explaining a symphony. I don't have the words anyway. He needs to experience it free of my account. I would have had trouble explaining the images I had seen of birds and death while my brain was losing its bearing at altitude. I leave it as a repeated suggestion: find the sky burials north of Lhasa at dawn.

His advice: go to Beijing. Take the train to Europe.

We down Irish whiskey and promise each other we will do the same in Laramie by summer.

4

Trans-Siberian Economics

FLOWERS WERE NOT EASY TO FIND in Beijing that winter. But I found a dozen roses during a cold March day in 1985, and with those red flowers—which I could barely afford at eight dollars—I at last secured a Soviet visa. After I had tried for two days, my application finally passed the stern visa gatekeeper, a buxom Soviet Embassy bureaucrat. I considered the roses an investment, not a bribe. The flowers also brought a smile to her face that cash could not buy.

The woman's "nyet," delivered without eye contact a day earlier, transformed into the stamp I needed. I was desperate and down to my last $300, which was enough for a ticket on the Trans-Siberian railway from Beijing to Moscow. Without a credit card, I didn't have a choice; a ticket from Hong Kong to Los Angeles or San Francisco ran $500. From Moscow I would go by train to Warsaw, then to Berlin, and then somehow, home. It was definitely a long route from Beijing, but it was my only option.

The Soviet visa was the necessary starting point for the succession of visas I needed: first for Mongolia, then Poland, and finally East Germany. I obtained them all in two hours within a few blocks of Beijing's embassy district, an island of European architecture in the city's sea of austere Communist buildings. The area had no bicycles, in contrast to the mass of black bikes throughout the rest of the city. It was a beautiful neighborhood of tree-lined lanes, not in any way like the rest of bustling Beijing.

With visas in hand, the train ticket was an easy purchase: $145 (287.50 renminbi) for the six-day train trip to Moscow. My remaining cash, $140 in a hundred-dollar bill and two twenties, plus Chinese bills totaling about $15, would have to get me from Moscow to Warsaw and then Berlin. The $15 in FEC (Foreign Exchange Certificates), the currency China makes foreigners use in their country, would soon be worthless on the train. I had traded it for regular Chinese renminbi on the black market in cities such as Shanghai, with men of a Muslim minority ethnic group known as Uighurs who were from the autonomous region of Xinjiang, on the edge of the Soviet Union's border with China, near Pakistan.

The exchanges had allowed me to stay in China longer than I could have using the FEC alone, which would have confined my spending to foreigners' venues like expensive hotels. I would not have been able to buy from the street food stalls and neighborhood restaurants I loved and depended on. Once I got to Germany, I planned to sleep in parks I knew in Munich or Frankfurt. I would find a one-way flight from Europe, I hoped, for under $150. But first I had to get through Mongolia and the Soviet Union.

Six days and five time zones to Moscow. Then two days to Berlin through Warsaw. Eight days and eight nights on the train: this was the bargain I loved trains for—the opportunity to both move and sleep safely, a hotel on wheels. I kept my cash, train ticket, and passport stuffed in a pouch down the front of my pants. This security I had learned the hard way. Once, sleeping on a beach in Sitges, Spain, I lost my backpack, which held everything but the clothes I was sleeping in. A beloved bicycle was stolen another time, and my only shoes disappeared in China. I lost them all in different countries, inches away from where I slept. So I learned to sleep in safe or hidden places, with my shoes on, an arm wrapped around what I could not lose, like a backpack, bike, or skis, and my passport and money hidden in my pants.

But I needed the train for more than cheap travel and a safe place to sleep. After two months of freedom, traveling alone during the winter in a Communist land, I craved the camaraderie and human connection that I found lacking in China as a non-Mandarin speaker. Except for meeting a traveler, occasionally, and Jeff in Chengdu, I had gone weeks without saying more than a handful of practical Chinese words and phrases. The Chinese trains, however, had offered more connection than I found anywhere else in China.

In the forced proximity, boundaries between people gradually broke down. I would show people sitting next to me a photo of my family, a map, or my passport. They would pass around to each other whatever I had handed them. Words in Chinese, smiles, modest understanding, and something shared.

But then the train would stop, and people raced from train to platform like floodwater, dispersing in all directions. And I'd start all over, again and again, meeting people on the train, barely saying hello before saying good-bye, and accepting as I stood on the train platform alone that I would never see those people again, their faces then as real as the sun but becoming a blur as soon after they departed.

I had been alone too long. I had spent two months moving among strangers, free to observe, undistracted by a traveling companion, or shopping for anything but food. I had anticipated that it would be much like an extended backpacking journey in the wilderness, alone with no rules or negotiations, just me finding my way. But not sharing experiences, stories, or questions with anyone for this long had taken something out of me. Being confined to my own interpretations of all that I was seeing gradually became less satisfying, more of an endurance stunt. I was bored with myself. I began to understand how hermits could go crazy. I needed to talk to someone, anyone. The train was my solution, and it fit my budget.

The Trans-Siberian's route is the longest in the world. It is 8,000 kilometers from Beijing to Moscow, then another 1,900 to Berlin. I calculated that it is the same as three round trips from Laramie to Eugene, Oregon, where I would go to see Jennifer as soon as I could get on US soil. I was attracted to being contained on a predictable course with a start and an end.

The platform of the Trans-Siberian Railroad is unlike that of any other train station in China. For one thing, there are few Chinese people, and none of the typical Chinese assemblage of chickens, vegetables, and bundles of goods. No one pushes or jostles to get on board. People of all shapes and dress carry large suitcases, chests, boxes. No passenger is traveling without multiple bags except me. Everyone keeps to themselves, focused as if on a mission.

I smell perfume, then a draft of cigarette smoke that smells of herbs, unlike the searing black smoke that engulfs other Chinese train stations.

I notice Chinese students, all men, and surmise that they are returning to universities in Eastern Europe, because one man carries a duffel bag manufactured in Poland and another bag has a tag with the
word "Praha" (Prague) on it. A few Mongolians, evident by their long
coats, are apparently on a shorter haul from Beijing to Ulaanbaatar,
not insignificant but only 1,553 kilometers from Beijing. I overhear an
Australian and his young family. A skinny British man who looks like a
teenager hauls bags with locks on them. People fumble with their tickets
and seem collectively nervous, as if taking a chance. Maybe some are.
Maybe I am, but I feel calm and ready for the long trip.

I settled into carriage 9, seat 35, in a cabin for four. My cabin
mates included a Polish woman who cried and didn't look up and a
well-dressed Polish man, looking like a diplomat in a suit and tie, who
had brought aboard two large bags that took all the storage space. He
fidgeted and, after a quick hello, did not talk with the Polish woman or
with me. The fourth seat was empty.

Most of the passengers stayed in their cabins for much of the half
day it took us get to the China-Mongolia border. We traveled alongside
the Great Wall for about fifteen minutes, as the track swept close on a
long bend. The sight brought people into the corridor that ran down the
length of the cabins on one side of the train. After we passed it, the train
huffed forward toward Ulaanbaatar and people settled back in their
cabins and rested.

As we approached Ulaanbaatar, the conductor banged open our
door with the force of authority and started sorting through the baggage
stored above the door, a space for large luggage.

"These yours?" he asked as he gestured to me, opening a duffel bag
stuffed with tennis rackets and chocolate.

The Polish man nodded quickly to me from behind the conductor.

"Yes," I said, acting on instinct. The conductor grunted and left. The
Polish man pulled out his wallet and handed me a note of Mongolian
currency. He opened the duffel to show me the tennis rackets and chocolate and shrugged. We arrived in Ulaanbaatar shortly afterward, and
he raced off the train with his duffel and gave me a quick wave, almost a
salute, from the platform. Behind him was a huge paneled billboard, like
an advertisement, that featured the painted faces of Karl Marx, Friedrich Engels, and Vladimir Lenin looking over the train station. I would

The Trans-Siberian train passing the Great Wall of China, 1985.

see images of those three men in various sizes, always hand painted, at train stations along the entire route. From the corridor, where I observed the station, there was a break in the train's movement, a pause in the churning of the train that gave me the opportunity to feel as if things had stopped for a moment, a deep breath on the Trans-Siberian's long route. But when I turned back to my cabin, I discovered that the Polish woman had disappeared. I didn't see her leave and had not seen her on the platform. Was she with the tennis racket smuggler?

Her long dark hair had draped over much of her face and she was, I sensed, elegant, though worn down, her face white but for her red eyes. I wished I had been more open with her, but she had seldom looked up and was now gone. The train, with the addition of another engine, started picking up its pace as we left Ulaanbaatar.

Alone again, I started walking the length of the train, down the corridors and through the banging doors between carriages. Each carriage felt like a new place, almost like a new nation, each expressing the character of the loudest person standing in the corridor. Most of the doors to cabins were closed to the corridor, a trail in the wilderness that I darted through.

I had no idea of the value of the Mongolian currency the Pole had given me until I entered the dining carriage that evening and ordered dinner as the train neared the border between Mongolia and the Soviet

Union. It was too large a denomination for the waitress who brought me my dinner to accept. She took a step back from my table and harangued me in Russian. She did not seem to be a happy person in general and was less so because of the large note I had offered. She apparently had little Mongolian currency and would not exchange it for Soviet rubles. I could buy anything I wanted with the money, but it was clear I was not getting my change in rubles.

"Nyet rubles," she said, wagging her finger at me.

My Mongolian money would become useless at the Mongolian-Soviet border, which we were approaching in a matter of minutes, so I added a bottle of vodka to my tab. This was still not enough to spend down what was owed me. So I ordered a second bottle of vodka and then offered to pay for the dinner of three women I had overheard speaking English at the other end of the dining carriage. The prospect of having useless denominations of currency induced my spurt of generosity. After the waitress, who seemed to be the boss of the dining carriage, walked to the end of the carriage and motioned to me, one of the women walked up to me. "Why are you buying us dinner?" she asked.

"My name is John," I said, reaching out to shake her hand. "You speak English and I have Mongolian cash I need to spend now," I explained.

"Robin," she said and shook my hand. "Well, thanks, but my friends are very uncomfortable with this."

The waitress took the money.

"Why are you uncomfortable?" I asked.

"We work for Senator Bill Bradley," she said.

"The New York Knicks basketball player?" I asked.

"The US senator from New Jersey," she corrected me with a quick smile; then she left for her table with her New Jersey coworkers as the stern and sturdy dining carriage waitress-boss returned.

The woman, who had grown even more severe since our first encounter, handed me my change—two Mongolian bills that, I finally accepted, would be bookmarks. She also pointed to the two bottles of vodka I had purchased and said "dobro, dobro," which I understood as "good," because she nodded with approval as she spoke.

I soon discovered why my purchase was so "dobro." At the Soviet border, the Trans-Siberian became a dry ride with no vodka or any other liquor, even beer, available for sale. This strict condition was enforced on the sale, but not the consumption, of alcohol and had apparently been made in response to problems related to drinking and associated drunken behavior on all Soviet trains.

I hadn't known about the dry rule, but now I understood the caches of beer I had seen a few people bringing onto the train in Beijing.

The situation had come to "unfairly represent the country as a nation of drunks," according to a British diplomatic mail courier, the young man with wild hair I had seen boarding the train in Beijing and whom I met in the dining carriage. He told me he made this journey regularly, carrying documents from China to Moscow on behalf of the British Embassy. He said he was "sort of posted in Moscow." He had seen fights, vomit, and assorted poor behavior from both men and women on his previous Trans-Siberian trips.

"Are they a nation of drunks?" I asked.

"Of course," he said. "It's the vodka. But I like beer better than Russian vodka," he added. "That is why I have beer in my cabin. I buy it in Beijing. Come by," he offered.

"I will," I told the Brit and shook his hand.

My vodka proved to be valuable the following day when we crossed into the Soviet Union. The dining car was changed at the border from a Mongolian to a Soviet carriage, though it was staffed by the same Soviet attendants. But the Soviet carriage was shy of food, even borscht, which is supposed to be a national staple. A hearty deep red with beets and meat in Mongolia, it was diluted to a pale pink broth as we moved into the Soviet Union. I had no rubles, so I donated a bottle of my vodka to the kitchen crew via the same server who had sold it to me the day before. She raised her eyebrows and took the bottle to the cooks. That trade provided me and those sitting with me—a German student traveling home from China and my beer friend, the skinny and disheveled British courier—with a bowl of borscht on the house for dinner that night and, the next morning, semolina cereal for breakfast, a meal they otherwise offered only to the Australian children. I was happy to be eating for free but dismayed to see the train's supplies growing thinner by the hour.

Later that day, we stopped at the city-town of Ulan-Ude, where the train moved from the Trans-Mongolian route onto the main cross-nation route, the Trans-Siberian. We were two days from Beijing and not close to halfway to Moscow. As I watched the workers add another dining carriage to the train, along with more Soviet passenger cars, I felt sure we would finally get provisions as well. I was wrong.

The Soviet passengers joining the train carried bundles wrapped in cloth and tied with straps for their voyages from one nondescript outpost to another. Past Ulan-Ude and into the southern edge of Siberia, food became so scarce that the dining carriage served only potatoes with nothing but salt. But there was plenty of hot water in the heated urn, or samovar, located in each carriage. If the train's staff was elusive on customer service in every other way, they were diligent about keeping us in hot water.

Three Chinese men in the cabin adjacent to mine were traveling by the Trans-Siberian to universities in Warsaw, Prague, and Paris. Hsu, an English speaker, had found me earlier on the journey in the corridor and wanted to talk in English. He told me he was studying medicine in Paris. The two others were studying engineering but did not speak English, so Hsu translated for them. The men had purchased their own food for the trip: ramen noodles, dried fish, and barbecued pork. This was a financial necessity for them and a lucky break for me, because they shared what they had.

As we ate noodles together, I gathered myself to ask the men what I had planned to ask Hsu when we had first met just outside Beijing. I asked them whether they would consider exchanging the small amount of Chinese FEC currency I had left for rubles. Hsu was happy to take my fifteen dollars in FEC that had the same denominations as Chinese yuan or renminbi, but they cost about 20 percent more with the black-market premium to exchange them for the equivalent Chinese currency. We traded at face value, a transaction that pleased us both. He wanted my FEC because it could be used in stores established for foreigners, the state-owned "Friendship" stores that had specialty foods from the West such as Snickers and Coke, and crafts aimed at foreign travelers. It surprised me, however, that he wanted the FEC while traveling to Europe, where he could not exchange it. It wasn't much money, but it would be valuable to them only months or years later when they returned to China.

Hsu asked me about my travels in China. He seemed fascinated that I had traveled alone without being able to speak Chinese. "How did you get train tickets?" he asked me. I told him I waited in line like everyone else and wrote Chinese characters for my destination and departure date on a piece of paper. He wanted to know why I went to Tibet, and what was there that I cared to see. I told him I wanted to see the people and the land. He did not understand my attraction, but he was pleased that I liked the lake, gardens, and tea in Suzhou and Hangzhou, both small historical cities near his home in Shanghai.

Hsu pressed on, asking me how I could travel alone and without a job. At first, I explained that it wasn't easy financially, but that I traveled on a budget. I added that I traveled alone because I thought I could better experience China that way.

"Good method," he said. "You see more."

The financial means for my travel continued to perplex him, however, and I sensed that my explanation confused or frustrated him, too.

"No school?" he asked.

"University, yes," I told him. "I studied business, finance."

"You do not work business?" he asked. "You are on the train to Berlin?"

"I am traveling for fun. I will work one day," I told Hsu. "I must."

"You must," he concurred.

I left Hsu and maneuvered from car to car up to the first-class carriages to talk with the Americans. I had not seen them again in the dining carriage, and they had not wandered the carriages to the back end of the train. At the door of the first-class carriage near the front of the train, a Soviet woman stepped in front of me, shaking her head. Each carriage had one of these women, dressed in a white apron, looking like a cross between a middle-aged nurse and a plump nun. They cleaned and filled the samovars, monitored their carriages, and generally kept to themselves. But this one was also tasked with keeping others out of the first-class carriage.

I smiled, spoke English, and laughed, pretending she was joking with me. I did a quick fake to the right, then left, and got past her. She didn't fight me and I didn't look back.

Robin met me in the corridor, almost as if she had been waiting for me. She was standing alone and looking out the window in the corridor on the north side of the train. The corridors were like a road between carriages, except for first class, where it was quiet with little traffic.

"Where have you been?" she asked.

"End of the train, past the dining carriage, down several to where the Chinese and Russians are."

"Are we the only other Americans on this train?" she asked.

"Yes, I think so, but there is a British guy, a German, and the Australian family."

Robin explained that they were on vacation, with their arrangements made through the diplomatic connections of their boss, the senator. She seemed proud to be associated with Bradley, and though I had never known a senator outside Wyoming—men who were fathers of friends, men who'd shake your hand at football games—I felt some pride in knowing Bradley just through talking with Robin. She told me about the senator as we looked out the window.

From Robin's stories of his dedication to his young daughter, I began to admire Bill Bradley for more than his politics, which I also heard about from her, and his basketball skills, which I had grown up watching on television. I became convinced over many miles of stories that he would someday be president.

We were passing through the taiga of southern Siberia. The mostly evergreen forest went on and on, its trees still in snow at their bases, but waiting on the front edge of spring with their limbs free of snow. The landscape had not changed for most of the day, as the train passed village after village without stopping. Log homes with worn roofs surrounded by dilapidated fences. Periodic birch trees with peeling bark. Sturdy fir and spruce trees standing tall against the wind and cold. Village churches and homes built of the wood of the forests, covered in coal dust over snow that had melted only slightly and refrozen in layers. Large trucks on rutted, snow-lined roads. Men and women bundled in heavy clothing who glanced at the train, then turned to whatever work they had been doing. Places and faces here and then gone.

"Wild," Robin said.

"Yes," I agreed. "I wish I lived right there," I said, pointing to a home with large shutters that were built to be closed to the cold and ice in winter, but had been opened to the sun.

"Are you crazy? You want to live here?" Robin questioned. "Take a picture instead," she suggested, as she leaned into my shoulder.

"I want to jump off the train to see more," I clarified. "Spend a day or more digging through the ice, uncover a road, shovel coal, cut wood, do any physical work. I want to get off of this train."

But the train didn't stop, and villages passed as if we were watching a film on a movie screen in Laramie showing scenes of the Soviet Union. I craved walking into and touching these beautiful and rough places, lost in the Siberian forest.

The other Bradley women eventually joined us in the corridor. The New Jersey women were, like me, fairly fresh from college. They talked of the politics of Trenton, New Jersey, a place I had never heard of, and Washington, DC.

They were advocates for their state and told me, like travel agents now, that I could take a train from New York City to Philadelphia across a narrow part of New Jersey in a couple of hours. I became enamored with New Jersey, a state they explained was shaped like an hourglass. I saw New Jersey as sand flowing like time from north to south and mentioned this to them.

"That's about right," one of the women said. "The north and south are completely different."

I told them I needed to get home from Europe via New York City, where I thought I could get a cheap flight to Wyoming, or Oregon, where Jennifer lived.

"Newark," the women told me at once. "Go to Newark, not JFK," one of them said. "Take Virgin Atlantic to Newark from London for ninety-nine dollars one way."

I was stunned. Ninety-nine dollars for a one-way ticket? "Beautiful," I said and looked at Robin. "I am going home through New Jersey."

The New Jersey women told me they appreciated the meal I had purchased for them on the second night of the journey and were friendly because of it. But they became uncomfortable when I explained the origin of the cash, coming as it did from the Polish tennis racket smuggler. I could tell that Robin thought the story was interesting, but the other two were not amused and immediately began asking questions.

"Why aren't you traveling in first class?" one of them asked.

I turned from the window to look into their cabin, and I could see dark-red paneled wood with nightstands that held real lamps made of brass. The white drapes and tasseled blinds reminded me of my grandmother's old, clean, and comforting home in Evanston, Wyoming.

"How much was a first-class ticket?" I asked.

"Only twice the price of a regular ticket," she said. "Cheap. Why didn't you go first class?" she asked again.

"Budget," I said.

My soft sleeper-class cabin felt fairly first class to me, especially after Chinese trains, which were always crowded and had a hard-seat class that was just that. There was also a hard-sleeper class on the Trans-Siberian. It was mostly full of Russians, although a few Russians were also in soft-sleeper carriages. The hard-sleeper class, which should have been called the no-sleeper class, was stuffed with smokers who seemed to light up day and night.

The Russians in my carriage didn't seem to care about the poor service that perplexed the rest of the passengers, especially the New Jersey women, and didn't complain about the train's sparse fare. Mostly they stayed in their cabins or the carriage corridor and ate whatever they had brought, which they kept in bags hanging out the windows and in baskets stuffed under their seats. The remainder of the passengers, however, had reached the breaking point in their annoyance over the empty pantry and the dismal and dismissive staff in the dining carriage.

The Soviet men in my carriage shrugged when I tried to explain the problem but offered me a slice of their gelatin-encased pork. They did not seem embarrassed by their compatriots and, I assessed, harbored little nationalism or pride in the Soviet train; they were clearly indifferent to my, or anyone's, poor impressions. They had plenty of food for themselves.

In Irkutsk, a large city near Lake Baikal, the world's largest lake, we saw only a few crates being loaded onto the dining carriage. I sensed we were living off the bleak remnants of the last harvest while traversing the beautiful, wide but cold Siberian landscape. This train was the USSR superpower's pride, connecting the port of Vladivostok to Moscow to St. Petersburg and Europe. How could it not have food?

Food became even more bleak and bland after Irkutsk. The train trip illuminated aspects of Soviet life I could not have imagined in a political science or economics classroom. The women from New Jersey agreed and talked about the politics of the Soviet Union—détente and the changes after Brezhnev died on November 10, 1982. How did they remember that date, I wondered, and scribbled it in my notebook along with other details I learned from them, as if I were in class. They talked about the Warsaw Pact, Yuri Andropov, and names I had never heard of. During this, my first conversation with Americans in months, I felt like the slow student in a class of book-smart overachievers. I tried to turn the conversation to Bruce Springsteen, but they continued to talk about Soviet politics and economics.

I finally put forth some practical Chinese economics to try to counter my ignorance of Soviet politics. I told the women that although I had failed to exchange my FEC for rubles in Beijing, I had traded with a Chinese student on the train named Hsu. I explained the FEC currency and the black-market premium I was able to get in Shanghai, trading with Chinese men from the far west who did not look Chinese but were.

"The area of Xinjiang is south of us now," I explained.

"Black market in China?" one of the women asked.

"China is nothing," I said. "You should see Nepal, if you want to see a black market. The Indian government limits the import of gold from Nepal (and everywhere), but the country has huge demand for gold to use in marriage dowries. The price is extreme, and enterprising Nepalese take advantage of it."

I told them that I had made $800 carrying gold in my hiking boots from Bangkok to Kathmandu for Nepalese businessmen. "And they bought my plane ticket," I bragged.

"Isn't that illegal?" one of them asked.

"Maybe," I responded. "But no one in Nepal cares. No one in Thailand cares either, and who is hurt but some caste in India manipulating the supply and market for gold? I wasn't carrying gold over the Indian border."

"Eight hundred dollars is not worth the risk," one of them said.

"Well, first, it wasn't all that risky," I explained. "And with the extra money, I lived for three months in Nepal and Thailand, with money to spare to keep traveling. I would not be here otherwise," I explained. "I'd be home painting houses or baking bread if I didn't smuggle a little gold."

"Smuggle a little gold," one of the women repeated with a condescending tone. "Where do you draw the line?" It was less a question, I felt, than an accusation. She intimidated me more than the police at the Kathmandu airport.

"With gold," I stated firmly.

I paused for a moment, because that was not my answer. I wasn't traveling train routes and smuggling gold to avoid baking bread in Laramie. I wanted to move in the world, and this was the only way I knew how to travel without spending a fortune. I didn't have a fortune and I didn't work for a senator. I baked bread, waited tables, and painted houses after college so I could do this. Traveling on the cheap was like hitchhiking. It was a practical matter.

Many of my friends from Laramie were doing the same thing, or had been, or would be. Most of us had discovered new options and opportunities for inexpensive travel that we shared with the others when we got home. We also tacked up notes for each other or anyone else on what was the information hub for travelers in Southeast Asia in 1984, a bulletin board on the seventeenth floor of a travelers' hostel at Chung King Mansion in Kowloon, Hong Kong, a cheap, crowded dive that, despite rats and drugs, was like a poor traveler's UN.

Waves of us were leaving Laramie, returning, and leaving Laramie again. I had discovered thirteen others from Laramie in Kathmandu several months earlier. Traveling alone or in pairs, we were all surprised to see each other there. We'd met up and drunk beer on Halloween night. The Laramie crowd included the young, beautiful Stacy, a woman my mom had taught in first grade, and her boyfriend, Chris, a guitar player who was roaming with the same guitar he had played in Laramie coffeehouses. Ted, a guy I waited tables with, was there. And Jeff, whom I baked bread with, was also in Kathmandu with his girlfriend. I was with Jennifer.

"We never left Laramie," my friend Matt Lane said, looking around at us.

I'd had no idea Matt was planning to travel to Nepal. But here he was. He had also smuggled gold from Hong Kong into Nepal by making a cast for his leg, with a tube from midthigh to knee to hide the gold.

He bought us all another round of beer, like he always did in Laramie. The beers came in tall dark bottles imported into Nepal from India. The candles in the room crackled with bugs that were attracted to the light and flew in through the open windows. We had beer that went down easy in the sharing of stories, in a night I wanted to never end.

"Here's to luck and Nepal. And Indian beer," Ted cheered.

"And here's to Laramie," someone added.

"Laramie," everyone said to the clank of beer bottles.

I had felt resourceful and on top of the world in Nepal. But now, traveling alone, months after I'd secured my stash of cash, calculating how I was going to best use what little money I had left, my confidence in myself and my options was waning, and the scrutiny of smart women from New Jersey wasn't helping.

"Look," I finally said to the women, "people and gold and vodka, like wind and like water, will always keep moving beyond political borders, somehow and eventually."

Not twelve hours later, facing sparse dinner fare for another day, the women were beginning to accept that their economic intelligence, like that of the average Soviet bureaucrat or train worker, was not suited for following the Soviet government's rule book.

They had convened in the empty dining carriage and allowed me and my scruffy British friend to listen to their ethical dilemma. They finally agreed that "breaking the law" was acceptable given the circumstances. Breaking the law for them meant allowing me to get off the train at stops—which was supposed to be a no-no without a visa and generally unwise in other ways—to buy something edible. There had been vendors at most of the train platforms, though they sold only stale biscuits, hard candy, and tea.

The women and a few hungry others encouraged me to make quick forays to search for food. I was antsy on the train anyway, tired of walking the length of it and wanting to get some exercise. I also wanted to see more of the towns and the few cities we had been passing through. I judged from previous stops that the Trans-Siberian halted for three to five minutes at each station, and sometimes as long as twenty minutes in larger cities. Fortunately, the New Jersey women had small ruble bills, a prudent part of their trip planning that I had failed to think of in Beijing. I had only what little Soviet currency Hsu had exchanged with me.

My first run at the city of Krasnoyarsk produced a loaf of dark bread, yogurt, hard cheese, and smoked fish, preserved since summer from Lake Baikal. The prices were modest, if not immaterial, to everyone who gave me small bills to buy them whatever I could find. I began to run at each stop. The circumstances at the end of winter in most Siberian towns provided few food choices, however; the smoke-filled villages with crusty snow covered in coal dust were usually as empty of food as the train.

Nevertheless, it became a sport. Whether I found food or not, my runs though towns and cities in the wintry Siberian landscape were a thrill. Then they became a necessity, not for food but for the runs themselves. I had trouble being in the train all day. I wanted most to be in the forests we were traversing, or in the small struggling hamlets we passed. Siberia looked like the Old West railroad towns in Wyoming, with coal stoves and people digging snow or dirt, sawing wood, pounding sledgehammers, like the landscape I knew at home, like towns around Laramie, like Hanna, Centennial, and Rock River. It was all familiar to me, the patched-together homes with wooden doors, wind-worn and worn-out vehicles in dirty snow. As the miles passed, I saw Wyoming over and over and, for the first time in months, felt the pull to be home.

Then the train would stop and I would run and find some dingy kiosk or store with root vegetables, noodles, hard candy, or if I was lucky, the beautiful dark bread.

The Soviet men in my carriage began to appreciate my dashes into the towns. "Dogonya, dogonya!" they hollered out the window at me. None of them joined me. I doubt they could run very fast, and even if they could, I knew they thought the act was ridiculous, maybe pointless and undignified, but certainly amusing. I wanted to run alone, anyway. I began to live for the leap off the train and for the fast dash. I ran every time the train stopped.

Playing carefully with train politics, which were overseen by the Soviet attendants in white uniforms, I returned to the train after each sortie to show the boss what I had purchased. I didn't have a choice. She waited for me at the door of the train. She was looking, I believed, for alcohol, and never took anything from me. I would then take the men something of what I had purchased. They would slap me on the back and offer me eggs and pork paste.

Much of what I brought back, especially the hefty dark bread, was the perfect supplement to the Russians' pork paste, a greasy pâté they called holodetc, which apparently needed only the refrigeration provided from hanging the bags out the window. The men also had hard-boiled eggs, which they produced from the storage spaces beneath their seats. They had an endless stash of them, which made me wonder whether they had known we would be short of food or had brought their own to avoid paying for it in the dining carriage. I declined the eggs, but their holodetc went well with the bread and the vodka I shared with them.

The Soviet women, on the other hand, grew progressively displeased. They stayed at one end of the carriage, mostly in their cabins, while the men roamed the corridor, looking out the windows and smoking. My New Jersey friends, like the Soviet women, would have nothing to do with these men and their holodetc pork gelatin and vodka.

The men were lovable and swinelike, I had to admit, particularly toward the end of the day, and more and more as the days wore on. They walked the carriage in their underwear and smoked, drank, spit, and smiled. I liked them. They were physical and friendly with me. Firm handshakes, hard slaps on the back, and punches on the shoulder after my runs. They did the same with each other. They laughed. They yelled. I sensed they were making fun of me most of the time, but I liked that, too, coming from winter-whitened men standing around in their underwear, smoking like overheated incandescent lightbulbs.

"Whoop, whoop," they yelled.

I jumped off the train again in Novosibirsk and almost got lost circling an extra block that had more to see than our other stops. The train stayed longer than usual, maybe twenty minutes, and I leaped from the platform back onto the train as it started moving, its door remaining open while the train rolled. I was exhilarated, relieved. My friends in their underwear howled like I had scored a goal at a hockey game.

The men never managed to pull any money out of their pockets, however, and I never asked them for any. But eventually, my sharing with them became a point of contention for the New Jersey women, because they were bankrolling my runs. They would not eat the pork products in yellow plastic bags. It became clear that it was not the pork itself but the unsavory men who ate the pork that made the food unpalatable.

Then, before I was forced to selectively distribute food, to our amazement, the dining carriage reopened. The restocking of the train satisfied everyone's appetites and put the conflict to rest. I guessed that Novosibirsk was the place that had finally allowed the dining carriage to replenish its inventory of potatoes, beets, bread, kefir, yogurt, and meat, as I had seen more food there.

The staff became moderately friendly with the first meal they served, before degenerating to their earlier habits, stomping around and somehow unable to hear. The senator's staff couldn't have been happier with the carrots in our soup, and I was relieved not to be bartering food between the various appetites and attitudes on the train.

We passed an obelisk in the town of Sverdlovsk, in the Ural Mountains, which marked the end of Asia and the start of Europe. The obelisk was beautiful but appeared to exist in isolation, representing a transition that had no corroborating physical evidence in the landscape, a monument in a forest passed only by a train and wild animals.

Senator Bradley's women of New Jersey told me of their itinerary in Moscow, arrangements I envied. Moscow was still over 1,500 kilometers away, about a day, but was becoming a magnet for us all. They would be met at the Moscow train station by US Embassy staff and taken to a hotel, their reservation prearranged. No one but the people I had met on the train even knew I was on the Trans-Siberian Railroad. My family probably thought I was still in China. But I planned to call home on my birthday, in April, once I was in Europe.

The train got to Moscow the next morning. The city seemed huge, judging by the time it took to get to the main train station from the edge of the metropolis. We pulled into the Moscow station and as soon as the doors opened, the passengers left the station fast, just as they do everywhere—like water through a broken dam. Quick good-byes, no good-byes, glances, waves, a hug here and there, and just like that, I was alone again.

I navigated to the city's subway system, which is deep, deep underground. "Bombproof," the New Jersey women explained before they departed. The subway was clean, quiet, and meticulously constructed. I finally saw Superpower. In the city center, Moscow's subway is like a museum, with art, statues, ornate tile, and marble floors, and is absolutely free of graffiti or litter.

Eventually, though, someone in Moscow will try to buy the pants right off your body. My opportunity happened ten minutes after coming to the top of an escalator out of the subway, an ascent that went on and on, taking many minutes to get to the city level from the subway's depth. I was wearing worn red Patagonia pants and had a pair of Levi's jeans in my pack.

A man near the exit pointed at my pants and flashed cash. I asked to see all the cash. He obliged and even let me hold it. This is the man to have a transaction with, I decided. It was a lot of money in rubles, maybe over one hundred dollars' worth. I held up two fingers, indicating that I had another pair of pants. He pulled out more cash and directed me to a side street just down from a huge glassed-in shopping mall. He pointed to the mall and handed me a few smaller ruble bills, acting on faith that I would buy new pants and return to sell him the ones I wore.

I bought a pair of wool pants in a shop in this enormous mall, which looked more like something in Paris or Hong Kong than anything I had seen thus far in the Soviet Union or China. I liked my new pants, which were of far better quality than what I was selling. I sold both pairs of my worn pants to the man in a quick flash of cash, and he stuffed them into a briefcase. With about $200 worth of rubles in my pocket, which was many times what I had paid for the pants back home, I considered getting a room, a shower, and a nice dinner. I felt instantly rich and deserving of a good night in Moscow.

I decided to go to the Hotel Mockba, where the New Jersey women were staying. It was large, glimmering, clean, and close to Vasily Blazhenny Cathedral in Red Square. The hotel had the look and location to accommodate foreign dignitaries, famous ballet dancers, and diplomats. I was desperate to stay there for the experience of it more than the obvious comfort. I talked with the women from New Jersey, whom I found in the lobby, about staying there, and Robin suggested I stay in her room, a nice gesture that the other two immediately vetoed.

"You cannot do that," one of them said to Robin, though Robin had a room to herself.

"Nyet," the woman at the hotel desk then told me when I inquired about getting my own room.

I had no reservation, which was a problem. She turned to another person at the front desk for guidance, though it was clear from the nearly empty lobby that the hotel had plenty of available rooms. Her coworker and then another talked, went back to paperwork, came back together and talked again, looking over at me periodically and, it appeared, having nothing else important to do while they talked and looked at me for over an hour. That I had only a transit visa was another, larger issue, one that I did not disclose to her, and I knew she would eventually check my passport. A regular tourist visa required that you spend a minimum of $50 per day, and I would have had to obtain one back in Beijing, when I only had $140. But now I had rubles.

I pulled out the rubles and offered to pay the woman at the Hotel Mockba reception desk.

"Nyet," she repeated.

I wished I had roses or another pair of pants. I left the hotel and decided to do what I could, which was to walk the streets of central Moscow into the evening. As night fell, I circled the same blocks, cold now, burning time and jumping up and down now and then to keep warm. No one approached me. Few people were out, and those who were I avoided. I sensed that it would be unwise to be discovered without a visa. But I had a story and ran through my explanation over and over: "I missed the train. I have no room. I am alone. I leave for Warsaw tomorrow."

I walked back into the hotel after midnight and quietly slid onto a bench near a dark side-exit I had scoped out earlier in the day. I thought about the rooms upstairs and Robin sleeping on white sheets. I didn't need clean sheets, but I had wanted to experience the hotel beyond the bench, though the bench was a blessing on a cold night in early April.

Early the next morning, I raced out of the Hotel Mockba, wishing I could say good-bye to Robin. I went straight to the train station, where I exchanged my rubles and pocketed Polish zloty. My two pairs of pants turned into a bundle of cash that I would now need to use in Poland, where I also had only a transit visa. The train and the carriages were like the Trans-Siberian, four people to a room with bench seats that turned into beds, and an upper shelf on either side that folded down to make two upper bunks. I had a cabin with one other traveler, a Chinese man who, like Hsu on the Trans-Siberian, was returning to college, in his case to Warsaw. My bed was comfortable; I was exhausted and fell asleep immediately as the train left Moscow.

I felt the train stop in the middle of the night, the clank against the rails and the screech of the brakes, sounds you learn to identify after traveling on trains. I awoke with the sensation of moving up, not forward. I got out of bed and looked out the window. We were in a building, and the train was indeed high above the ground.

"Gauge change," my cabinmate told me. He had been on the route before and spoke English and Polish and probably Russian. He was not curious and was less conversational than Hsu, so we had talked little.

Out the window, I could see that we were not in a station but in a warehouse. Men with rolling jacks, like those that lift a truck with a flat tire but several times as large and on wheels, moved from carriage to carriage as if on a factory assembly line. And like that, in the middle of the night, we were down and moving toward Warsaw. The night work of the railway men would have been easy to sleep through, but now I was wide awake, thinking how the change in the width of the rails, starting in this place, was once a principal strategy of the USSR in World War II to prevent the use of the rail routes from Poland into the Soviet Union. I might have easily slept through the place that was once the chief impediment to Nazi expansion to the East.

We passed another obelisk, a larger one, marking the end of the Soviet Union and the start of Europe, just as the obelisk in Sverdlovsk had marked the end of Asia and the start of Europe. We were now on the narrower gauge that could take us through all of Europe.

By noon we were in Warsaw, a city of smoking taxis and horse-drawn buggies, both parked at the train station. With my transit visa, I had most of the day to kill before my train left for Berlin. And I had a pile of local currency. I considered exchanging it for deutsche marks, but the commission would eat too much of the cash, and I was planning to get to West Berlin, not stay in the East, so I wouldn't need East German currency. I looked around the station for something to buy, but I did not need or want fine crystal glasses or the vases that seemed to be everywhere. My birthday was the following day, so I decided to splurge on a horse-drawn ride around Warsaw. The city was sunny and in bloom in early April. Spring was coming and I couldn't wait for it. Thrilled with the sun and headed home, I took a buggy tour of the city.

We circled old streets, around buildings reconstructed after World War II and newer ones reflecting spiritless but functional Communist architecture, and into a central square where the buggy waited while I ate lunch at what the driver indicated was the finest restaurant in Warsaw. If it wasn't the finest, it should have been. I ate meat and cheeses, drank wine, and indulged in a huge dessert crepe with honey, cream, and chocolate.

Back at the station, with Polish zloty left in my pocket, I pressed the remainder of my cash into the horseman's palm. The money was some multiple of what the ride was supposed to cost me. The remaining cash from my two pairs of old pants probably paid his living expenses for a few months. I shrugged. He nodded, a man doing what he did and doing it well. He barely smiled but held my hand for a long moment as we shook hands. I felt as if he saw right through the exchange. I was poor; that was evident in everything but the cash and my new Russian pants. He was poor, maybe, because he did not have a car and had no customers but me. But I had money I could use for nothing but a gift. He turned from me to his horse. Poland was behind me.

I left for Berlin with exactly the same amount of money I had left Beijing with over a week earlier. I was a rich man with $145 in my pocket and a route to the Berlin Wall, where I planned to walk to Checkpoint Charlie. I thought I could cross there, which turned out to be a naive plan. The American flag flew not fifty yards away, a sight that surprised me. I started toward a gate with a kiosk where men held guns. They did not look at my passport. Instead, they waved me away and back toward the train station. They shook their heads while eyeing me and said nothing. I walked back to the station and passed without scrutiny or cost from East to West Berlin, then by train to Munich, then by thumb to London, then by a ninety-nine-dollar one-way flight through Newark, and a slow route home by short-hop flights and by bus. I spent the night of my twenty-sixth birthday, the eve of Easter Sunday, sleeping in bushes in a Munich park called the Englischer Garten. I made it home with thirty-seven cents in my pocket.

5

The High Road

EIGHT MONTHS AFTER I HAD LEFT EUGENE with Jennifer, I was back in Eugene with her, arriving with small change in my pocket and a plan to go back to Tibet. She had managed, during my time traveling, to fabricate that we were married and had secured cheap accommodations in the university's family housing, a pleasant maze of World War II–era grounds filled with grass and the children of graduate students. It was perfect for us, and we quickly made friends with other students, most of whom were our age and had children. I could see Jennifer's heart wander to the children we met. Mine did, too. We shared a vision of having children together. Jennifer didn't fault me for not returning earlier, and while we both knew the truth that we had aimed to be parents together, we accepted that the timing was wrong for both of us.

I began painting houses and selling Nepali earrings, which I had carried for months, at sorority houses. I visited Pema's pawnshop to tell him I had followed his advice to trek around Annapurna. I mentioned that I had gone to Tibet and was planning another trip there.

Pema walked to the front door. "I will return soon," he said as he locked the pawnshop door behind him. I looked around the shelves of his shop, where everything was either useless or valuable or both, depending on life's circumstances. But today I had no taste for the interesting clutter. I was not selling anything and needed nothing in the pawnshop. I sat down on a couch near the back of the shop and thought about my time in Tibet.

The door opened and closed with a thud. Pema locked it from the inside and set a bag of tea on the table. He picked up loose tea with his hand, placed it into a metal pot, and moved the pot to a small electric burner he had taken off a shelf.

"Tell me a story," Pema finally said. "Something from Tibet."

With the pawnshop door locked, I felt something building in Pema during his precise procedures with the tea. He kept his head down as he watched it come to a boil. He rose, poured my tea and then his own, and settled the pot on the table before sitting calmly, looking me in the eye as he picked up his cup.

"Give me a story," he repeated.

"I'll tell you something," I said. "I saw men feeding the dead to birds. To vultures on the northern edge of Lhasa at sunrise."

"I know those birds," Pema said. "They come to take us back. They bury us in the sky."

Pema explained the ceremony to me as if he had been there. But he had never seen a sky burial. Few do. No families, no friends. Only the rising sun, a small group of men, and the birds.

"Those birds come to the hill behind the monastery," he said.

"What monastery?" I asked.

"Drepung." Pema told me that he had once lived in such a monastery in Tibet, given to the monks by his mother when he was a boy. Many families allowed one son to be in the monastery, he explained. He was placed there when he was five years old, and this was when I learned of his walk through the mountains on the Tibet-Nepal border with the Dalai Lama.

"Nineteen fifty-nine," Pema said. "Long ago." He laughed and said he did not know dates back then. "I knew many things but not the time, day, month, or year," he said.

Little information had escaped or entered the remote land during centuries of geographic isolation. Then the Chinese invaded, first in 1950, followed by a final clampdown of its borders in 1959 that cut Tibet off from the world. Until 1984, only a handful of people—mostly climbers able to pay high prices and willing to endure choreographed itineraries—had made it into Tibet.

Pema told me how he had moved from his home with the Dalai Lama in Dharamsala, India, to Nepal, where he worked guiding foreigners (usually Americans, he explained with a wink) on treks. Now he was selling used everything to college students in a small American town.

"I have photos of Drepung," I told Pema. I promised to return the following day with photos I had taken in and near Lhasa.

I came back the next day and spread the photos on a large wooden table Pema had cleared of the clutter of kitchen utensils. He touched and studied each one slowly and intensely before moving to the next. He ignored his customers and stopped joking with me. Eventually, he asked whether he could borrow the photos. I agreed and told him I was planning to return to Tibet in a month: six of us from Laramie—two teachers, two carpenters, and two bread bakers—to ride our mountain bikes from Lhasa to Kathmandu.

"China," Pema said. "They will never let you," he said. "Never."

Undeterred by my experience with altitude sickness, I began discussing the logistics of traveling by bicycle to Nepal via Tibet with my friend Jeff back in Laramie. I could find no precedent for gaining permission for such a trip, and I suspected the Chinese government would never sanction it. The availability of food and water in Tibet concerned me, too, but the uncertainty of navigating the Communist bureaucracy loomed larger than the altitude.

With slim prospects of pulling off such a trip, Jeff was already scheming. After we had met in Chengdu, he managed to travel by hired minivan from Lhasa to the Tibet-Nepal border—so he knew the route I wanted to take. We compared notes at Jeffrey's Bistro in Laramie, where we had both baked bread over the years.

Jeff was a bread baker who traveled. Or, more precisely, a traveler who baked. He wanted to write and was constructing a vision of making a living baking, writing, and traveling. He had the skill of blending into places without being noticed—even in Laramie. He grew up a few blocks away from my home, but I had never seen him and didn't meet him until we baked together after college. If Jeff was overlooked in Laramie, his way of keeping a low profile served him well as a traveler. He maneuvered Communist bureaucracies, dangerous borders, and obscure roads as easily as he could come and go from a small Wyoming town.

With years of traveling informing his strategy, he knew how to turn a short trip into a long journey. Jeff had taken watches to the Philippines, smuggled gold into Nepal, and always carried a bottle of Johnnie Walker or Jameson for trade in whatever circumstance it might be beneficial—like crossing a border at night with sketchy, incomplete travel documents, or avoiding a search.

"A bottle of Johnnie Walker equals no search," he once told me.

From his time traveling the interior of Southeast Asia, Jeff had learned that a stack of officially stamped paper—regardless of what was written on it, or in what language it was written—was as good as, if not better than a single verifiable approval. He knew we could not gain specific approval to bicycle across Tibet without giving up time and the serious money that climbing expeditions pay, and maybe not even then.

I did not have the patience to plan such a trip. But I had Jeff. I trusted he could somehow figure out how to get us into Tibet with bicycles. With Jeff at the helm, a team of six formed over the summer: three natives and three who had landed in Laramie, all of us itching to move. We all had Laramie in common, and that was enough to form an expedition team.

Stories are currency in Laramie. Stories of journeys are what count the most, like tales of a last trip into the woods or somewhere in the world. They were all stories to be built upon, like the history of people who arrived in Laramie before the railroad. Like Jacques La Ramée, a French trapper after whom our home—a former seasonal camp area for various native tribes, turned railroad town, turned university hamlet—was named.

In the Buckhorn Bar, you'll hear the one-line philosophers: "You can leave Laramie, but Laramie will never leave you." "Laramie has just enough missing to push you out and just enough good to keep you coming back." The young, just like the old-timers from whom you'd expect these words, say such things in Laramie, adhering to a story line of a place built on a path to somewhere else.

Jeff had constructed a story, and a path, for himself. He studied English and wrote his master's thesis at the University of Wyoming about bread baking as a metaphor for home and exploration. The thesis was a wandering essay about yeast, flour, and travel that alluded to the inspiration of an unnamed drug. It was good enough to earn Jeff his degree, though if such writing tends to gather dust on a shelf, Jeff's thesis was a plan to travel and learn, and to learn to travel.

I understood it best one night at his house with a group he had invited over for dinner. He and his girlfriend had baked fresh, hot bread and had scrounged everything on the dinner table from a dumpster behind the Safeway store two blocks away. This included a bouquet of flowers. He made a meal from discarded food but augmented it with spices he had brought home from his travels. Jeff told us stories of the ground spices he kept in glass jars. He told us how he had created our feast from notes taken on the road in Nepal, Thailand, the Philippines, and China. We all agreed it was one of the best meals we had ever had. With stories of his travels as currency, Jeff was a wealthy man that night—over a dinner he had paid no money to prepare.

By the end of the summer, with Jeff's guidance, we had aggregated six stamped documents—none of which gave us permission to bicycle across Tibet, but which in sum could be taken as permission, should it come to that with officials in China. We each got a three-month Chinese visa and permits that allowed travel in a "B" restricted travel region of China, including Lhasa, but not the rest of Tibet. We each also had a Nepalese visa, an exit permit to leave Tibet by road (without travel means identified), a piece of paper that allowed us to exit China from a different place than the one we entered, and documentation of our bicycles, which focused on preventing us from selling them in China. The combination of papers, Jeff assured us, would convince or confuse the police, military, or public security officials who would surely stop us.

■ ■ ■

I returned to Eugene and visited Pema at his pawnshop to pick up my photos of Lhasa. Pema said, "I have a letter for you to take." He had apparently suspended his doubt that the Chinese would allow me into Tibet on a bicycle. Or hope had taken over his skepticism.

He had also drawn a map of an area he had lived in as a young boy. "A day's walk from Lhasa," he said. It was a place he called Nedong Chukawa. The letter, Pema informed me, was for his mother, whom he had neither seen nor had contact with since 1959. He did not know whether she was still in Nedong Chukawa, or even whether she still lived.

Along with the letter, which he had put in an envelope with her name written in Tibetan on the outside, Pema gave me photos of himself and a gold watch to give her. I left Pema with a mission to find his mother.

I felt an obligation that distracted me from the concern I had had for what we would face in Tibet—like finding drinkable water and fighting altitude sickness while cycling above twelve thousand feet for six hundred or so miles.

It was improbable that I would be able to locate her, but I could not bring myself to tell Pema my doubts. And he did not share his own, which he surely must have had. It would be an unlikely journey within an unlikely journey.

We flew into the Lhasa airport six months after my last visit and gathered our bikes, which were still in the boxes from the manufacturer that had sponsored us. Lhasa is the lowest point on the high road across the Tibetan Plateau to Kathmandu.

In the intervening months, the Chinese had put their touches on the airport, with the same square corners and cement austerity of their architecture nationwide. There was no indication of the culture or colors of the country. The Chinese were also putting pressure on the Tibetans in less subtle ways. I met a Chinese geothermal engineer on the bus ride into Lhasa. He spoke English, which was a skill I welcomed—but which made me wary of him, too, especially when he informed me that the Chinese would soon control this land's electric power potential. He explained that after working for two years he had received six months of leave to return home, paid by the government.

"I hate this place. Look at it," he said, sweeping his arms toward the window. The Tibetan landscape is wind worn and isolated by a high-altitude plateau edged by the highest mountain ranges of the world: the Karakoram to the west, gorges and forests to the east, raw distance in every direction. The Himalayas south of Lhasa outline the border with Nepal, a craggy white fence that appears impenetrable from a distance. "This land is behind. But the money, for my family, it is worth it for me. The geothermal potential," the man added, "is unstoppable."

The likely prospect of having our travel intentions scrutinized and our mountain bikes confiscated weighed on us. We were taking our chances and we knew it: six Americans without permission to bicycle in Tibet, but carrying new mountain bikes donated by an American company that manufactured them in Taiwan, a detail we had belatedly realized needed to be scraped off our bike boxes before Chinese security inspections at the airport. We were just one step or stumble ahead of the authorities. We made it out of the airport, but the Chinese in blue Jeeps were everywhere on the road into Lhasa.

We packed into the Snowland Hotel, a hostel-like compound with a sunny courtyard and shared outhouse. We put our bikes together, sorted bags of gear, and began riding in the hills around the city to acclimate to the altitude. Between Lhasa and Kathmandu are five passes rising to nearly nineteen thousand feet. The altitude worried me. What would I do—in fact what could I do—if headaches hit me on the road, as they had on my last trip? I kept my worries to myself, not wanting to admit that I had been worn down and maybe on the edge of death the last time I was in Tibet.

While the rest of us had flown to Tibet from Hong Kong via Chengdu, Jeff had traveled overland from Hong Kong to Guangzhou to exchange dollars for the currency China requires foreigners to use, the FEC. The FEC, however, maintained a black-market premium to the equivalent Chinese currency. Working the arbitrage opportunity, Jeff took the FEC in exchange for a greater number of renminbi. He then took the Chinese renminbi to Lhasa to exchange for Nepali rupees with men desperate to unload the rupees they had earned selling Chinese cigarettes and matches in Nepal. He planned to work the black market between rupees and dollars one last time once we got to Kathmandu; his profit from the four currency exchanges would pay for his plane ticket (with some dollars to spare).

I roamed the streets of Lhasa searching for food we'd need on the ride, while Jeff was trading currencies and counting and bundling his money, all worn and dirty bills in low denominations. Once he joined us in Lhasa, he would stuff one of his four panniers with rupees.

■ ■ ■

Finding Pema's mother was another improbable pursuit. But dreamers could find their compatriots in the early days of independent travel in Tibet, and I met Linda Bella Lau. Twenty-eight-year-old Linda was from Hong Kong and traveling solo. She spoke good English, liked my story about Pema, and agreed on the spot to help me find his mother.

First we found a driver who spoke Chinese and Tibetan and hired him and his rickety old van. Unfortunately, no one we met in Lhasa had heard of Nedong Chukawa, the place Pema had told me was his home. But we headed downstream along the Tsangpo River anyway, following Pema's vague directions that his home was a day's walk from Lhasa and not far from the river. After an hour, we crossed a bridge over the river and went up a valley to the southeast, operating on instinct alone, and found trees and pastures. After we asked Chinese people living along the road, it became clear that Nedong Chukawa was a name that predated the Chinese presence. We needed to find old Tibetans to help us locate it. And even if we could discover this place—probably a family compound, not a village—how likely would it be to find a woman who had given her boy to the monastery a quarter century ago?

Toward evening, now hours from Lhasa, we came upon two old Tibetan women wearing long woolen skirts, walking along the road. The driver stopped, leaned out of our van's window, and said the name "Nedong Chukawa," the only words spoken. Linda handed the women the envelope with the Tibetan words written on it. They handed it back to us and directed us down the road to a mud-walled compound nearby. The women walked next to us as we drove slowly to the compound, where they went inside a gate ahead of us. Then they waved us in and walked away.

I was relieved but apprehensive. I pulled Pema's letter back out of my pocket. There were several one-room spaces around a small court-yard, and a goat was tied to a post. The goat's dung had been pressed into clumps against one of the walls of the compound, for cooking fires. One was burning at the center of the courtyard. A large pot of steaming water hung above a heap of smoldering dung.

An old woman approached us. She looked serious and shy but was unafraid. I handed her the letter, which she took without expression and sat down on a wooden bench. In a moment a smile filled her face. She settled her hands on her lap and looked at me. She gave directions to a small boy, who dashed out of the courtyard. She rose and took the pot from the fire and prepared tea for each of us, moving as calmly and methodically as if she had planned for our visit.

My apprehension was evaporating, but I remained alert for her questions. What could I possibly say about a man I knew only from a pawnshop? The wait for tea was what I needed to gather my thoughts. Neither Linda nor our driver spoke with the woman as she poured us

Pema's mother with Haines near Lhasa, Tibet, 1985.

cups of tea. Her calm calmed me. I took a deep breath of fresh mountain air mixed with the smoke of the open hearth. I wondered whether she was Pema's mother or another woman who knew him.

A man raced into the courtyard, anxious and hyperactive, speaking Tibetan with the old woman between questions to Linda in Chinese. Linda talked with him as he sat down with a cup of tea and calmed. The talking stopped and Linda turned to me.

"This is Pema's brother," Linda said. "And she, of course, is their mother."

She was dressed in worn, dull-red wool, with a brighter, almost pink scarf wrapped several times around her head. After serving us tea, she kept her hands folded in her lap. They reminded me of a rancher's—all muscle with blue veins and stained by a life working outdoors.

She looked old. Math raced in my head. She could have birthed Pema at age fifteen or maybe thirty-five, I thought. Pema was ten years old in 1959 when he fled. Today, in 1985, that made her between fifty and seventy. She looked older.

I pulled out the photos Pema had given me and handed them to the woman. "Pema," I said.

She looked at the photos, stroking them exactly as Pema had done with the photos of Lhasa. Linda explained that the younger brother had never known his older brother. A smaller man than Pema, he sat with his mother as they lingered over each picture, slowly touching Pema in them and smiling at each other. The man finally said to Linda in Chinese: "He is in America now, an important man. We knew it."

I handed Pema's mother the gold wristwatch and she gave it to her son, who placed it on his wrist, holding it out and swaying it side to side with exaggerated movements as if the watch were heavy. I had prepared several envelopes with Pema's address and postage to the United States. I gave them to his mother.

"Nedong Chukawa is in Pema," the mother told me through the brother, then through Linda. She then turned her words: "Pema is in Nedong Chukawa."

She told me to tell him that he must visit, because she would die in two years. I reconfirmed through Linda and the brother what she had said and promised to tell him. "Two years," I repeated, and held up two fingers. She smiled and nodded. We left, keeping silent, knowing that the Chinese would not let Pema return to Tibet. It was a long moonless night ride back to Lhasa. The weight of the reality—the distance that separated Pema and his mother—cooled my enthusiasm for everything. Including our bike trek.

▪ ▪ ▪

We set off on our bikes from Lhasa early in the day to avoid the attention of the security men in their blue Jeeps, and we soon lost ourselves in the crisp air, bright sunlight, and view of the Himalayas. Each of us carried three bottles of water, food for what we estimated could take us three weeks, and warm clothing. The weight of my bike, especially that of the two panniers on my front tires, was strange to handle at first but became normal in only a few hours. The Tibetan Plateau, which I had expected to be high and flat, was anything but the normal plateau. The first pass on our second day—a five-thousand-foot climb—split our group in two. Three of us, including Jeff and Rick, a soft-spoken but opinionated carpenter, emerged as the strongest cyclists and made it to the top of the pass by nightfall. The other three did not. I was relieved to be on the summit, and surprised, given my problem with altitude earlier in the year. Each of our two camps had stoves, fuel, water, and food and were fine from a practical perspective. But the following day when we reunited, the others had been joined by Joseph Bossons, a Frenchman from Chamonix. He had raced his ten-speed to catch us out of Lhasa and carried a sleeping bag but no tent or stove. The conversation started with a challenge.

"Why did you go on?" one of the second party asked. Any one of them might have asked the question. The three faced us.

"Did you consider that we would not get to the pass by dark?" another asked.

The questions came as if they had rehearsed and repeated them the night before at their camp. Their unity had come from being left behind. Our answers had been calculated, too, because we knew that breaking apart so early would cause tension in our team, though we had concurred that they would be fine and had food and shelter.

"We thought you were okay. We knew you wanted to get to the pass, just as we did."

I had empathy for them. But my body got me to the pass this time, which made me accept that each day at altitude is a new experience with yourself and what your body might, or might not, be able to do. And on this climb up the first pass, I had wanted to keep moving, needed to keep moving, because I could. I knew I could be the laggard tomorrow.

Our homegrown solidarity had evaporated by the end of the second day. Altitude, it turns out, burns egos as easily as energy. What camaraderie we had had in preparing for the journey over beer and coffee in Laramie was lost.

The following night, this time all together, we were less taut with tension than worn out from exhaustion. But the tension was there, too. All eyes were cast down, and our talk had the terse precision of a staff meeting, all matter-of-fact tones. We shared only hunger and headaches.

"God-damned wind," someone said, though any one of us could have said it.

"Wind dehydrates my brain," Rick added.

Grunts all around acknowledged the comment. As wide and beautiful as Tibet is, it was nearly impossible to enjoy its beauty in the wind.

But the wind finally calmed as the moon illuminated our campsite.

"More noodles?" I asked as the cook that night.

Bowls shot to the rim of the pot out of the dark. Three days of exertion had already worn our legs and lungs and made our stomachs bottomless barrels for fuel. We ate noodles we had brought from home and augmented them with rice, dried yak-butter cheese, and onions that we had found in a Lhasa market. Our best provision was Chinese army-ration biscuits in army-green wrapping marked 761.

We needed each other. Though we shared little during the day, in camp we pulled together in a legion of tasks—pitching tents, cooking, purifying water, and working on bicycle chains gummed up with dust. It was how we did things back home in Wyoming, where the landscape is similar to that of Tibet, and people's stubborn ways compete with sundry competencies, undisclosed incompetence, and the reflex to revert to self-reliance.

"You don't call a plumber in Laramie. You are the plumber," Craig said one night after wrapping up his work lubricating our chains. Craig taught industrial arts to high school students and, like Joe, a grade school teacher, had the patience for practical tasks like patching and pumping up tires. He would explain to us just how the chemistry of a substance he had brought for us in a tube was important for metal chains. He detailed how to adjust our chains for dust and wind, and the different way he would prepare them for ice.

The performance of duties, all taken without assignment, worked for us. Ask for help? Not in Laramie, not in Tibet. We each did what we could do best, whether filtering water, cooking, or fixing our bikes.

Above us was another pass. It looked ominous, higher and into snow. We felt the cold creeping into us by the mile. The difficult uphill climb and descent had been followed by another climb. I looked out at the Tibetan landscape and it never ended. We were in a higher Wyoming without end.

As days drifted into a week and then another week, the monotony of bicycling against wind and cold dulled my brain. I realized I had lost track of the day of the week but knew exactly where the moon would rise and how large it would be. The waxing and waning became my calendar on the Tibetan Plateau, and the moon's light made our nightly camps easier. Yak herders drifted into our camp with their dogs on bright nights but stayed away on the dark new-moon nights.

Hunched over my handlebars each morning, sucking air and staring at the dirt of the road, I could not summon the energy to look up and take notice of the landscape. We pressed forward like meaningless gnats against Tibet's wind. In the howl in my ears, I listened to my breath and could hear my heart thump, thump, thumping in my chest, its cadence becoming the drumbeat of my burning quadriceps and the rotational pushing and pulling of pedals, over and over. The sight of the long hill ahead of me helped me breathe in a pattern deep and deeper, as if I could force my lungs to enlarge, and I believe they did. The repetitive action helped me suppress my concern for altitude sickness, which crept into my brain periodically out of the thin air. I started to believe that the thought of altitude sickness alone could instigate it. Deny fear of the altitude and keep breathing deep. That was my way to move forward.

My toes had been so cold for so many days that they lost some sensation, but they tingled—a symptom of frostbite that would deaden feeling in my toes for a year. When my body drummed against the wind and the cold throbbed to the end of my freezing toes, my mind would go away from my bike.

I drifted away from my body and questioned why I was here, why any of us were here. What, exactly, was the point of this? And then I would drift home to plans I had half hatched, then to work baking bread, to cold beer, to more travel plans. I realized that no one in Laramie questioned the idea that put us in this cold wind with loaded bicycles. No one ever suggested that I stay home for once and do something serious, something that had more than cold toes and a story attached to it. It would be Laramie prodding me to go again, and I would. We all would. Over and over, we ran from Laramie to come back home.

There may have been an unstated status in Laramie to being a traveler, with remote or dangerous places like another notch on a belt. At the same time, I knew that the value of a journey was ephemeral once home and the stories shared. I came to think of it as reading a book that shaped my life going forward, as many books did, but that also led to the next book. Still, a book is one thing and a journey another. For me and many others, Laramie simmered with the energy of adventure, whether nearby or in a distant new place.

I had talked with friends from the university, usually at weddings or Wyoming football games, who had struck out from Laramie to meaningful careers as engineers, attorneys, and doctors. They would say things like "I wish I was doing what you are." But I still began to question the durable value of my passion for roaming, especially compared to friends who had become doctors, delivering babies and having their own children.

My father was blunt: "You just do whatever you want to do, don't you?"

I didn't have an answer except yes, but I said nothing as he stormed from the room.

"He is jealous," my mother said. "When he was your age, you were two years old."

Rick was ahead of me on the road and my mind wandered to how he never finished his construction projects, and never unpacked from a journey until, readying for a new one, he foraged through his backpack or a heap of gear in his garage. He had a backpack stacked against a wall next to an unused car in his parents' garage that, as best I could tell, was filled with clean pans and dirty clothes.

"What's in there?" I asked him once.

"Nothing I need, I guess," he said. "I don't know."

Team on bicycle trek from Lhasa, Tibet, to Kathmandu, Nepal, 1985. From left, Haines, Craig Angus, Rick Kent, Joe Bundy, Jeff Alford, Joseph Bossons, and Rick Smith.

Rick owned two houses in Laramie. He slept in one and worked on the other. But neither was really ready to be lived in. He bought one with a cash advance on a credit card for about $5,000 and it wasn't even worth that. But after a year, the house had plumbing, lights, and windows of all different sizes and styles salvaged from demolitions and dumpsters. The place felt like a show home for everything old and odd. His friends admired the place, though, and visited it regularly to see what nuance Rick's attention to a budget and design could produce—a nook in the wall for a single book, a handle made from a branch he found in the park after a storm, a floor pattern of tile discarded by contactors building an upscale home across town.

For the next week, we rode at our own paces, each facing the incessant headwinds and wrench of stomach pain alone. It was easier that way, and inevitable. The altitude drew out the differences among us, our varying physical capabilities spreading us out for miles along the road. Our unmanaged sprawl had its benefit, however, because it very likely confounded the Chinese public security men we would see every few days in their Jeeps. Over and over, they chose to ignore us rather than gather us up and be forced to make a decision about our presence. We confirmed with each other nightly that they did not acknowledge any of us with a nod, or even eye contact.

We gradually adjusted to whipping wind and bright sun that never cut the cold edge off the day. The extra ten thousand feet in altitude, however, had its own sinister system for enforcing its will on each of us, the impact of which varied by person, and by the day. A strong cyclist one day might be slow the next. The changes in strength and stamina were so unpredictable that they bred discontent between us. We were all proud and tough, but altitude, then competition, and finally superstition overtook us. How could a strong man become the weak one overnight? Was it what he had eaten? But we had eaten the same food, drunk the same water, and cycled the same route.

The exception was Jeff, whose lean body inexplicably absorbed thin air better than the rest of us. He had the lanky physique of a runner, more suited for marathons and high altitude than athletic Ricky, who was a strong carpenter like Rick but was burdened first with a headache, then wheezing congestion in his lungs. Ricky moved at a crawl on his bike. I worried that he would cough up blood next, and we would be without a way to get him down from this high, long road. In the dark of camp, however, his ailing condition never altered his nightly ritual of boiling us cups of tea and hot chocolate from his stash.

"This," I told him, "is something really good of you." Ricky's concern for us all left me without adequate words of thanks. I wanted to hug him but of course did not. I didn't know him well, and men generally didn't hug each other back home. Tibet was hardening me more than I realized. The cold, the wind, and a foul stomach turned me toward myself. I simply had nothing to give, physically or emotionally. I rode my bike with fear, pride, and pain at my own pace, as did the others. We pounded up inclines as alone as hungry coyotes on the wind-stripped high plains outside Laramie.

Each of us could hide our pain while cycling solo. At night, the pain would subside enough to get us dreaming of next projects and trips. Everyone had something brewing. Ricky told us one night how he envisioned building a group of people, planting a garden, and working together back in Laramie. It would be a place opposite of how he had grown up in Florida, the son of a man who became wealthy putting down asphalt.

If Ricky was formed in Florida, he was reshaped by Wyoming, the state where he landed because his parents had sent him to NOLS, the National Outdoor Leadership School, in the central Wyoming town of Lander. NOLS attracted teenagers, often from out of state, some of whom had come into trouble back home, whose parents imagined them adjusting from bad grades or delinquency by way of Wyoming's wilderness. It was an alternative to reform school and a life less oriented to nature and mountains. Some, like Ricky, who stayed in Wyoming, were the new pioneers. He was not unlike my great-great-grandmother, who left Missouri in search of anything—and found just enough in Wyoming's high prairie to call home. Something a little better has always been just ahead of us in Laramie, almost in clear sight.

▪ ▪ ▪

Chomolungma Feng—Mount Everest—had towered to the south of us for days. Against the bluest sky imaginable, the mountain had a plume unfurling off its summit, like a heaven-bound ghost. I could not take my eyes off it.

We were sixteen days and 483 kilometers into our ride (the Chinese had kilometers marked periodically on square whitewashed cement bricks along the entire Friendship Highway). Rick asked me whether I wanted to leave the road the following day for North Everest Base Camp. I had had a recurring bout of dysentery from drinking bad water and had little energy and waning interest in big mountains and adventure. I wanted to eat and warm my feet. But I told Rick I would decide in the morning. The next morning, I was feeling stronger and knew I had to go to the mountain. It looked so close, but it was eighty kilometers to the base of Everest. When would I be this close to the world's highest mountain on a bicycle again?

We split off from our friends, who had grown ragged and weary of each other, for our detour. We didn't know exactly how far it was to Kathmandu, but it was, we calculated later, 252 kilometers to the Nepal border, and another 114 from the border to Kathmandu. No one wanted to join us. We split food with the others to give us eleven more days, calculating it would take us an extra week to get to the mountain and then rejoin the road to Kathmandu.

The road to Everest became a field of glacial deposits, which would have been a delight to geologists but were a nearly impossible impediment to bicyclists. After two days, the macaroni in my panniers had powdered from the constant bouncing and vibrations.

After three days of weaving through streams of glacial runoff and rock rubble, without encountering traffic of any type, we reached a monastery at the edge of a wide valley that framed Everest about ten kilometers away. The grounds of the monastery were dilapidated, largely destroyed, and in a state of rubble. We were surprised to encounter this place, Rongbuk Monastery, though it is famous to Buddhists everywhere. A magnificent rebuilt stupa, white and clean at its base, with golden steps extending into the sky, was diminished only by the mighty Everest behind it. The area was empty but for a few women acting as caretakers. They greeted us with Swiss salami and Dijon mustard, provisions left by climbers.

We camped below the monastery on the dry grasses of the valley below Everest Base Camp. At nightfall, our tent became a village of wandering sheep, yaks, and a few herders in their long coats made of yak hide and sheep wool. Around us circled the men's muscled and wary dogs,

North Everest Base Camp, near North Everest, Tibet, 1985. Rick Smith, left, and Haines.

a mastiff breed with black eyes. They built fires of sheep dung coaxed into hot coals, using a small bellows made from hide and tin pounded into a small air funnel. They could ignite a small stack of a dozen sheep dung pellets into coals in a moment of effort. Their yak-butter tea was boiling before I could put together and fire up my multifuel stove (as essential as a passport because it could be powered by any fuel). These men in hide and fur, essentially wearing their tents and sleeping bags as clothing, were equipped for Tibet's cold wind better than we were in our advanced gear. We cooked macaroni, mostly powdered now, with yak butter the herders shared with us. They would eventually move away into the night to sleep in their coats, which appeared cumbersome as clothing but must have made stiff and sturdy shelter at night.

Above Rongbuk Monastery we rode to an empty base camp, a wide, flat moraine of tumbled rock at the end of enormous lateral moraines, and glaciers dusted on the edges by falling rock. Up the mountain was a steeper jumble of blue ice. It was evident from circles of stacked rock walls around us that this was the staging area for climbing expeditions in April and May, but in November the moraine was dead quiet—until early the next morning. A Land Rover drove up to us. We unzipped our tent as two Japanese men got out of the truck and circled our bicycles. They laughed with each other.

"Hello," I said.

"American?" a man asked.

"Yes."

"You are not on motorcycle?"

"No, bicycles," I told him.

The two men broke into smiles, waved, and left us without another word. Later in the day, more Land Rovers arrived, and an entire camp of Japanese men with large tents, video film cameras, and new motorcycles materialized as if from another planet. The motorcycles were a type designed to climb up inclines and over rocks, an aspect of the motorcycle sport that had apparently grown popular in Japan. We learned that they were there to establish an altitude record by motorcycle. One man confided that they had been worried, having heard back in Lhasa that Americans were ahead of them. They were relieved that we were only on bicycles and their record attempt up the mountain was safe from competition.

I felt as if it were nearly all downhill from Everest, though we had two iced-over and frigid passes to climb. Despite the inclines and cold wind, the route became less an exploratory path than a road to Kathmandu. I started counting kilometers to the city that would be warm and full of food.

On the way down and down from the final pass of the Tibetan Plateau, in a crease between peaks leading into the low valley of Kathmandu, we encountered an Indian man riding uphill on a single-speed bicycle. It was the heavy black bicycle one sees throughout India: the Golden Rooster. Solid and indestructible, these bikes last a lifetime. But in this environment, that cyclist was the equivalent of someone running a marathon in cowboy boots. He was the first cyclist we had seen. We stopped to talk. The man was traveling up the route we had descended, hoping to get to the Nepal-Tibet border above us. I might have dismissed his plan, except that here he was with a bag over his shoulder, wearing cotton clothing and carrying a jug of water strapped to his seat, having bicycled from India to over ten thousand feet. We were not about to diminish his energy by explaining the difficulty he would face with the cold and high altitude ahead. We judged from his bicycle that his trip was already a greater physical feat than ours, and we both admired him for it. I knew that his solitary journey, with the only bicycle and clothing he knew, was a personal one for him, a great story that would never be told. By contrast—though we did not imagine it then—in eight months, Rick and I would be on the cover of both American and Dutch bicycling magazines, our story and photographs filling pages of glossy publications at the grocery checkout line back home and in Amsterdam bike shops.

We continued downhill as a river, blue and gray with fine glacial silt, grew alongside us into a thundering torrent, creating its own cool breeze on the road's tight corners. Dropping from over eighteen thousand feet to four thousand feet in a few hours, the landscape was transformed with new plants and increasing humidity at each turn of the road. Sweat evaporated from our skin in the downhill wind. Wild monkeys ran across the road in front of us. Rhododendron flowered, and we shed our clothing hour after hour from thick coats to long underwear, then to shorts and short sleeves as we finally weaved into Kathmandu. There, we discovered that our friends had spread themselves around town in different guesthouses. They had disbanded in frustration with each other after we had left them under Everest's shadow. It would be months before we shared our stories with them.

By the time I arrived home, Pema had received a letter from his mother. She had repeated her appeal for Pema to visit before her death in two years. The arrival of the letter had surprised him but did not delight him as much as I had imagined and hoped.

At his house on the edge of town near a loud freeway, we dug in mud to the light of a flashlight, gathering garden potatoes for a curry he was preparing.

"The Chinese fear men who carry their own stories of history and religion," Pema explained. He pulled a last potato from the ground and laughed. "I know where the bodies are buried."

"They will never allow me to return home," Pema said. "But I never left my home, Tibet is still in me."

The letter comforted him, he explained, because he had long feared his mother had died. "Taken to the sky," he said.

▪ ▪ ▪

After four years of traveling, and going to Tibet twice in one year, I decided it was time to stay with Jennifer and find a job that had predictability, insurance, and a retirement plan. I was hired by a Portland bank, a job I was grateful for given my work gap after college. Jennifer, however, had other plans. She graduated and moved to Taiwan to teach English and learn Chinese. We remained a couple for five years. I made her student loan payments, three of them totaling $185 per month. I felt I owed it to her, and I loved her. She would come back for visits to Portland and Laramie, and I would meet her in Taiwan, Hong Kong, and India on short vacations every year.

I was enjoying my work, but the predictability I sought became a cage. At the same time, Jennifer and I began growing apart, the distance between us too far to bridge with letters and semiannual reunions. We tried until we could try no more. In Portland in 1991, we looked each other in the eye and agreed we were done as a couple. A month later, which was five years after I had settled into a career, my bicycling companion in Tibet, Rick, called with a notion to join a kayaking expedition of the length of the Niger River in West Africa with two other Laramie friends. I took a leave of absence and left for Guinea a month later. Jennifer was convinced I went to Africa because we had broken up. But for me, it was the kind of thing five years in a bank job drove me to do.

6

Finding Tembekoundo

IMPRISONED IN THE WET WILDERNESS and last long days of the monsoon season in early October in Guinea, we slip our way uphill on washed-out trails in search of the source of the Niger River. We are aiming to kayak the length of the Niger, provided we can find it. Provided it is navigable. Four Laramie men—Mark, Mike, Rick, and I—are wandering in a new universe of mud slurry and soggy green mulch that reaches from our toes to the sky. We march in the rain forest with persistence, but with diminishing imagination and waning faith that we will find the true beginning of the river.

We know we are on a long and uncertain journey, having prepared in just five weeks, searching for a river we had no maps to help us find, and racing two clocks. The first is catching the post-rainy-season flow of the Niger River, whose route could deplete to braided channels of mud far downstream in Mali and Niger during the drought season, though that dry landscape seems unimaginable now. The other is the timetable of Mark's and Mike's wives, who are both six months pregnant back in Laramie. The fathers-to-be need to be home by Christmas and are hell-bent to shoehorn this journey into their lives before they start changing diapers. Rick and I, on the other hand, have nobody waiting for us at home. I got a leave of absence for six months from my bank job, prepaid my bills, and crossed half the year off my calendar. Doing the simple math of the Niger's linear length—officially 2,600 miles but probably more like 3,400 in actual meandering river miles—I calculated that it would take us more than four months if we could cover about twenty-two miles a day without a break and without surprises. I was pretty

72

sure that we could not kayak the length of the Niger by Christmas, but we knew so little for certain. I kept my doubts to myself because the likelihood of traveling the length of the river in any amount of time at the moment seemed beyond belief.

Our imagination alone had gotten us this far: lost and lugging kayaks and expedition gear showered on us by outdoor equipment company sponsors. Mark had cajoled these sponsorships in a fast month of phone calls from Laramie. He sold our expedition using his credentials as a magazine writer and had lined up The North Face and MSR, both longtime supporters of expeditions, and Feathercraft, a manufacturer of small and sturdy folding kayaks that had never sponsored anyone for anything. All three companies bought into the prospect that we would accomplish the first continuous descent of the last long African river from source to sea.

These companies from San Francisco, Seattle, and Vancouver, BC, sponsored us to write magazine articles and provide reviews of their tents, stoves, clothing, and kayaks. They were companies with logos we knew, not people we had met. While most of my Laramie friends were satisfied with sharing stories of past and next adventures, our corporate sponsors wanted more.

"Exposure, period," Mark had told us bluntly. "Sponsors want pictures in magazines, photos for advertising and stories." And they wanted his book, which would detail the first continuous descent of the Niger River.

The expedition had not been Rick's or my idea, or even Mike's, and the sponsors were not ours either. They were Mark's, and he pocketed the cash they provided. Rick and I, on the other hand, had several hundred dollars on us and felt lucky to be in West Africa with kayaks and a tent. We were poor for tourists but wealthy for Africa.

The colorful tents and folding kayaks, however, are now as pointless as a gold wristwatch on a man being set into his grave. We are without a map, traversing the saturated sponge of the West African highlands with rainwater racing around our legs. Water is everywhere, but there is no river in sight.

Then, by providence or utter necessity, out of the rain emerges a man named Sori.

"Yes sir," he says. "You look, look. I find for you, good."

He informs us in succinct pidgin English that he once worked at the US Embassy in Gabon as a driver and shows us a crumbling, taped-together photo ID as proof. Sori Keita had been looking for us, it turns out, after word got out in the town of Banian that foreigners were planning to move through the forest on foot. He tells us he is from the Kissi area and the village Bambaya, which is where we think we need to be headed.

It is clear: Sori is our map.

Sori offers us his services to find the forest trails to the Niger's source, a place he calls "Tembekoundo." We pay him half his charge up front— 27,000 Guinea francs, or about thirty-two dollars, for him and the four men he will find to carry our kayaks to the next village.

"You walk, walk. I find," he says. "Three day, two night, Tembekoundo."

"You have been to Tembekoundo?" I ask Sori.

"No, sir," he says. "Tembekoundo eats people." He swings his body around to greet a man who has walked up to us.

Sori Keita, Guinea, 1991.

Sori introduces us to the area's village chief, who had arrived out of the wet green as if conversations and plans had been circling through the forest ahead of our arrival, and explains our plan to the chief.

"Chief say, no river your country?" Sori asks us.

"Yes," Rick says, after a pause to consider, as he always does, a thoughtful response. "But not like your river," he explains to the chief through Sori.

The chief nods.

"Ee barabo ee bara, ee barase ibara," the chief says in Malinke.

"You left your home, you

found your home," Sori translates for us. "Chief offer place to sleep inside."

■ ■ ■

We had found a dry home, which is comforting in this inescapably wet landscape. Finding the Niger River's source, however, the elusive place in the deeper bush known as Tembekoundo, remains another matter.

Getting to West Africa with kayaks in five weeks had seemed to be half the journey. That challenge led us to choose folding sea kayaks over canoes because we could take them as regular baggage on a commercial flight and carry them in backpacks in the forest. With double loads of gear and kayaks, we were grateful to have the help of Sori's men, and not to be shuttling our gear in the rain. But now that we were here with boats and gear, the reality of weather, food, our health, and finding the river became the overlooked other half of the journey.

Although we knew the Niger's length, we had not managed to get much more than basic data about the river and the historical accounts of a handful of early explorers. Useful information was hard to come by, and we could not, in the short time we had to prepare, find anyone who had been in the Niger's highland area. I had found US Defense Mapping Agency maps, but the available sections were incomplete, as if we had about a quarter of a complicated jigsaw puzzle in scattered pieces on the table in front of us.

Mark's research indicated that no one had ever done what we were attempting, which was his driving motivation for constructing the expedition. Two centuries earlier, in 1805, a Scotsman named Mungo Park died on his second attempt to find the Niger River's course—referred to at the time as "Africa's last geographic secret." Park's first mission in 1795 and his second expedition ten years later had garnered the financial patronage of the explorer-turned-benefactor and exploration sponsor of his time, Sir Joseph Banks and his African Association. At about the same time, Banks dispatched another explorer, George Vancouver, to lead what became a discovery of the new botany, unrivaled beauty, and deepwater port potential of the Pacific Northwest on the distant Pacific Ocean. Vancouver and his team of scientists documented meeting native coastal people of the Pacific Northwest who traveled by canoe and kayak and ate from the abundant resources of land and waters.

Sir Joseph Banks's directive for Mungo Park was to find the mysterious Niger's course across the continent. His colleagues in London imagined that the Niger's route might be the trade route across Africa, quite possibly linking the continent's West Coast to the great Nile in the east. They dreamed of the Niger as the potential source of new wealth, greater than the more distant travels of George Vancouver.

In 1805, Mungo Park disappeared on his second journey on the Niger River's long route, a sweeping arc, they would later learn, shaped like a question mark. Park was close to, but forever short of, his life's obsession of reaching the Niger's mouth at the Atlantic Ocean. The world eventually learned that he had likely died at the hands of regional chiefs in what is now Nigeria. His rural hometown of Selkirk, Scotland, has mourned his disappearance for over two hundred years and celebrates him annually by dressing up a local man as the blond-haired explorer and closing the town square for one day. Outside Selkirk, the name and legacy of Mungo Park are almost completely unknown.

That fate was not for us. Mark had a vision of putting us on the map, with a book contract in hand and a cash advance in the bank in Laramie to write about what he referred to as "the last great river journey." He was pleased with himself, and why not? He had not only a book deal with a cash advance, but also a wife who tolerated his untimely travels. Rick and I were excited to be with Mark and Mike. It seemed to us, even lost in Guinea's mud and rain, a privilege to be with friends attempting something larger than our lives back home.

But I had trouble believing that no one had traveled the length of the Niger River. What about the Africans who lived along its route? They traded goods, moved between ethnic and tribal areas, not yet nations. And yet, I reasoned, most people in Africa had no reason to descend an entire river, let alone for the sole purpose of accomplishment. This is the irony of our time in the world: we are traveling without much of a purpose but to have the experience, and to leave home and come back with stories. Descending a river is not a worthwhile venture for most people.

We had all grown up within blocks of each other in Laramie, but this was the first trip for the four of us together. While Mark and Mike had many shared adventures under their belts and could finish each other's travel stories, Rick and I had only our one long journey together on mountain bikes across Tibet.

Rick was our trip philosopher—whether we needed one or not—a disheveled, lovable guy with a swimmer's lean athleticism (yet harboring no opinion of himself as athletic) and an alternative view on most everything. He asked questions of everyone he met but, with innate modesty, shared little of his own stories. He had barely pulled together the necessities of the expedition, which as far as we could tell were stuffed without thought into a backpack, still in the wrapping from their manufacturers.

Mike, on the other hand, was the planner we needed. Since his wife had become pregnant, Mike had become a practical man, and that made him the best of traveling companions. He had carefully created a medical kit that, he told us, "can handle everything." He clarified, "That is, everything but sewing your arm back on."

He was also our humorist, which we needed as much as the medical kit. His sturdy smile turned to a wry smirk as we experienced the malfunctions of Guinea. The lights had gone out at the airport when we arrived in the capital, Conakry, at night. Then the cab we took from the airport drove without its lights. "This is just Laramie in a blizzard," he said. "I can't see whether it's all white or all black. But it's warmer here, just like a vacation."

Our expedition leader was Mark, who was physically strong and consistently competitive. He looked to me as he got older like Mick Jagger but with a bulkier body. I had known him since we were twelve years old, and though he was now a grown man, he had not changed an inch since then. He was possessed, even when he was laughing, with one-upping everyone on any story. He was as driven today as he once was in gym class—to do more sit-ups, more push-ups, or more of anything than any boy in our school. Mark was always trying to be a better man than his friends, physically and mentally, and he liked to let everyone know how that was developing.

He brought along two Ruger semiautomatic 9mm pistols (given to us by the gun company), which he smuggled into Guinea in the nose of his kayak. Fortunately, the brisk passing of two twenty-dollar bills to the official poking around our gear helped us pass airport security in Conakry. Mark insisted that we needed guns, based on a bad experience he had had bicycling in Yugoslavia, when he was jumped in the night while camping with his girlfriend. He shared the other gun with Mike, who also once needed a gun to ward off bandits on the South African coast after they threw rocks from a cliff onto his campsite below. Rick disagreed with the need for guns based on his instinct that guns helped to incite rather than avoid conflict.

"Not with hippos," I pointed out.

That's what I was concerned about—hippos, not people. I had brought along a flare gun, thinking it could be used to frighten them, since they might be able to take the shot of a gun. The flare gun might frighten a man, too, should that be necessary.

I had also brought a few paperbacks of African fiction and a history book on the Niger, The Strong Brown God, by Sanche de Gramont, published in 1975. I had also found Mungo Park's journal of his first Niger exploration, Travels in the Interior Districts of Africa, which was published in 1799. A reprint was easy to find, which surprised me given the lack of current books or travel information about the Niger River.

Although Laramie was our base camp, I was living in Portland, Oregon, where I spent a great deal of time in the library, at Powell's Books, and on the phone back to Laramie with my friends preparing for the trip.

We had organized our expedition into two teams of two: Mark and Mike, and Rick and I. It made sense given the practical disbursal of two-person tents and gear such as water pumps, stoves, tools, water bottles, and food provisions. But I sensed after our first phone call that we were all on Mark's one-man expedition, just along for the ride.

For instance, he had talked the company that makes Cutter insect repellent out of $10,000. We knew, however, that the bug dope would provide no benefit against malarial mosquitoes. Nothing but antimalaria drugs could. The money was in his bank account, waiting for his return. Mark would focus on himself in Africa, as he did at home. Mike, Rick, and I would need to keep an eye on each other.

■ ■ ■

Or Sori Keita would watch out for us. We wake to him praying before sunrise in the village where we slept inside at the direction of the chief. Later that day, walking in mud in search of Tembekoundo, we stop in a downpour for his ritual, in which he takes off his hat and shoes, kneels, and honors Allah.

Sori's route to Tembekoundo is more like fording a tributary than walking a trail. We move with our faith in him but with rainwater plunging downhill around our ankles and flowing behind us in a muddy muck. Sori assures us that we have not lost the path.

We encounter few people, and after three days we have passed through only two villages. In the first village, we see an active school filled with boys, their books, and soccer balls. Nearby, next to mud huts with perfectly thatched roofs, women and girls are singing and pounding millet in a circle, with thuds of wooden mallets into a wooden mortar that stands sturdy in the middle of the women like a hearth.

In the second village, Foraconia, we meet a tall man with a rifle and a nice man with a book. The man with the gun pulls Sori aside, while the man with the book comes over to us and tells us in French, which Rick translates, that they had been posted in the forest to watch for people coming through the area from Liberia. Liberians had been fleeing their warring country through the forests of Sierra Leone nearby, and then into Guinea in search of safety. These men were to lead Liberians from the border area to refugee camps deeper in Guinea. Their presence here seems an ad-hoc assignment and, though we are not sure (and they may not be either), not a military one. Their job is clearly not to restrict people's passage, but rather to welcome and assist Liberians with the wave of a gun and the calming words of the man carrying only a book.

The man with the book tells us he is a schoolteacher. He carries a taped-together book of Montaigne but apparently no change of clothes or a gun. His shirt is in tatters, as are his shoes, but his eyes are alive with questions. "Why are you here? Where are your families?" he asks and smiles, amused with us and at what is happening.

"Why you, a teacher?" I ask the man.

"Because I would do it," he says, his willingness apparently his primary credential for being posted in the roadless highlands.

His sole role, as far as we can tell, is to translate the languages of the border people, mostly Malinke and Kissi, into French, possibly for government officials who speak French, though Guinea separated from the French in 1958. And to translate for the escaping Liberians into whatever language they speak—Malinke, French, and, to the extent he speaks it, English.

> Human understanding is marvelously enlightened by daily
> conversation with men, for we are, otherwise, compressed
> and heaped up in ourselves, and have our sight limited to the
> length of our own noses. —Michel de Montaigne

But their work is slow. In the monsoon rains, there is little foot traffic
from Liberia through Sierra Leone and the two men are clearly bored
in the deep bush. The man with the gun indicates that he will join us on
our walk to the Niger's source, his daily monotony apparently winning
over his initial urge to use his authority to turn us around. Like Sori,
neither of the men had been to the Niger's source.

Sori agrees with the man with the gun, indicating he wants both men
to join us. We follow Sori's instincts and also agree. The simple protocol
means something to all of us. As we walk, Sori tells us he has a gun.
"From first white man. English, eighteen thirty-seven." He adds that he
also has masks and animal skins he wants to sell.

"You have the gun?" I ask Sori, simply to see what he will say about
it.

"Yes. That's it," Sori replies and immediately gives instructions to a
few young boys in the village where we had stopped, a place with only
a few huts, who jump up into action.

I wonder how Sori knows the date, and how this gun will appear out
of the bush for us to purchase. How is it that such a gun is even here, in
someone's home, wrapped in rags, a useless relic without bullets, waiting for a purchaser for a century and a half?

"No, Sori, I do not want the gun," I implore.

"Yes, good. No problem," he says. The boys have already run away
from us, long gone from the huddle of mud huts. I imagine the boys
searching for the gun, or some old gun from a chief or elder, or maybe a
relative of Sori. The people of the highland villages so far seem to know
Sori. He is clearly an important man to all those we meet.

Sori tells me that he let an American take masks some years earlier
and was sent $1,400. "You take. Pay later," he explains.

We start walking again before the boys return with the old gun. Sori
continues offering, despite our objections and lack of interest, items for
sale as we pass through other small, nameless hamlets. A leopard skin

in one village, a monkey pelt in another, and old rock implements he tells us were once used for woodworking, softening animal skins, and making masks.

If the white man is in this forest, the people seem conditioned to believe he has come to take something—artifacts, animal skins, and once even people. We are here for something, for sure, but not artifacts, though Mark is mining for stories. I came to West Africa looking for an escape and to explore. I have no interest in carrying anything but what I need.

"How many children do you have?" a chief in the village of Kissadji asks us.

None of us have children, but Mark offers that he and Mike will be having children soon. "We have waited to have children until we can afford them," Mark explains to the chief.

The chief's response, again through Sori, hints at confusion. "Chief says children not cost money," Sori says.

"Oh no, tell him we need money before having children, and we have fewer children in America," Mark says. Sori interprets patiently as the man with the book stands close to listen and take notes. The chief responds to Sori.

"What does he say?" Mark asks.

"Chief says you love money more than children," the man with the book explains.

"If God gives you children, how you not take?" Sori asks us.

Mark is scribbling in his notebook and does not answer.

Finally, the chief says, "Ee barabo ee bara, ee barase ibara" (You left your home, you found your home).

"Chief give chicken," Sori says.

"If chief gives you chicken, how do you not take it," Mark says, snickering.

Around a fire, eating chicken, bananas, and oranges, the man with the gun tells Sori, who explains to us, about their work in the highlands.

Whole families, with children in their arms, had walked past these men over the past year, traversing the roadless forest with nothing but their clothing. They were in search of a city for safety and food. Camps for the refugees had been established in Kissidougou, several days' walk away.

The man with the gun had been letting people pass through the forest toward the small towns where they could find a road to areas such as Kissidougou. Some Liberians, the men say, try to go to the capital, Conakry. We had heard on our shortwave radio that Liberia was in chaos and uncertainty, with what the BBC reported as warring bands of men and loose alliances of young boys with guns coming out of the bush. The chaos moved from the rural bush to the capital, Monrovia, the city named after US president Monroe, in a country resettled by freed slaves from America.

The men blame the traffic of Liberians into Guinea on a man named Charles Taylor. "He is taking control of Liberia," the man with the book tells us.

The next day, after a long walk in mud but under a sunny sky, Sori stops us in a clearing, a boundary in the deep bush made evident, he explains, by the trees stripped on one side of what is otherwise an indecipherable frontier in a region of porous borders. We are along the border between Guinea and Sierra Leone.

Sori motions with his hands, without saying a word, toward the dark green, densely forested Guinea side of the border. Below us sturdy bamboo is circled by and interspersed with tall leafy trees. Sori and the other men stop and variously squat or sit on the ground. We had arrived at Tembekoundo, where they would go no farther, no closer to the Niger's actual source. The men even avoid eye contact with us, a hint of their concern, which might have made us worry but does not.

We are at last this close to the Niger's source, and enthusiasm has overtaken judgment or concern. We are moving with the water now and do not look up at Sori or the other men as we fall with the gravity of the land and our excitement into the dense bamboo forest to Tembekoundo.

We immediately drop from the tree-stripped Sierra Leone side of the border into the bamboo in search of something. But what, exactly? A geyser, a spring, a small creek? We have no idea. Bamboo grows thick and in tight clumps if it is not cut, and it is as unyielding here as the metal bars of a prison. We pull our way through notches and climb up slots of picket lines of stiff stalks, whose fronds wave high above us in the wind like something teasing us. With the prospect of our river expedition starting, Tembekoundo is large in our minds. And it is before us.

Thinking big but following each other into a narrow space of interwoven bamboo, limbs, and vines, we pull branches aside for each other. We plow with our bodies while twisting through branches we bend and break as we go into tighter and tighter spaces. I hear monkeys yap. Then I hear something barking, maybe the same type of monkey farther away, then another sound, then another unknown yowl layered in the incessant buzz, a beautiful blur of sound in the wilderness. In the sparsely populated highlands, I feel surrounded, almost crowded, by wildlife. Tembekoundo is the complete opposite of the silent solace and wide view of wilderness we know in the high altitude of Wyoming.

We are not that much above sea level, maybe a couple of thousand feet in elevation. We are at the start of a river longer than those that start near our home in Laramie at 7,220 feet to become the river of our continent, starting with the Laramie River, then the North Platte, which joins the Missouri, which meets the Mississippi. Yet the Niger runs farther. We know that. But where is the start of the river? The highest point? The farthest? The one of many creeks with the name that continues to the sea?

We come to a small, dark chasm, a ten-foot-deep divot in the steep ground that harnesses a small constant stream of clear, calm water. We

Team at Tembekoundo, source of the Niger River, 1991. From left, Mark Jenkins, Haines, Mike Moe, and Rick Smith.

climb into the chasm, which captures a spring. The air is cool in the green shadows, and quiet, as peaceful as a place of worship. The green bamboo stalks tower above us like a cathedral in the bush.

Tembekoundo.

We drink from the spring and pause, but only pause. It may be a perfect moment here where the Niger begins, but our enthusiasm to finally go with the river pulls us out of the green, wet church. The rain has stopped. The loud pattering of water on leaves has ceased, and the sounds of insects, animals, and birds take over.

7
Never Leaving Laramie

The continuous work of our life is to build death.
—Michel de Montaigne

SORI JOINS US AGAIN WHEN WE LEAVE the chasm of Tembekoundo. He wants to move, and so do we. We are moving with the river but walking, imperfect for us but evidently fine with Sori, who, having skipped seeing the actual source of the Niger, seems energized to walk with us while we find a place to start kayaking. The early Niger is a brown thread wandering loose through the green woven blanket of the highlands. We meander through every imaginable hue of green, periodically pulling back limbs along the Niger's bank to see whether the river is wide and deep enough yet for our kayaks. The river pulses, testing its banks as it circles back on itself, pushing soil from its banks, breaking the limbs of bushes, and finding its course. It looks unpredictable.

The Niger River has always started in this highland place, but a millennium ago the river ended, after a thousand miles, in the interior desert of the continent, not at the sea to which it flows today. It ceased in an inland delta that remains unique to the world and that still exists, downriver from us in the headwaters. The Niger no longer stops there because it asserted itself, during a flood or earthquake or both, pushed the inland delta deeper into the desert, and joined another river that came out of the mountains on the desert's northern edge. This expanse is known as the Sahel, stretching through the nations of Mali and Niger. The two large rivers grafted into what is now the tenth longest river in the world, a geographic conundrum, as it flows away from the coast for over half its length and then arcs back to the ocean. Knowing the geologic history of the Niger makes the early river seem young to me, and as alive as an animal growing daily in the womb.

Two days down from Tembekoundo, descending still by foot as the Niger gathers streams and strength, we arrive at the village of Dougoulema and the river's first bridge, made from riverbank trees and wide enough for a truck. The people of the village have hacked a wider path with machetes on the other side of the bridge in an effort to invite traffic. We greet the chief, who asks us whether we are there to bring a road to his village. We walk onto the bridge with him and look for the first time at the river, now wide enough for our kayaks. "No," we tell the disappointed chief as Sori steps in to explain that we have boats in our backpacks, a fact that perplexes the chief until we unzip the backpacks and show him our roll-up kayaks.

The thread of the Niger has grown wider and it is now a darker brown, as beautiful and sleek as the skin of the young kids in the village, and moving as fast and flat as a serpent through grass. The Niger's bank remains part river and part foliage, a tangled space between land and water. I see a break in the bush on the bank where limbs are ripped, almost shredded, and the grasses matted in a path over a yard wide. I ask Sori about it.

"Crocodile," he says, as four naked boys leap off Dougoulema's bridge into the river and swim against its stiff current to a place under the bridge where they can climb ashore. Mark strips off his clothes and swims with the village boys. The chief smiles.

"Ee barabo ee bara, ee barase ibara," he says, repeating the comforting greeting we had heard in every village.

We pull our kayaks from our backpacks and begin assembling them. Sori marvels at the colors—two red, one blue, and mine, fuchsia. He picks up the aluminum frames that we pull the colorful skins over. We put our boats together under the watchful eyes of Dougoulema's men and boys, who have surrounded us. As we assemble them, Sori purchases us forty oranges and twenty bananas for 800 Guinea francs, just shy of a dollar. Outside the circle of men and boys, I see water jugs moving on the heads of women and hear the dull thuds of millet being pounded and the raspy sifting sound of grain being separated from stalks.

Mike Moe, left, and Rick Smith assembling their Feathercraft kayaks in Dougoulema, Guinea, 1991.

Sori realizes our time together is over. We pay him and also offer the chief money for the village school, where we had seen, just as in other villages, only boys studying and playing. Sori bids us farewell and flees on his swift feet across the bridge and down the wide trail as quickly as he had appeared days earlier.

I feel his loss. But the river is pulling us. Without Sori's guidance, our map is now the Niger River. After six days and hiking some ninety miles, much of it reversing our course into the Niger's source, we leave Dougoulema in the afternoon in our kayaks, with the entire village gathered on the bridge and bank of the river. We hold our paddles over our heads in salute to the people and round a bend into wilderness, with no sign of the village or of human beings. After only an hour, we discover that what eats people is not at the source, Tembekoundo, as Sori told us; it is what lives in the river immediately downstream from Dougoulema: crocodiles. They are living missiles. The first one we see moves without creating a wake, more like a bird in the air than a reptile in the water. Then its tail whips a hard slap on the water and the creature accelerates toward Rick.

With gun drawn, Mark readies to fire at the crocodile plowing through the water on target toward Rick's kayak. The crocodile is five yards from Rick and is surging. Mark is ten yards behind Rick. Fire it, I think. Fire now!

Time accelerates to the point where it could not move faster. Mark aims. But as suddenly as it appeared, the crocodile drops below the surface and into the dark pull of the river.

It is gone.

I am pulled by the river's current directly to where Rick's boat had been, and Rick is now downriver. I look around and paddle hard. The river pulls us onward. We move without speaking, as if we had seen nothing, and I wonder whether the encounter with the crocodile has really happened.

I consider whether we are we in denial of danger. Or is denial a way of enduring fear? The wild crocodile is unlike anything I had seen on television, in magazines, or at a zoo. We are invaders in their world. The river and its banks are not ours. If the crocodiles are hungry, they will get us eventually. I question our ability to thwart crocodiles, and I doubt our sanity as we pull into the tall grass along the riverbank to camp.

We spend our first night only a few yards from the river, in tall reed-like grasses that wave above our heads. Like soldiers on a mission, we tamp down a modest clearing by bending and breaking the grasses to make space for our tents. Mike suggests that we put our kayaks in a flank around the tents in case crocodiles come ashore. I agree, but Rick argues that crocodiles have no reason to consider us or our kayaks a threat. Rick is unconcerned with the crocodile that, in front of my eyes only twenty yards away, had had a bearing on him as food.

I tell him, "Rick, that crocodile was at least twelve feet long, in case you didn't see it. Its head was the size of our cockpits."

"Danger is in your mind," Mark tells us.

"You had your gun drawn," I remind him.

"You saw boys swimming in Dougoulema," Rick says. "They were not afraid. Besides, kayaks have never been on this part of the Niger. They don't know we are food and don't need to eat us," he finishes, assured in his opinion.

"Which means that, not knowing we are prey, they wouldn't try to eat us?" I ask.

"Bamako means 'bay of crocodile' in the Bambara language in Mali, which is like Malinke," Mike interjects, referring to the local language. Bamako, the capital city of Mali, is five hundred miles downriver.

"How do you know that?" I ask Mike.

"National Geographic," he says. "That means we may be seeing crocodiles until we reach Bamako. Maybe crocs will know how tasty people are by the time we get there."

When I consider the prospect that we may have to deal with crocodiles for weeks, I decide I want one of the guns. Yet having seen the speed of the crocodile approaching Rick, I doubt that a gun would be useful most of the time. Everything had happened so quickly, and that time we had a warning: we saw the crocodile. Mark could have shot it. But could one shot stop a crocodile? And would we have time or even be in a position to see or shoot the crocodile next time?

I try to sleep, but my mind is trapped in the moment and convinced that we could just as easily be camping without Rick and planning how to get the hell out of here. Next to me in our tent, he is fast asleep.

My mind roams to the rivers I had been on in the United States, where my sensation has always been of being pushed by the water. It pushes in the Colorado River in the Grand Canyon, in the fast-moving Rogue in southern Oregon, and in the Northgate Canyon of the North Platte near Laramie. The Niger River, unlike other rivers, pulls. Even after just one day on the river, I felt the Niger pull as if it is tethered to a longer, deeper force, like a river close to a tide. But we are nearly three thousand miles from the sea.

I realize I cannot look back over my shoulder on the Niger River. When a bend of the Niger has passed, it is over. What is behind me is gone, because I shouldn't look back. The crocodile is gone, but another one is very likely around the corner. Going with the Niger is like listening to a symphony, or climbing: you pay attention to the moment and reflect later. Ahead of us is a meandering river, flooding over its banks and moving fast. I must focus on what is next.

Day two on the river, a troop of baboons chase us from tree to tree along the bank, screaming and baring their teeth at us. I see five, then twenty, maybe more as they fly in and out of the green tree limbs. Golden and gangly, but nimble in the trees, the baboons are snarling warriors. I immediately fear them more than the crocodile, because they are aggressive and tribal and there are more than I can count. Baboons are lanky and large, and as extraordinarily fast on foot as by tree. They mirror our speed for many minutes. I take their reaction as part curiosity, but more as a territorial warning not to come near. If we were to touch land, I sense we would be shredded.

We are alone here. People in the Guinean highlands do not use the river for travel, except to cross it here and there, as evidenced by boats tethered to branches and sunk along the shore to keep the wood swollen so the boats don't crack in the heat. They don't use the river for daily life, either, relying instead on side streams for drinking water and cleaning. We see one village in sixty or so miles. I hear a village one day, through the bush, somewhere out of sight and with no visible trail. There is no escape from our kayaks, which are small islands unto themselves. And we find little negotiable space on the riverbank. The river, too, is entangled in downed trees, green limbs, vines growing in all directions, and, periodically, baby crocodiles sunning themselves on larger limbs along the riverbank. My compass indicates that the meandering brown river doubles back on itself over and over. Miles of travel on the water equate to negligible progress in real distance.

Crocodiles may explain why there are no villages directly on the river. Two lunge out of the water like explosions onto a worn path of matted-down tall grass. It seems from their reaction that we have frightened them, but I doubt it. They are huge and it is impossible to imagine them below anything on the Niger's food chain.

"You see," Rick points out, continuing his earlier argument, "crocodiles think we are pursuing them. They won't come after us."

We clear a camp in the tall grass above the Niger's bank and beneath a dense, tall tree canopy. It is a good camp, but we have no food. We sleep hungry and rise early to get to Faranah, the town on the road from Conakry that had been our first stop and our first sighting of the river before we got into the forest and found the river's source nine days earlier. We gauge it to be a half day or so downriver.

The forest in the morning buzzes and hums with birds and insects above us as we break camp. The hum, it turns out, is mostly from bees. The buzz of a bee becomes a hum when they swarm in a swirling tornado. Thousands of them circle in a gap between the trees above us, a beautiful yellow and black swirling cloud that we pause to watch as we pack our tents. Then, like a shot of lightning from the cloud, one finds Rick. He yells, slaps, and is engulfed immediately by hundreds of bees. In desperation, he runs to the Niger and dives in. When he rises from the water, his head is again engulfed in a cloud of furious insects. Stunned and unmoving, I watch him, until one bee hits me in the head, and then hundreds attack me in response, just as they had attacked Rick. I dive into the Niger with Rick. Then Mark is swarmed. We strip naked and put our pants over our heads to protect them, our mouths barely out of the brown water. Bees still pound our covered heads. The ominous sound of thousands of circling bees is relentless and inescapable.

"See any croc?" Mike yells to us from the riverbank, safe and not stung.

"So this is how we go?" I ask Rick.

He laughs. "The headline reads, Three naked Laramie men enter the food chain to be eaten by crocodile after being bombarded by killer bees."

Mark laughs, too.

"Welcome to Africa, men!" Mike howls.

We wait. Then wait longer. It is our only plan. The bees slow and spread out but remain everywhere around us, though they act less as an organized storm than an uncoordinated meandering of individuals. I move slowly and do not swat the bees that land on me. The answer with bees, it turns out, is to move with them and not anger them to provoke a sting, which, I later learned, emits an alarm pheromone that brings the hive to attack the spot of the first sting. An animal can die this way when bees swarm its mouth or snout. Be with them, and they will be with you, became our only option. One by one, we move slowly out the water, naked but for our shorts draped over our heads, and get into our kayaks. Bees swirl around our heads, gradually circling away as we proceed down the river. I count thirteen stings, each a small, sore welt on my face and head.

Two hours later, not two weeks after entering the highland forest, we reach Faranah, the first small city between the Niger's source and Guinea's border with Mali, which is another three hundred miles downriver. We welcome our return to Faranah and civilization. We have hiked and kayaked nearly two hundred miles but have, realistically, barely begun the long river.

On our earlier trip through Faranah by road, we had befriended employees of a Norwegian telecommunications company called Nera. They were pleased to see us return and offered us cold beer and a small aboveground swimming pool. A small team there, led by a couple from Oslo who had worked in Guinea and West Africa for many years, lived in a walled compound that also contained equipment to build transmission towers for wireless telephones. They invited us to camp and store our kayaks in the compound while we rested and purchased provisions for the next leg of the river.

Free of the river and my kayak, I long to be alone for a while. I walk into town, located at a crossroads, with trucks and cars honking on the main road a mile from the Nera compound. Circling the perimeter of a huge open-air market, I hear a few men speaking English amid others speaking French and the languages of the highlands. One of the men is delivering small round loaves of bread to a merchant along the dusty road, who displays the bread alongside wedges of French cheese wrapped in thin aluminum foil in a glass case.

I approach the men and ask them about their bread.

"Ee barabo ee bara, ee barase ibara," I say, repeating the phrase the chief said to us in Guinea, to the tall man holding a bundle of bread in a bag. He smiles, walks over, and shakes my hand.

"Baguette?" I ask.

"This is sugared bread, not French. Fifty francs," the man says in English.

That is about five cents, and I buy one and eat it immediately.

He observes me as I eat. "Excellent," I tell him and ask on instinct, because he is speaking English, whether he is Liberian.

He nods. "I am Mohammed. We are Muslim and speak the Mandingo language," he explains with an unexpected openness. "We were unsafe. Guinea is safe. There are many Muslims here." He tells me that those who could escape in the night, a year earlier, left like a blast that dispersed the family and everything thereafter. Others in the family stayed behind. "We left by bus and road and we kept moving, then we walked and carried each other."

Their first stop was Sierra Leone, and then Guinea. They were early escapees of a fast-boiling war that spread to all corners of Liberia. They had traveled the same area we had traversed, in search of a place they hoped would be good for them. As time passed, and before refugee camps had been established elsewhere in Guinea, the family found Faranah and started a bakery.

I ask whether I can see their bakery. Mohammed seems pleased with my interest. He and another Liberian man lead me to a quieter area not far from the busy market, which I am anxious to explore again later. Their bakery is one large room, housed in a mud-walled building with a stove made of mud and flat stones from the Niger's bank nearby. The room is dark but for daylight from windows, and smoky. Men work shirtless while young boys tumble between their legs. Several men turn from the oven to a table, moving round loaves into and out of the flaming fire with wooden tools. Small tree limbs are cut and stacked by one man while another stands ready to replenish the hot coals with new wood.

Round loaves the size of a child's fist rise quickly in the oven's heat as if they are balloons being inflated by a deep, long breath. They brown as fast as they rise and are pulled out of the oven, in batches of ten or so at a time, by an assembly of the men working as precisely as a conveyor in a factory. A man hands me a hot loaf, more like a large bun than a conventional baguette. It is transcendent in taste and in the circumstances of its production, coming from these dislocated people, pushing forward simultaneously with simplicity and aspiration. I

Liberian refugee Mohammed in his family bakery, Faranah, Guinea, 1991.

am hooked on the people and their bread.

I learn over the next few hours that the Liberians are an extended family of sixteen, aged two to thirty-two. Mohammed tells me he is thirty-two, which is my age, too, and he is also the apparent leader, as he observes the operations of the bakery more than he works. In this stifling room, I count the production, about 350 loaves that day. I calculate that this will garner eighteen dollars in revenue before the cost of yeast and flour. But it supports the family.

They have the radio tuned loud to the BBC. Charles Taylor was reported to be meeting with an emissary, Jimmy Carter, a step at initiating discussions and possibly a resolution of the conflict.

"Jimmy Carter. He is great man," one of the men tells me.

Charles Taylor's name alone caused grunts from the Liberians.

Mohammed explains that his country is controlled by a man who uses boys with guns to create chaos and uncertainty while siphoning off the nation's cocoa, rubber, and minerals. It seems incomprehensible, all of it, and unstoppable, from the look in Mohammed's eyes. Not sure what to believe or what to say, and overwhelmed with his situation, I turn to the children.

"Where are the mothers of these children?"

"Some with grandparents. My mother, maybe. We don't know," he admitted.

"These children," he pauses, "did not cry until we arrived here." He pulls a toddler to his feet and strokes his head while the boy wraps his arms around the man's bare leg like a tree trunk and hugs it. "Today, they cry. You hear?"

I had not noticed the crying and still could not hear it. I cannot hear anything over the hot hissing and popping of the oven's fire, the kneading and pounding of the bread, the movement of bare feet, and the pulling of soft round loaves of white bread from the oven with long wooden sticks onto worn wooden tables. The dulled colors in the room—from the wood to the people to the bread—are those of an old photograph. There are no reds, blues, or yellows. Only black, white, and brown clothing covered in flour, which billows like quick clouds in the hot air to settle onto sweating bodies. It is very nearly a dance, the orchestration of individuals guided by the movement of baking bread. I leave Mohammed and his family's bakery, inspired by their durability and spirit. I am reinvigorated for whatever the next leg of the Niger will bring.

Back at the Nera compound, I see Mark and Mike talking, their heads huddled together, and I realize they are not really here. For them,

West Africa has been a series of days languishing from one to the next. Sori, the hippos, the crocodile, the bees, these would be the thread of stories they would carry home. But nothing made up for the stories they had left unexplored with their wives back home. I had sensed this early. It had been evident in their laughter at danger. Accepting danger was a part of their lives. A slip or a slide on a mountain could have ended things for either of them on climbing journeys, or expeditions like this one. But this time they laughed at the irony that we could die doing something that we wanted to do but could just as easily have done without. It was evident on the long nights when they talked and talked in low voices in their tent. Their minds were more on what they were missing at home and what changes awaited them than what they were experiencing. They were in Africa. But they had never left Laramie.

I, too, returned to Laramie. The smoking-hot bakery brought me home. Baking bread was a job for me between excursions. I relied on baking to feed myself easily and cheaply. I could share and sell bread and rolls, which proved a practical way to restart my life in Laramie or anywhere. I did this over and over for years before taking a career job at a bank. I never felt as good as I did when I was working alone, starting yeast in warm water at sunrise in the summer in Laramie at a small restaurant, smelling the bread bubbling with yeast, the soft dough building itself before my eyes before I kneaded and baked mounds of it. As the bread cooled, I would rest on the bench outside the restaurant with a cup of coffee, alone in the sun while stacks of bread waited to be eaten. For this reason, I was immediately drawn to the Liberian bread bakers.

Their bakery is not the place of quiet or solitude I had come to know while baking at five in the morning alone in a Laramie restaurant kitchen. But it is alive with what I loved most about baking bread: each day had a refreshed start, an effort, and an accomplishment. The baking of bread, I realized while visiting Mohammed's bakery, feels a lot like our mornings on the river. Each one had a simple and repeated pattern: breaking camp and brewing something hot to drink and then eat, followed by the drift of the river, pulling us into the day that in this region has a twelve-hour span of light and dark.

A map in the Nera compound showed just two towns in more than two hundred miles downriver in Guinea—Kouroussa and Siguiri—and nothing in between. We convene and make a shopping list, alert not to run short of food as we had on the first leg of the river.

The market is sprawling with aisles of booths, tables, and baskets holding everything from clothing to pots and pans to all the food grown in, or imported into, Guinea. A man waves me over to a table of T-shirts boasting logos from American universities (Texas, Missouri), companies (Coke, Pepsi, a bank in Ohio), and bands (New Kids on the Block, U2). Next to his table is a busy covered booth with an enormous stack of Chinese porcelain-covered metal cups and pans, colorful plastic tubs and pots, and all varieties of plastic utensils.

I narrow my list of provisions based on the space available in our dry bags and boats. I must purchase food for ten days, which is about how long we estimate it will take to get to Kouroussa. I buy sixty cans of sardines in tomato sauce from Tunisia. Two large cans of beef from Finland that were marked for government assistance. Four large bags of dried pasta from Italy; four cans of condensed milk from the Netherlands; a hundred tea bags from England; a bag of hard candy from Poland; two bags of cookies from Colombia; and eight small cans of tomato paste with no manufacturing country listed. We load other dry bags with rice, dates, sweet potatoes, peanut butter, onions, oranges, and bananas. All of us fill liter bottles with regular gas for our two stoves. We are set for the next leg.

We leave after two nights in Faranah, sensing we are on a long leg of the expedition. The river is smooth and brown, calmer than above Faranah. It is also wider and rolls without breaking into a splash or sound other than the hiss of water rushing through tree roots and branches along the bank. The Niger meanders with a constant current. Some turns are hairpin, others sweeping; nothing is straight on the river, and each bend provides a new view that is just like the one we have passed. The uncertainty we felt on the upper Niger has abated. Perhaps we will cruise easily on flatwater current all the way to Kouroussa.

Then, "RRRRGHHH!" A deep, hollow roar erupts from somewhere, everywhere. It could have come from the sky or behind us, in front, either side. The sound paralyzes me before I see a wave the size of ocean surf coming at me. A hippo has lofted itself from nowhere several feet out of the river right next to Mark and me. I stare at it and see the animal spin away from us. I brace to avoid rolling. Mark is paddling ahead of me like a man possessed. But the hippo has gone back under-water, beneath us in the wake of waves.

We all paddle away hard without speaking or looking back.

Hippos, like the bees, are upon you without warning. But there the similarity ends. Adult hippos weigh two tons but are nearly impossible to see on the Niger because they spend almost all their time—includ-ing breeding, birthing, and sleeping—in the water. They are the shape and color of the rocks in the river. They do not smell, or they smell the same as the river. They wander the bottom with lungs the size of oxygen tanks. Unfortunately, we learn this later.

"You frightened it," Rick finally offers as explanation. And we are off on another debate about an animal we have absolutely no experience with or knowledge of.

"Why was it frightened?" Mike questions.

"Maybe it had a baby," Rick offers.

"If the hippo had come in our direction, we'd have been swimming," Mark exclaims.

"Hippos kill more people than all other African animals combined," Mike tells us.

"How do you know that?" I ask him.

"National Geographic," he says.

"We shouldn't surprise them," Rick says, somehow an instant expert on hippo behavior, and suggests that we tap our paddle blades on the coaming ring, the hard fiberglass rim that surrounds the cockpit seats of our kayaks for a spray skirt that we do not need on the river. I try it. We all try it.

"The sound will travel underwater," Rick says. No one argues, and we paddle forward on the brown glassy water, periodically tapping our paddles against our kayaks. It seems ridiculous, like singing on a trail in Wyoming to avoid surprising bears.

"RRRRGHHH. RRGHH, RRGHH." We hear another hippo, and again we do not immediately see it until it surges out of the river ahead of us. It is like an explosion. Then it moves upriver toward us. "RRR-RGHHH." The sound rumbles as if from the heart of the earth, shaking my body like the crack of thunder.

An adult hippo is larger than a cow or even a bison, and it looks hairless. This one has pink around its ears and nostrils, a natural balm secretion that, I later learned, protects its skin from cracking in the sun. It snorts in long grunts that are more like deep roars. They last and last, as the animal's lungs are built for spending long periods underwater. Are they water animals that move on land? Or land animals that forage at night but live in water? No matter, these creatures are plucked from the Pleistocene and own the river.

We all steer away from the hippo, who moves upriver but on the other side of the Niger, only twenty yards away. On its other side, close to the bank across the river from us, I see a baby hippo, then another baby, both the size of the biggest pig you can imagine.

"Oh shit, a mother," Mark yells back to us and paddles downriver. I want to do the same but the mother hippo is still too close for me to make a safe route away from it. I pull onto the left bank and scramble out of my kayak up a steep bank and lose sight of the others.

"It's a mother," Mark yells again. "Get clear, get clear."

From the riverbank, where I try to get up a tree, I watch the mother slow momentarily for one of her young. She keeps moving with her baby upriver, away from us. I think of bears again, which I had been told over and over not to run from. You can't outrun a bear, and if you run, it may consider you prey. We had no such guidance on hippos. I agreed with Rick that warning them of our presence was smart, but escaping them? Land seemed better than water.

Once the mother is out of sight, I get back in my kayak and regroup with my friends. We paddle for a few hours uninterrupted by anything, putting miles of river away on the glassy water. We find a good place to camp midriver on rocks the shape and color of hippos. It is exposed but feels safe, and it is beautiful beyond any place we have seen on the Niger as the sun sets and the smooth rocks cool. Rivulets course through the rounded rocks and we bathe in the warm water.

We arrive in Kouroussa after four full days of pushing down the river, covering, we estimate, 110 to 120 miles since Faranah. It is Halloween night. The town's buildings are in costume as an old French city. Dressed in old, worn threads, Kouroussa's roads are lined with trees like a boulevard, and behind those trees stand European houses. But they are windowless, and many are falling down. I aim for a train station at the end of one boulevard and find it abandoned but for a family living in the corner of one room. Parched grass fills the space between the rail lines, which are rusted and unused. There are no trains or remnants of trains. This place used to be something but seems not to want to be anything now. The old French veneer accentuates the spooky, too-quiet aspect of the city.

I meet a German aid worker at a shop along the main boulevard. "Guinea is shit," he spits. "You understand? Shit." He tells me he has been in Kouroussa for two months. He had been posted in Chad for four years, Thailand for four years, and Senegal before coming here. "I asked people in Senegal about their brothers in Guinea," he tells me. "They told me the people of Guinea don't like to work."

"What are you doing here?" I ask him.

"Nothing," he says. "There is nothing to accomplish here."

I walk back to the river, where we had found a flat place to pitch our tents, and see a railroad bridge that has fallen apart, pieces apparently taken from it. At the river, Mike is listening to the BBC on his radio, and Mark is writing in his notebook. "Stories," he says. "I need stories."

Rick is talking with a local man nearby.

"This man tells us not to drink the water here," Rick tells us. "See that down there, past that old rail bridge?"

"Yes," I say. "It looks busy."

"That is the public toilet," he tells us.

"Welcome to Africa," Mike sighs. We leave the next morning.

The Niger widens below Kouroussa where a large river, the Milo, joins it. The Niger is now more like an enormous linear lake than a moving river. It flows, but barely, though I still feel its pull, like the inevitability of falling asleep. The banks are drier and more savanna-like than the dense forest we had left behind in the highlands, and the sparsely populated stretch between Faranah and Kouroussa.

We see hundreds of wading birds—stilts, plovers, crocodile birds, egrets, and ibis. I am enchanted with the variety of kingfishers, especially the tiny bright blue and orange pygmy kingfisher. Above us are raptors and an eagle, the West African fish eagle, much like our American bald eagle except with a bronze-colored body and the pronounced white of its head extending down its chest. We camp on sandbars for three straight nights and see no one on the river until we get to Siguiri, which is Guinea's last town before the border, 143 miles from Bamako, the capital of Mali. We have traveled about 200 miles in the previous seven days, an average of almost 29 miles a day. Over beers, we talk about the total distance we have traveled, about 300 miles, an accomplishment we toast that night in Siguiri, and then sigh at the time it will take to paddle another 2,300 miles. The calendar math is simple: if we are able to move as swiftly as we have the last week, it will take us three months. That is, if the river is as easy as it has been since Kouroussa, and the actual river miles equal the "official" recorded distance, which is probably a linear measurement, not a measurement of the length of the river's winding path.

Outside a café the next morning, over Nescafé with lait sucré, Mark and Mike tell us they are going to jump on a truck for Bamako and go home. They leave before finishing their coffee. Just like that. Mike returned home to his wife by Thanksgiving. Mark purchased a motorcycle and took it to Timbuktu before returning home to his wife by Christmas.

We sit at the café watching the truck carrying our friends as it rolls in dust, out of sight.

Expeditions are like relationships. Each one preconditions a response to the next. You gain some specific wisdom and greater confidence but, inevitably, greater apprehension. Each one provides the next with a context for expectations that, like falling in love all over again, make the next journey less likely to be as surprising because, after many expeditions, you always know exactly what is new but also what is missing. And we do not easily get over what is missing, even in the midst of something new.

This was the Niger River for Mark and Mike—a series of expectations unmet and a series of encounters unrecognized and unexplored. Like a young lover grown old, they lusted for a last hurrah. What they had imagined, they had not found. Mark left the expedition he had conceived, and Mike, his closest friend, joined him.

"Let's have another one of these great coffees," Rick suggests. And we do just that. We do not have to be anywhere anytime soon. I realize that Rick and I left the expedition that morning, too. But the journey has begun.

"Where are we going?" Rick finally asks.

The river pulls onward and we get into our kayaks the next morning on a journey to Bamako, Mali.

8

Travels into the Interior

MY FIRST IMPRESSION OF THE RIVER without Mark and Mike is that it is bigger, and quieter. The Niger does become wider by the day, even the first three days out of Siguiri, as the landscape flattens without hills and the riverbank foliage diminishes to a border of grasses and fewer trees. But the distance between the river's banks is also accentuated by it being just the two of us on the water. Neither of us is a big talker, as both Mike and Mark had been, so we paddle without much conversation. And while the four of us had moved more like beads separated on a necklace, Rick and I begin to paddle with less of a tether between us. I check where Rick is more often. He will be in front of me one morning, far behind in the afternoon. We pass each other quietly, sometimes fifty yards apart, and without a word we will navigate back together for lunch, and in the evening to camp.

For the first time we see wooden pirogues, some many feet long and stacked with goods and goats, moving downstream with the aid of small sails or men with long bamboo poles, pushing them off the river's bottom. We stop in a village just inside the Malian border, a border we learn of only when we try to use Guinean currency to buy fruit and are rebuffed but are given a few oranges anyway, out of kindness. Behind the fruit vendor's wooden stand is a delicate small mosque made of compacted mud, its spires adorned with white ostrich eggs.

Everything in the first days without Mark and Mike becomes easier and less dramatic. In the two and a half days since leaving Siguiri, having covered 143 miles, I calculate that we have averaged five miles per hour when we get to Bamako.

We hear Bamako—the whine of motorcycles on its streets—before we can see it. The river is quiet and boat-free even as we paddle into the city, spread far and flat on both sides of the Niger. The river is connected by a bridge, the first bridge we have seen crossing the river since Dougoulema. There, the Niger had been more a wilderness for crocodiles than a river to bridge for humans. Bamako claims a population of 1.5 million, though that figure does not include the region's seminomadic people and traders from throughout West Africa who travel there to buy and sell. We will see more faces in five minutes in the West African metropolis than we have in a month in Guinea.

Bamako had not always been a bustling trading hub. It had been settled by the Bozo, a nomadic river people who fished and hunted. The dangerous crocodiles that gave the city its Bambara name, Bay of Crocodile, are long gone from Bamako, and the Bozo, too, have moved away, downriver a few hundred miles to a quiet area in the interior, where they fish for the Niger's two hundred–plus species of fish.

Now, Bamako has a few tall buildings, skyscrapers ten to fifteen stories high that tower in contrast with an otherwise horizontal city. One new building closest to the Niger is a branch of the West African Central Bank. It hovers over the city like an exclamation point, constructed of cement yet colored a dull orange that mimics the glow of mud mosques. This international development bank is positioned next to a cement plant that gets its sand from a dozen or so men who dive with buckets into the middle of the Niger. Bucket by bucket, the men work without pause to provide raw material for structures in the city.

Just before Bamako's bridge, we see a dock connected to a green lawn sloping up to a white building with wicker chairs and large windows facing the river. Things are quiet and secure at the dock, empty but for one speedboat loaded with gear for water-skiing. A sign identifies the place as the Bamako Yacht Club. We paddle up and get out of our boats.

Three men meet us outside the club as we walk up the lawn. Then they welcome us into the windowed room, with enough seating for forty people and a stocked bar. The men talk with us first in French, and then quickly in English after hearing us talk to each other. They speak with each other in Arabic. They are from Beirut, home of the pragmatic entrepreneurs of the globe, spread so widely worldwide that more of the city's people live outside Lebanon than within its borders. We had experienced Lebanese entrepreneurs early on in Conakry, at a restaurant owned by a Lebanese family.

Another man, the only customer in the club, is sitting at a window table. He introduces himself as Jean Pierre.

"I work until one every day," Jean Pierre says immediately, as if to explain his drinking at midday. "I work for the French government, aiding Mali. Who are you?" he asks us.

"Rick," I point, "and I am John. We are from Wyoming," I say.

"Where?"

"Americans," Rick said.

I notice the Lebanese have walked to another corner of the club. But Jean Pierre has a volley of questions for us, all of which we could have anticipated: Why are you traveling on the Niger? Where are you coming from and where are you going? Then, finally, the practical questions: Where do you sleep and what do you eat?

Jean Pierre is friendly in that enviable way that some people are; they can move in a crowd at a cocktail party and have something worthwhile to say to everyone. But I sense he is lonely and bored, as I suspect most men who drink alone at midday are. But he speaks quickly and easily in English and with animated gestures before pausing, taking a sip, and shaking his head at us. We wait for his next question, which hangs on his lips between sips. He tells us, as if answering a quiz, about the club and its members—a small group, he says, all men and all foreigners, and one with a speedboat. The bar, Jean Pierre points out, is stocked from the world—but only with what the members drink.

"A drink, gentlemen?" Jean Pierre inquires.

We decline, telling him we want to walk into Bamako.

"For me, it is gin," he says. He then swings his arm from the bar to point out the windows. "That bridge is filled with traffic all day, every day," he starts, settling back in his chair to tell us more.

Jean Pierre, commanding our interest and attention, launches into the history of the bridge: it was conceived in 1912; construction started in 1936 but stopped during World War II; and it was finally completed in a 1957, when it fit the needs of a city of roughly a hundred thousand. The Malian government renamed it the Bridge of Martyrs in 1961, for those who died during Mali's battle for independence from the French. Jean Pierre says that trucks must wait until night to cross because of weight restrictions. The traffic has induced the Saudis to build a second bridge, but population growth outpaces bridge building. "The Chinese are constructing another bridge for Bamako, with Swiss engineers," Jean Pierre tells us.

Jean Pierre stands and waves down at our kayaks, shaking his head again, and puts his hand on Rick's shoulder while looking back and forth between us.

"We will meet here at four," he says. "A museum, a drink, maybe a film," he adds.

Before we leave, one of the Lebanese men, the one I sensed was the manager, suggests that we can sleep there in our tent. "You stay here as you wish," the man says.

Our needs were clear, our situation framed by how we had arrived and how we were dressed. Our shirts and pants were ringed in dried, white salty sweat, and our boats with our mobile lives sat on their dock. The lawn at the club would have been as nice as anyplace we had camped, but we didn't stop to consider his offer or start spreading out our tent. We did feel comfortable and safe there, however, and asked whether we could leave our kayaks and gear there while we explored the city.

"As you wish," the man repeats.

We clean ourselves with river water and a bathroom sink in the bar. We are free of the river and our boats, finally, with space to move on foot, to wander any direction on streets full of people. The city presents us freedom we had not known, bottled up on the river. I look at our kayaks and feel as if I had tied my trusted dog to a fence post and walked away. But my guilt evaporates quickly because the boat is anything but my own legs. And I am dying to walk and keep walking.

We leave through a metal gate, guarded by a man who locks it behind us. Immediately down a quiet road, the main thoroughfare approaching the bridge is clogged with stalled traffic. A man and a boy push a small car to the side of the tight knot of vehicles while other people wander among the puffing tailpipes. A table next to the bridge sells bottles of gas in square Johnnie Walker bottles—an indication, perhaps, that the yacht club sells a lot of Scotch whiskey. It seems that all of Bamako comes to the bridge. Twenty more feet of width would uncork the city to move over the river. Below the bridge, the Niger River is empty of boats or people.

Bamako is a dust bomb that buzzes at eye level with every conceivable sound of motor, from wailing squeals to growls. A motorcycle weaves around us without a glance from the rider. Another cuts between Rick and several camels tied with handwoven rope to metal poles pushed into roadside dirt. Drivers of cycles, three-wheeled carts, minibus taxis, and cars all honk incessantly, not in annoyance, but for warning or by habit. No one seems angry.

The roads are ripe for collisions but collisions aren't happening, even though the road and the bridge are shared by trucks, animals, motorcycles, animal-drawn carts, taxi buses, taxi cars, and pedestrians of all ages. We weave and dodge our way down the road as unpredictably as flies in the wind. Rick suggests we move with the same instincts we used with hippo: walk calmly and be predictable. Don't dodge them; let them move from you. But as with the hippo, if trucks don't move, you must move away from them, and quickly.

Groups of men stand to the side of the main road wrapped in the darkest of blue robes, an indigo that shimmers in the sun like the surface of a lake under moonlight. But it is hot, and I wonder how they can tolerate turban-extended head wraps veiling their mouths and often their noses. Stately and solid, like statues in a town square, the tall men are Tuareg, the most famous of Malians. A mention of Mali in any book will highlight the nomadic Tuareg. They cluster together, staying to themselves. The Tuareg travel to Bamako from the desert that stretches north of the city to Mauritania, east to the country of Niger, and beyond to Algeria and Libya, a borderless area of borderless people. They are not river people. They walk or travel by camel and have come to sell wares such as leather and jewelry before provisioning for their trek back into the northern desert. The men have no women with them.

I hear people hiss as they pass them, but there are few Tuareg to hiss at. They present an aura of confidence that exceeds even that of the few polished people driving the streets in Mercedes. I learn, as we walk and see more small groups of Tuareg, that they do not hide themselves in the city. They choose not to blend into Bamako and capture, as a result, a presence incommensurate with their numbers.

The sight of them fuels an urge to explore Mali beyond the river. The only way, if there is a way, for us to see how they live is to get into the desert. I consider taking some days to walk north of Bamako alone.

Our first stop is the US Embassy, where we check our visas and document our entrance into Mali. I ask about the Tuareg.

"Tuareg are dangerous again," a man wearing a suit and tie tells us from behind a counter with a window that separates him from a small, empty waiting room. The window is the single public interaction point of the embassy for us and those seeking visas. The man, a foreign service officer, is more unfriendly than a bored minimum-wage worker at McDonald's and is utterly devoid of advice, let alone inquisitiveness about what we are doing. All the man says is, "Tuareg are dangerous."

"How long have you been in Mali?" I ask him.

"Too," he says.

"Two years?" I ask.

"Too long," he says, sliding my passport back to me across the counter.

I felt as if I could explore Bamako for months, circling the same area daily, and not face tedium. Bamako buzzes and wanders. I had fallen for it.

Rick and I can both use time alone, though neither of us mentions it. We had rarely been out of sight of each other or out of reach of our kayaks for weeks. Now we were in a city that moved as unrestrainedly as the river, but in all directions.

We leave the embassy in search of a good cup of coffee, disheveled but exhilarated. I eye a tall hotel in a lush park off Avenue du Fleuve, down a narrower bush-lined lane. The hotel appears elegant, not old but already dated in an exuberant mix of styles that transformed it from shiny-new to tacky-dated almost overnight. It is noticeably isolated, with walls and gates for diplomats and careful tourists. I have no intention of spending a night in a bed there, but I am curious about such a place and want a cup of real coffee, a deviation from tea and the powdered instant Nescafé we boil on our stove every morning.

Despite our wrinkled and worn clothing, a guard lets us through a gate without question before a doorman with a smile welcomes us toward a tall wooden door and into a garden. A rock path takes us into the hotel and its café overlooking Bamako and, just beyond rows of one- and two-story buildings, the Niger River, as wide and docile as a lake. Looking at the river from a distance makes me feel disconnected from it, and I feel fine with that. Being on a river for 450 miles has been enough, but I do not share my thoughts with Rick. The hotel is clean and offers shelves with books, mostly in French but a few in English. I look around the café, searching for a traveler to talk with, but the place has more potted plants and waitstaff than customers. It is well past lunchtime, apparently a lull in the day.

"This is an island," Rick assesses, looking around the hotel's almost empty café.

I don't think he is complaining, because Rick seldom complains, but he is right. The café is quiet and disorienting in its cleanliness and order. The hotel is veneered in dark hardwood, probably from forests south of Mali in Burkina Faso or the Ivory Coast. It is so completely isolated in its entire makeup that I could have believed we had left Mali. The view, however, confirms that we remain dead center in Bamako and close to the river.

An extraordinary cup of coffee arrives, exactly as you'd get in Paris, except the coffee tastes even better and smells as rich as the wet West African forest floor. At that moment, in a state of craving, my coffee is as perfect as any coffee anywhere in the world and is precisely what I wanted. We had made it to Bamako, an accomplishment, and an end of a journey if we let it be that. The river landscape had been drenching then dangerous, hot then lethargic, and altogether more than we might have been willing to accept, had we known what to expect.

"You want to go?" Rick asks after we have lingered long enough that I begin considering a second cup of coffee.

"Where?" I ask.

Rick stands up. "Bamako," he says. "A bakery," he adds and walks out.

Living without a daily visit to a bakery had been a difficult endurance for Rick. If anyone could find the semblance of a bakery with a cinnamon roll in Mali, a land without cinnamon, Rick would. He needs a place to sit and strike up conversations with strangers. I need another cup of coffee.

I sit back, completely alone for the first time in weeks. I am without a care for what I might do next in Bamako or on the Niger. I am satisfied to sit still without a concern or a plan. We had not discussed what we would do if we didn't quit our river journey in Bamako, though the decision was waiting for us to make, eventually, after coffee, after walking the city.

The waiter explains that the river was once on the hotel's edge. I look outside again. The Niger is now about a mile south of the hotel. He tells me it had circled the hotel for some years but then "the river found its way." He corrects me when I refer to the river as the Niger.

"Djoliba," he says. "Blood—Djoli. River—Ba."

"Why blood?" I ask.

"The river is our blood," he says. "You," he says, pointing at me, "will not die in water because your soul lives in water."

"How do you know that?" I ask the man.

"I say to you that I see," he says.

"Thank you," I respond, stunned. If I project anything it is relief, because I am not a man born for water. He has no idea I cannot swim.

I leave the hotel and walk along a dusty road, though it is paved under the dirt, where I find women lined up under tarps cooking food for sale. One woman's stall has both fried plantains and baguettes filled with skewered meat cooked over charcoal. I pick her because of the smell, hot and sweet, and the extra space she has under her tarp. It provides shade that I need to eat hot food on a hot day. I have explored as far as I need, and I stay in the shade with the woman as she serves people baguette after baguette wrapped in newspaper. No one pays attention to me, an anonymity I relish. One after another, customers, mostly men, wait for their food. Then a woman dressed in sweeping colorful cloth with automobiles on it comes to the stall with two children. She splits two baguettes between the three of them but, unlike other patrons, stands with her children to eat and does not choose to squat in the shade.

I find Rick at the club. He had located a nine-dollar-a-night hostel in a former Christian mission that, like the yacht club, is run by Lebanese men. Jean Pierre had also returned to the club to pick us up in his car and tour the city.

He weaves and honks through traffic like a seasoned taxi driver while picking up our conversation from earlier in the day. First he takes us north to Bamako's art museum to see an exhibit of Malian puppets. "You will meet a fine man named Xavier, a Belgian, at the exhibit. He wants to meet you."

At the show, a tall man approaches us. Jean Pierre introduces us to Xavier Van der Stappen and leaves us.

Xavier tours us around the exhibit, explaining that he is writing about the show as a journalist for a Belgian magazine. Xavier is tall and lean, dressed in pressed pants and shirt without the sleeves rolled up. He appears to be more a movie-star version of a journalist than a man anyone would mistake for a real journalist. But he is inquisitive, as I would expect of a journalist, and he asks us questions similar to those Jean Pierre asked, but with more specifics.

"Why are you, Americans, doing this river journey?" Before we answer, he wants to know about our "canoes."

"Sea kayaks," Rick tells him.

"How did you get them into Guinea?" he questions.

He listens with calm intensity, leaning forward to hear every word we tell him about the benefit of sea kayaks over canoes, including details, which he presses us for, about the internal frames that allowed us to carry the kayaks as backpacks in Guinea and as regular luggage on airlines.

"That is the way," he says and pauses. "Smart men."

As we walk through the show, he explains the painted wooden puppets, which were strung to perform with dark threads hidden in every joint. The Malian puppets are so detailed and full of mixed colors that they dance without moving. The Belgian enjoys explaining Malian art, as soft spoken as a museum curator.

We sit down after the tour, and Jean Pierre arrives with a cool ginger drink for each of us. Xavier continues to listen to us explain our trip in the Guinean highlands. He looks at us closely as if assessing us, sits back in his chair and says, "You are doing something, really something," and then toasts us with the ginger drink. As our glasses touch, he says, "I also canoe Niger River. Six years ago."

"Six years?" Rick asks.

I cannot utter anything in response, remaining alert to his next words, in shock that he had preceded us so many years earlier. Rick laughs uncomfortably for a moment and then shifts to a true laugh.

"Yes, like yesterday," Xavier says. "Djoliba never leaves you."

"Djoliba?" Rick asks.

"Blood-water," I interject.

"Yes. You know," Xavier says.

Xavier canoed the entire Niger River over a three-year period. He says he finished in 1985, after leaving Guinea and returning three times from Brussels, with different partners each time, picking up the river where he had left it. On his first trip, a lunging hippo bent his canoe in half in Guinea. Then, during a drought year, the Niger simply ran dry in northern Mali. Finally, on his third trip, Nigerian officials would not allow him to pass a river checkpoint. After three years, Xavier made it the 2,600 miles to the ocean from Tiro, a village on the Milo, the major tributary of the Niger in Guinea.

I sense he does not want to tell us too much, choosing his words much more carefully than he did when talking about puppets. He focuses on specific facts about his journey at certain places along the river and speaks mostly about the water, the animals, the food he ate, but not about himself.

"Did you see the pygmy hippo on the upper river?" Xavier wants to know.

"Hippo yes. Pygmy no," Rick says and tells him that we started on the main stem of the Niger after hiking to its source.

Xavier says he chose the Milo River because of the pygmy hippo, which he explains is small, bright pink, and very rare. "They are said to be only on the Milo River," he adds. "I did not find one. I want to, still."

Xavier tells us that he hunted monitor lizards and monkeys to eat in Guinea. He used a powerful compound bow he had brought partly for hunting but also for safety.

We had eaten what we found to cook in village markets. Xavier had eaten from the land. I look at Rick, who is mesmerized by his stories. I know that he feels as I do, like an intramural adventurer compared to the Belgian journalist-hunter-adventurer.

I am not deflated by Xavier's disclosure. Disappointed, yes, yet also inspired. This man had accomplished what we had admitted to each other in our tent at night was improbable if not impossible. We had wondered why no one had traveled the length of the Niger. Overlooked? Not documented? I had kept in the back of my mind that, despite Mark's research that indicated we would be the first, someone must have gone from source to sea on the Niger. Xavier confirmed my hunch. It was a relief, if only because it would focus us on continuing for the right reasons—to see the river itself, and its people and animals. Experience for its own sake instantly trumped our beginning with Mark and Mike on a quasi-conquest "first descent." Rick and I were no longer on the expedition we had started with the four of us. If we still had the motivation to accomplish a first descent, Xavier had put that prospect to rest.

Although we had admitted to each other since arriving in Africa that we were not the self-driven expedition types who could pull off such a journey, we had gradually accepted the illusion of ourselves as versions of eighteenth-century explorers. I had a notion of us as modern-day versions of Mungo Park, whose book I read at night in our tent. That illusion vanished after meeting a man of our own time who had hunted and eaten wild animals and reptiles on the Niger.

While we hadn't decided what we would do after Bamako, Rick and I had talked in Siguiri about the possibility of quitting in Bamako, still upstream of more than two thousand miles of river. After the highlands in Guinea, our goal was to get to Bamako, where for pride and practical reasons, we could end our journey. There was an international airport there and we were sufficiently satisfied with what we had already done—hiked and kayaked all of the Niger through Guinea into Mali, and avoided being taken by crocodiles, hippos, or bees.

"Where did Jean Pierre go?" I ask.

"He will come," Xavier says, and I understand, as if being played like a puppet, that our meeting with Xavier had been arranged by Jean Pierre from the moment we had arrived at the yacht club. Jean Pierre, to his credit, was not one to spoil our arrival to Bamako with the fact that another man had preceded us.

"But for sure, for sure, be careful of the five-meter fall below Bamako. I could have died there," Xavier says. "You are really doing something," he repeats, without offering us further advice.

And as if he had timed his entrance, Jean Pierre arrives to invite us to an outdoor showing of *The Last Temptation of Christ*.

"I must go," Xavier says, excusing himself from joining us. "You go your way." We would not see Xavier Van der Stappen again.

"There goes the expedition," I say to Rick.

"Good," Rick says. "First, first, first. I can't wait until Mark finds out."

People arrive for the movie by foot and motorbike. If there is any semblance of organization or a boundary, we cannot detect it, but people queue at a table to get into the movie in the flat, dusty ground between buildings. Some have mats to sit on, and others seek the few trees to sit against. But most people sit in the dirt. The film, with French subtitles, is shown on a big outdoor screen, like a drive-in. Jean Pierre fuels us with cold beer as the heat of Bamako eases into a bearable warm night. I am absorbed in the film's themes of recirculating doubt and fear, but also longing.

The following morning, without ever discussing our options, Rick and I begin provisioning for a week on the river. If I let my mind roam home to food, the approaching football season, and skiing, I'll be headed to the airport. When I start thinking that way, I pull myself back. Or Mali pulls me back.

Buying food in Bamako is a luxury of choices, and the options for cooking our dinner while camping reenergize me. If Rick wants to stop, I decide, I will, too. But Rick never mentions quitting and neither do I. We leave Bamako early in the morning, five days after we had arrived.

The Niger had been backed up like a lake in Bamako but becomes a real river again below the city. It surges through miles of dark water-worn granite channels that first constrict the river and then carry it into passageways walled with sheer, polished rock.

Once into the river's flow in one of these channels, "blood water" takes us with it. We have no choice. No place to stop. No way to scout ahead. No time to second-guess. Everything I do with my paddle is a reaction. We move at the will of the water, trapped on either side by black river-polished granite.

To my left, I first hear and then see a whirlpool, a deep hole that sucks water like a tornado at its center, creating a monstrous slurping sound that burps and gasps every couple of seconds. The river is being punched in the gut as half the channel is pulled into the hole. We brace with the current pushing us past the whirlpool against the opposite wall. I imagine a deep canyon under the river creating hydraulics that bend the river in all directions below us.

No one is on the river or along its banks for miles until we pass several people, men and women dressed in bright clothing up on a high ledge. They stand in a circle around a goat in what appears to be a cere-mony. We pass so quickly that they do not notice us. There is no looking back for us while we brace against several more circling black holes in the fast-moving water.

After many miles of moving as the river decides, we pass a dead goat swirling without end in one of the whirlpools. It would easily trap us, too, if we were caught in it, but there is no time to imagine the worst.

Below us, we hear as thunder, but do not see, Xavier's waterfall. We grab an edge of rock along a low bank to escape the current and eye the falls as best we can. They appear to be only ten to twenty feet high but likely fall into jumbled large rocks like those we can see downriver beyond the falls. The channel widens at the falls, as the rock walls come down to river level, and I realize, looking behind us, that the Niger has carved many channels through the granite, each captured in its own turbulent, rock-encased canyon. The area was once certainly a natural dam of the river; it remains, as it has for centuries, an impediment to travel, too furious for fishing, a place left for worship rituals, goat sacrifices, and little else.

A smooth edge ahead of us pours over a precipice, and the sound of crashing water reverberates like pounding bass drums that I feel in my chest and stomach. A calm river, the old, slow, lakelike Niger we had known at Bamako, is visible in the distance beyond the falls.

The falls are a half mile wide and composed of not one but many waterfalls. The river seems almost indecisive here, as it seeks space between boulders to slither over the falls. We locate a way to the edge on foot, leading our boats over rock and lowering them down in one area where the water is not falling, in a boulder field in the middle of the river. In higher water, this entire precipice would be deadly, as it had almost been for Xavier when he canoed this section.

Below the waterfalls, the river is, as we expected, a jumble of boulders, but it grows wide again and becomes slow and steady, and as brown as the surrounding landscape. We are soon out of the adventure and back to the Niger we know. I take off my life jacket.

Beyond the spray and wind of the falls, I can feel the heat of West Africa again. Inside the channels of the rock swath the air seemed cooler. Or had I not noticed the heat in the spinning and pulling of the river?

"Why did we do that?" Rick asks.

Here we go again. "Did we have a choice?" I sigh. But I know we could have skirted this section of river by road from Bamako, and probably would have if we had thought or talked about Xavier's warning about how dangerous it could be.

"Really," Rick presses me, "what's the point? Why are we here doing this?"

Because this had not been a question in Bamako, I know that Rick is not frustrated or frightened. He is not seeking a pro-con analysis, or a plan with alternatives. His question is The Question.

"Tomorrow," I say.

We have been down this conversational path many times before, on this and other long trips together. Rick resurrects it when, facing the absurdity of our circumstance, the question is not irrelevant. A never-ending question is better than a black-white answer for Rick.

"Besides, we have nothing better to do," I say. Rick has heard this before, too, and I know what he'll say next.

"This is the best thing to do today," he agrees.

Days strung together without quitting are becoming our way on the Niger. It was the same for us when we bicycled in Tibet in 1985. The wind, altitude, and dysentery wore us down daily, but we'd wake up the next day and keep bicycling. We were repeating our conversations from the Himalayas six years later.

"But what are you accomplishing?" I had asked then and repeat now.

"I imagine Segou," he says. The next stop, or the next page of a book, is what drives Rick, not the end of a journey or the end of a book.

Tomorrow. Crocodile or cinnamon roll, each day presented what would make the next day better for Rick. Safer—maybe. Wilder—maybe. It didn't matter, so long as the next day was a fresh start. If Rick values the continuity of going to a bakery every morning, he relishes meeting someone new each time. A turn in the plot. A place to camp on the river.

That evening, we fight back mosquitoes (and malaria) during dinner, eating a variation of noodles with tomato paste, okra, and onions. As a surprise, I add a can of corned beef from Finland that I had found in Bamako. Rick says our meal tastes better than ever, though it tastes largely the same as it has every other night. I believe the day makes our meal taste better.

The sunlight fades to a greater descent of bugs. Hundreds swarm us as we climb into our tent. As we kill mosquitoes one by one in a nightly ritual as consistent as our dinner, toads come onto the sliver of sandbar where we have camped. With no place to go on the narrow landing, toads the size of a fist shove themselves under the floor of our tent to rest under our warm and worn-out bodies. They begin to croak, safe beneath us, where they would otherwise have buried themselves in sand.

"Now this is living," Rick says.

I agree: the presence of fat toads under our bodies is far more comforting than repelling. We are part of the river this night, not visitors. After the cataracts and river hydraulics above us, I feel grateful that we are living.

We had seen no river traffic for two days below Bamako, but it becomes a highway at Koulikoro. The small city is Mali's port, which connects to Gao, another small city hundreds of miles downstream, near the border with the nation of Niger. Wooden boats with motors line a dock at Koulikoro. The town is nearly a suburb of the ever-creeping capital. It is known throughout West Africa as the place that produces Hippo brand soap, its logo as ubiquitous here as Coca-Cola in America.

We find a cool beer at a mobile pushcart that uses only the evaporation from wet cloth bags to chill the bottles and sit for hours watching wooden pirogues slicing through the Niger's water. All the pirogues are of the same design we've seen since entering Mali. They move like thin knives through the water, though many are forty or more feet long and none have motors. Both the bow and stern of the boats extend over the water, with a plank on which men stand with bamboo poles.

One after another, pirogues pass the dock area. Men push their bamboo poles behind them against the river bottom and then, in a sweeping movement, throw their poles forward and reposition themselves to grab the poles and push again. The cadence of the movement appears so effortless that I imagine it must take years of training. Then a boy passes doing the same rhythmic, sweeping push with his body. Then two women work their pirogue, in a mirroring of each other, twenty-five feet apart at the front and back of their boat. They all move the same way, with the weight of their bodies arced back in the push, followed by the pull of the pole into the air and the body sweep forward to repeat.

One boat carries a dozen white goats. The goats all behave, standing in one direction and at attention as if trained for military service. The boat moves out of sight up the edge of the river. Another pirogue is stacked high with gourds that will be made into the calabash bowls that

Traveler sailing with open palms and hands raised, a common way people greet others with a reference to a peaceful passing on the Niger River near Segou, Mali, 1991.

are used in every rural home. Another holds pottery, and one next to it is stacked high with fish traps made entirely of woven reeds.

Larger boats of similar design but with motors have a wide girth to hold travelers and their goods—melons, millet stalks in bundles, the same golden gourds. Grass mats shade the decks, and cross braces support seats for passengers and their smaller baggage of fabric and plastic bags holding dried okra, rice, and freshly picked onions. Meanwhile, the two dozen or so pirogues that brought people and goods to the dock area have quietly moved downriver on human power.

Men motor their pinnaces, which are just larger and motorized pirogues, to the middle of the river, while pirogues, guided by men and women alike, hug the bank where the water is no deeper than the fifteen- to twenty-foot length of the bamboo poles they use to move their boats. To cross the deeper center of the river, they put their bamboo poles down along the inside of their boats and use their wooden paddles, made of one piece of carved wood.

Traffic increases with each bend of the river as we near the historic city of Segou, 150 miles below Bamako. Alive with river commerce, a different Niger River has emerged in front of us. The quiet movement is interrupted every so often by larger motorized pinnaces, but we do not hear the whir of traffic we heard in Bamako. The river is a highway as busy as a road but is nearly silent. I hear individual voices in the distance, somewhere on the bank.

Segou descends to the river without flood walls or barriers. Women carrying containers of dripping water leave an ephemeral dark sprinkling of color on the hard soil. Children's wet footprints rise from the water's edge up into Segou. Unlike in Bamako, there is no bridge. The city-town rests on the south bank of the Niger, while the northern bank is open to the wide Sahel, stretching to the Sahara.

Men build boats by hand with ax and adz out of dark wood, and we angle our kayaks toward them, assured that the camaraderie between people with boats, whatever the design, will provide a friendly landing and men to watch our kayaks.

The boat builders do not have a building, but a temporary grass mat–roofed area that serves as a staging place for the boats they construct like puzzles from various sizes of wood. Boys stack slabs of lumber in the sun. The work site has no electricity or storage. The people not working on boat building walk through the area without distracting the builders.

Two boys run to us and help pull our kayaks onto higher ground but go immediately back to work at the small boat-building enterprise. A man approaches and, without words, moves his extended arms and hands slowly up and down, nodding his head to convey that our kayaks can stay there. He points to his eye and then to our boats, an indication that he will watch them.

The river is shallow on the banks of the small city. Women wash clothes and children wash themselves in knee-deep water. This relationship with the Niger makes Segou seem more like a town than a city. The place smells of soil and smoke, not traffic, and I notice birds on the riverbank—egrets, long-legged shorebirds, geese, and the ubiquitous sturdy crocodile birds, which have become the defining birds of the Niger River. We see them daily on every quiet or peopled sandbar along the river.

We look up from the boatyard to the market just up the bank, a quilt of women dressed in reds, yellows, and blues. Tarps and tables of goods weave with the women into the center of the small city. The people of Segou flow back and forth from the river to the market. Buildings around the edge of the market are constructed mostly of earth-brown brick worn and faded by sun. Bamako had newer buildings, an aura of an African capital that Segou does not have. Yet Segou is a long-inhabited regional trading nexus and is much older than Bamako.

We are surprised that we do not see any Tuareg in Segou, as we did in Bamako. Even after walking to the outskirts of Segou, an easy trek in the small city, we find no Tuareg, which is a disappointment. The BBC report on the radio the night before had given us a clue to their absence: the Tuareg had reportedly taken a busload of children hostage near Timbuktu and had released them. The BBC covered it quickly in its African Report but did not explain why it had happened, except for a reference to long-standing Tuareg efforts to achieve independence from the Malian government. The British reporter had sounded almost nonchalant, because no children were harmed. But a Peace Corps volunteer we met later told us that no American volunteers had been posted beyond Mopti, a town downriver from Segou. International foreign aid workers had had their vehicles stolen around the Timbuktu region and had been evacuated. Though the US Embassy had not mentioned anything specific about the Tuareg situation, the Peace Corps volunteer advised us to immediately check in with the embassy back in Bamako.

Other Peace Corps volunteers, who kindly offer us a place to shower and access to their bookshelf, are surprised that we had been not only on the river in kayaks, but in the river itself. They uniformly advise us to avoid the water, having been counseled under the threat of expulsion from the country not to get in the river because of the risk of, among other maladies, the water-borne schistosomiasis, a snail-propagated parasite that causes chronic pain and eventual failure of internal organs. We have made reasonable efforts to avoid this well-known disease, pouring iodized river water (which we also drank) onto our legs every now and then. But we are in the river daily. While Rick shrugs at their advice to contact the embassy and stay out of the river, I begin to feel as if maybe we are being too dismissive, even naive, about the threats.

So far, the water we'd been drinking from the river had not caused us any problems. Neither of us had had even a stomachache for weeks. Maybe the risks were overstated. Maybe they were not. Whose opinion should we trust? If schistosomiasis is prevalent, we figure we probably already have it. But when you feel good, and we do, the threat of an unseen parasite is difficult to fully accept—compared to hippos, crocodiles, or swarms of bees.

We are seasoned by the time we reach Segou, I reason. Here and healthy, with over 650 miles of river under our belts, we have been durable enough thus far. We have also been lucky. In any case, we are moving, and Timbuktu is downriver. I come to find it increasingly unpalatable to question a next day that is not on the Niger.

9
Moving with Mungo Park

TWO CENTURIES EARLIER, the Scottish explorer Mungo Park and many people in England and Scotland knew of the Niger River but had not seen it. It was more an aspiration than a river, an idea built on mystery and myths formulated out of several generations of ambition and nearly a century of losing men attempting to find it. Some thought the river was connected to the Nile, others to the Congo. Some believed that it flowed to the east before inexplicably submerging and emerging again hundreds of miles away in East Africa. All believed the Niger held wealth and resources. But in 1795, no one from Europe had safely returned to establish the truth.

Finding the elusive river had become a preoccupation among the wealthy leaders of England. They were competing for colonial superiority with the French, Belgians, Italians, and Portuguese, all of whom had been scouring the edges of the continent for over two hundred years. But the interior remained a void on their maps, a space the mapmakers filled with references to gold and fertile lands, visions of wealth that kept eating good men alive. Monsters conjured in mapmaker minds also began appearing on the maps of interior Africa. Jonathan Swift wrote, well before Park's journey: "So geographers, in Afric maps, with savage pictures fill their gaps, and o'r uninhabitable downs place elephants for want of towns."

England and Europe needed a new generation of overland explorers who could move alone or with little support to penetrate the interior of the continent. Over the quarter century between Mungo Park's birth and his arrival onto the explorers' stage, some thirty men had left

England for West Africa. Year after year for twenty-five years, not one came back.

Europe was restless at the end of the eighteenth century, and England especially so, having lost its American colonies. Many men, young and old, were feeling constrained on the British Isles, a corner of power becoming smaller and smaller around them in a larger, unknown world. England was as competitive for new trade as it was desperate for renewed prestige. The wealthy benefactors of London's African Association had sent, over a decade, three men in search of the deep interior of Africa, believing a river route might connect the west coast in Gambia with the east coast of Africa. Three notable explorers of Park's generation undertook the challenge: John Ledyard, an intrepid wanderer originally from Connecticut, in 1788; the Irishman Daniel Houghton, in 1790; and finally the skilled Arabic-speaking German with a French passport, Friedrich Hornemann, who was sent in early 1797. They had variously approached the interior from Cairo and Tripoli in North Africa or through the Gambia River route on Africa's west coast. In a slingshot of men into Africa over many years, word would gradually return to London on the fate of the explorers. Of these last three, two died early in their journeys, and one was never heard from again.

On the heels of Hornemann, the African Association next chose the young doctor Mungo Park. He was to go by way of the Gambia or Senegal River along well-worn slave-trading routes before entering dangerous tribal country controlled by territorial bands of Moors; through this land, they assured Park, he should find the Niger River.

With the young Park on his way by ship to West Africa, the gentlemen in London, cigars in hand and timepieces tucked in their waistcoat pockets, sat back once again to watch their calendar. Their latest man, this twenty-four-year-old Scottish doctor from rural Selkirk, had proven himself on earlier expeditions by ship to remote locations to document botany. Park was credentialed, schooled in medicine, and stood steady for this assignment. Long before he was chosen, he had chosen himself for the experience.

Men like Park did not do it for money. There was little money in it. The benefactors of the African Association, men who had pooled their funds to finance the expeditions, had decided over dinners that their explorers would receive a sum of one hundred pounds, rational-izing that "in such an undertaking, poverty is a better protection than wealth." Some of the explorers with debt and families were given inter-est-free loans, but their engagement was entirely a transaction built on the explorers' willpower and desire for prestige, not wealth. Explorers "acted without gold to challenge nature" on journeys urged on by bene-factors and mapmakers alike. They sought to gain fame unattainable by any other of life's paths.

Just shy of Segou—downriver from the swath of igneous rock that might have stymied our journey—fourteen months after leaving Lon-don, Mungo Park at last found the Niger River.

> One of them (referring to his guide) called out "Geo affile!" (See the water!) and, looking forwards, I saw with infinite pleasure the great object of my mission: the long sought for, majestic Niger, glittering to the morning sun, as broad as the Thames at Westminster, and flowing slowly to the east-ward.
> —Mungo Park, *Travels in the Interior Districts of Africa*, July 20, 1796

It would be nearly another year before Park could recount his sight-ing of the Niger to the men who had supported his journey. By the time he again set foot on English soil, he had been gone for two years and seven months. He returned with several stories of barely escaping death. His book, published in 1799, cites the African Association for its sup-port, referring to himself as "their faithful and obliged humble servant." The book was widely read and reprinted numerous times to meet the demand. Copies of the old book remain available in antique shops in Edinburgh, Scotland. But Park never found the river's terminus at the sea on his first journey. Although he resettled back in Selkirk, became a doctor, and started a family, he could not let his dream die and left for the interior of Africa again in 1805.

We understood Park's restlessness. An endemic urge of the young in Laramie is to leave. Laramie is more than enough for a kid. Until it is not. Getting out of Laramie by road led to places by plane thousands of miles and months away. We would eventually leave town and keep going, and we did it over and over. It didn't matter how far from home we were. Once you are past the city's limit, you have left. Gone.

When you leave Laramie, you trust that you will return to the same place—that bright sunlight, the university's tall trees and old buildings at the heart of town, the sound of trains rolling through at night, familiar family names on retail businesses. It makes leaving easy, knowing it will be there when you return. It makes returning home as predictable as the morning sun rising over the Sherman Hills east of town.

"I haven't seen you in a while. Where you been?" people would ask.

People assumed that another journey was half hatched as soon as any of us stepped back home. "Where next?" they'd ask automatically. Laramie is a base camp, a warm tent from where we could map routes into the rest of the world, wherever that was. In some ways it did not matter where the next trip was—a lake to fish in the nearby Snowy Range, or a river to kayak on a continent thousands of miles away.

Like Mungo Park, we also had our own version of benefactors. Our relationships were not with wealthy and influential men, but with consumer companies that made the gear we needed. If Rick and I felt some responsibility to the sponsors, we certainly had no obligation to them. Our sea kayaks and our tent alone were so valuable and beloved to us, however, that we would likely do whatever the companies asked of us. These sponsors, however, were a world away while we were on the Niger. Taking pictures of the gear, or documenting the performance of our tent and kayaks, was a task for eyes and ears so distant that I had absolutely no motivation to do it. At the same time, however, I kept a daily journal detailing everything I saw or thought. Mungo Park inspired me.

Yet 196 years earlier, Mungo Park had kept his focus, writing detailed notes of his findings, which he tucked into the brim of his hat. Park's ability to maintain that discipline amazed me. He did so despite nearly starving when captured by Moors, slogging through the monsoon, approaching death from dehydration during the dry season, and enduring near-fatal fevers.

Park traversed over a thousand miles on foot through constant danger for nearly a year before he located the Niger. The man was built in mind and body for such endeavors, though Park's journey almost killed him.

Worn down by sickness, exhausted with hunger and fatigue, half naked, and without any article of value by which I might procure provisions, clothes, or lodging, I began to reflect seriously on my situation . . . the tropical rains were already set in with all their violence; the rice grounds and swamps were everywhere overflowed; and, in a few days more, travelling of any kind, unless by water, would be completely obstructed.

By comparison, we had it easy. For the most part, we knew where we were going. We had a few maps. We had malaria pills, iodine to purify water, a tent, and a plane ticket out of Africa. Unlike Mungo Park, however, we had few people but friends and family back in Laramie who would care about where we were. Probably more people in England and Scotland in 1795 wondered about what was in the interior of Africa on the Niger River than Americans did two centuries later.

For me, though, the expedition's purpose had always been more personal than public, and the obscurity of the Niger River was as much an attraction to me as the challenge of navigating its entire course. Five years in a banking job had been enough for me. Perpetually lacking commitment to a job or to relationships, I was looking for another opportunity to dodge a predictable, static life. The prospect of sticking to the Niger River was a mirage I could accept. I had committed to the river, whatever it would bring, for as long as it would take and as long as I could take it.

"This river ends?" Rick often said. It was a joke. Then it wasn't. The river was a way of life, a lifeline, a conundrum.

The concept of moving down a river for the sake of moving down a river was perplexing to those we met. In 1796 in Segou, the chief wanted to understand why Mungo Park had come to see the river.

The chief, Mansong inquired if there were no rivers in my own country, and if one river was not like another.

Nearly two hundred years later, the same question was asked of us in Guinea, and then in Segou. An old man on the riverbank where we left our kayaks in Segou asked, "You do not have a river in your country?"

It was nearly a challenge.

Rick answered as he had in Guinea. "Not like your river," he said.

The man responded in Bambara with the same phrase we had heard in Malinke in Guinea. "Ee bori ka sow, ee nani ka sow." You left your home, you found your home.

The full geography of the river—that it starts as a small trickle and ends in the ocean—remained an elusive concept for people. It had become a more elusive concept for us, too, after moving on the actual river compared to looking at a map back home, where the river appeared straightforward, a blue line. We pulled out maps and showed people the river's route, tracing it down past their village or town, past national borders to the Gulf of Guinea in the Atlantic Ocean.

The old man in Segou corrected us. Waving his hand at our map, he then pointed to the river to let us and the assembled people in Segou know that the river was in front of us, and not a blue line on the paper we had unfolded.

"My name Mamadou Sinayago," said the man who had translated the old man's conversation for us. "We build pirogue at this place, thirteen generations. My pirogue will take you to the sea."

Like a salesman, he told us his family had built eleven pirogues that year. He had two of those for sale and two under construction.

"Thirteen generations," he repeated. My quick calculation put his business as existing before Mungo Park arrived in Segou in 1796. We were seeing a boat, I immediately realized, made exactly as one Mungo Park might have seen.

"Come, I will show you," Mamadou offered.

He took us into his unfenced boatyard, which spread up a sloping hard-packed dirt hill from the riverbank where we had left our kayaks. We walked with him past several men and just as many boys using metal tools. A charcoal fire burned to heat a tool that made holes for the long, square nails that the boys forged and then pounded into shape. Other men and boys cut and fitted pieces of odd-shaped wood into the structure of the pirogue. The nails held the pieces together.

"We are Bozo," he said. "I teach my sons, not all the cousins."

Mamadou explained his secret as he walked to the bow of a boat on the river's edge being readied for launch. He pointed to what he had painted on the side of his pirogues.

I noticed the painted symbols, different designs on each pirogue. One, freshly painted, consisted of lines in white, yellow, blue, and red shapes and contours that represented the river, fish, the sky at night, and other symbols I did not understand. Mamadou did not offer to explain the painting's meaning when I asked. He ignored me, concentrating, his salesmanship put away for a moment.

"Hippo will not take this pirogue," Mamadou finally said. "Today I paint."

It took only twenty minutes for Mamadou to paint the right-hand bow of the pirogue, a span of two feet. He called the wood of the pirogue jalla, a dark-red mahogany, a wood that I imagine could be milled for fine furniture if it were not used for this higher and better purpose as a boat.

I asked about the pirogue he was painting. He had built it three months ago to be motorized but had closed the hole for the motor and propeller.

We would buy that pirogue.

It was as inevitable as falling in love—a spark that feels surprising but becomes a fire you had not imagined but then cannot douse. Traveling by pirogue felt as if it were meant to be, whether that had any basis in good judgment or bad. After five weeks and 650 miles on the Niger in kayaks, the river emerged as new again with the pirogue.

But love alone did not manage practical matters; its enthusiasm conceals, if not extinguishes, common sense. We needed to understand why the river was changing into a meandering weaving of channels that we did not know how to navigate. Our maps, made by the Institut Géographique, were scaled variously at 1:200,000 and 1:1,000,000, with detail that showed the river sprawling into channels through marshes. The land around the channels on the maps was crosshatched green and blue, indicating the uncertain and seasonal paths of the Niger. The river, apparently unguided by current, eventually moved into a main channel again before Timbuktu, 450 miles downriver.

I had not considered that we could find a guide to help navigate our way through what is now an inland delta of the Niger and was once the end of the river in the desert. But Mamadou understood this before we did, probably when he saw in our eyes that we would buy one of his pirogues, though we had yet to discuss a price.

"Bozo know Djoliba's way," Mamadou said to us.

A man in pink-framed glasses walked up to us as if he were part of our conversation. Mamadou turned and introduced us to another Mamadou.

"Bozo, like me. He will go with you."

Mamadou, our boat-builder friend, suggested we pay our guide 1,500 CFA (the West African currency tied to the French franc), about six dollars a day. He explained to us that the man otherwise rented a pirogue for 500 CFA a day and hauled what he could for people, usually grasses from across the river that he sold to mat makers in Segou.

Pirogue boatbuilder Mamadou Sinayago, Segou, Mali, 1991.

We learned that our boatman was thirty-seven, had an eighteen-year-old wife, Fatima, and a three-and-a-half-year-old daughter. He needed work and was willing to travel. While boatbuilder Mamadou commanded our respect through his confidence, boatman Mamadou embodied a more laid-back, less businesslike style.

He sat down under the shelter of a grass mat next to our boat and began to coax charcoal into a fire for a pot of tea. He put on his pink-framed glasses, which had no lenses, and motioned for us to sit down next to him. I glanced at his wrist to look at his watch. It had no hands. I asked him whether I could see the watch, and he showed it to me with pride, holding it in front of me, a piece of ornamentation but obviously not a functioning timepiece.

"Your partner," boatbuilder Mamadou had called him when introduced.

I admitted to myself that in uncertain circumstances, we needed a calm companion and tea as much as we needed a map. As with Sori in the Guinean highlands, we had found both in Mamadou. I would fold our other maps, sheets of colorful paper, and not look at them again for nearly a month.

We had a boatman before we had a boat. Boatbuilder Mamadou turned back to our transaction: the pirogue cost 175,000 CFA, $700, a bargain for the time and craftsmanship required to construct a pirogue built in a mosaic of thirty-odd pieces of wood. No contractor or furniture maker back home could have conceived, let alone built, such a boat from the assorted dimensions Mamadou had used. We could see that nothing was wasted in the pirogue-building yard. Any portion of wood left over from the last boat became a part of the next, the various slabs linked with reinforcing nails his sons and their cousins forged themselves in the charcoal fire in the sand. "Strong," Mamadou assured me.

We bought bamboo to cut into a deck for the middle section, and grass mats to shade the area where we would escape the sun during the day and sleep at night. This was fun work, like kids building a tree house. Rick started talking of Huck Finn. I ignored him because, as much of a good time as we were having, this was not fiction. We had to configure the pirogue into our movable home and we needed to learn from Mamadou how to move it to Timbuktu. I dismissed Rick also because he was exactly right. We were as naive as boys with a raft escaping onto a river in Missouri in 1840.

We put one of our kayaks into the pirogue and tethered the other to the pirogue's side. Our four lightweight carbon-fiber paddles, the cost of which equaled that of the pirogue, became baggage. With Mamadou's help, we picked out three bamboo poles, longer and fatter than those he purchased for the deck, for 500 CFA, about two dollars each. Boatman Mamadou showed us on land how to use the poles and had us practice.

Our pirogue slices through the water the first morning on the river, much slower than our kayaks but more elegant, a rhythmic dance as much as a method of movement. But the work with the bamboo pole is anything but effortless because to do it properly—throwing it forward, planting and pushing, and then pulling it out of the water—requires the entire body and concentration, at least for the first hour each day. It then becomes a repetitive pattern of movement that soothes. Mamadou nods at us with approval from the back of the pirogue, where he acts as our rudder, guiding us along the bank of the river.

A day downriver, we reach the Niger's first dam. The Markala Dam is small by any estimation, but it stops the mighty Niger for the first time. The dam provides irrigation, a bridge over the river, and electricity for the town of Markala, which unlike other Malian towns and villages is laid out in a grid following its electric lines. Despite such benefits, the town has the least human

Boatman Mamadou on our pirogue at the Markala Dam, Mali, 1991.

presence on the streets of anyplace we had been in Mali or Guinea. We walk the streets at night and see one reason why: the glow of televisions in homes, light pulsing out of open windows.

Above the dam, we camp along a lake created by the backed-up Niger, which is filled with blooming purple water lilies. The lake is surrounded by several enormous old mango trees that, unfortunately, are not in season. This unlikely shaded backwater is not the dry Sahel and not Mali. It is the oasis people imagine in dreams, except it is real.

It takes us several hours that morning to find a man who can help us through the lock, a drop of about five meters. The man we find, or who eventually finds us, is an unofficial-looking character dressed in billowing brown pants and a ragged shirt. The lockman charges us 3,000 CFA, about twelve dollars, and earns it many times over during the next two hours while our pirogue passes the metal gates to the Niger River waiting for us below the dam. The mechanical process of the old dam requires the lockman's human touch to move the gate doors and guide the water. He moves like a good fisherman working an eddy with his line. Mamadou, in his pink glasses, manages our pirogue as if he had done it before, adjusting our boat against the rising water to keep it from hitting the lock's gate.

Back on the river, we get ready to move again, but Mamadou has other plans. He walks into Markala and purchases Chinese tea and then fires charcoal into flames with dried grass in less than a minute. Mamadou prefers Niger water he retrieves from the river to our iodized Niger water in bottles, though we offer it. His blue pot, also made in China, boils and steams on two small charcoal chips. We celebrate our passing of Markala with three rounds of sugary hot tea. We stop shortly after the dam and Mamadou prepares to sleep in the stern of the pirogue and we find ground for our tent. Mamadou says, "Harra esseda" (May you wake up one by one).

In the morning, the Niger bends sharply to the south toward the town on the left bank, Sansanding, just ten miles beyond the dam. It gleams in the sand with old mud buildings and a central market.

On the edge of Sansanding, as we land the pirogue, children run up to us, both boys and girls. They jump up and down and then run circles around us after we step off the boat, unafraid and without a shred of shyness, as they squeal "Mungo Park, Mungo Park."

This shocks me, because usually we hear toubab or toubabou, which means "white man," or most often cadeaux, which is French for "gift." But Mungo Park? Did this mean "white man" to them, or did they have a story of Mungo's visit here? Their voices immediately warmed me, invited me into their town.

We walk into Sansanding on a market day. Mungo Park's journal had prepared us for what we would see, as if the clock and calendar had not moved in nearly two hundred years.

> Merchandise are exposed for sale on stalls covered with mats to shade them from the sun . . . beads of indigo in balls, cloth, copper bracelets, tobacco and salt . . . the people were everywhere employed in collecting the fruit of the Shea-butter trees, from which they prepare the vegetable butter. The

kernel is first dried in the sun, the butter is prepared by boiling the kernel in water. The kernel is enveloped in a sweet
pulp and the butter produced from it, besides the advantage
of its keeping the whole year without salt, is whiter, firmer,
and, to my palate, of a richer flavor than the best butter I
ever tasted made from cow's milk.

We had eaten the butter for the first time in Segou after seeing it
displayed in a mound on a table in the market. It has a slight herbal
smell and tastes rancid, with the texture of lard. It is an acquired
taste, perhaps, but not one I could imagine becoming fond of, despite
Park's assertion that shea butter is better than cow butter. But it can
be used for almost anything. Mamadou the boatbuilder had used it
to seal the wooden joints in his pirogues. In Europe, the French use
the silky substance in expensive cosmetics. In Mali, it is more often
called karité, the French word for the ubiquitous cloudy substance.
The stuff is magical and grows wild inside hard nuts on trees in and
around Sansanding.

In the center of the market is a large table under a tarp with a mound
of karité butter as big as a boulder. The vendor carves off pieces of various sizes for each person waiting in line; they will use it as a lotion, to
waterproof leather, to make candles and soap, or to cook with. The next
stall sells okra, yams, cassava, onions, and green melons.

But for the gas in rag-corked bottles and a handful of motorcycles,
we are in the same place that Mungo Park visited in 1796. Park left
his journey just beyond Sansanding, in Silla, after growing increasingly
apprehensive of the Moorish traders from North Africa.

> I was advancing more and more within the power of those
> merciless fanatics . . . I should sacrifice my life to no purpose;
> for my discoveries would perish with me. I saw inevitable
> destruction in attempting to proceed eastward . . . merchants
> are ignorant of the termination of the river; for such of them
> that can speak Arabic describe the amazing length of the riv-
> er in very general terms, saying only that they believe it runs
> to the world's end.

Park would return to London with his report and write the book that I read. So, down the river from Sansanding, we move beyond Mungo's journal and I put his book away. The loss of Mungo Park as a companion is a hole. The emotion makes little sense given the vast differences between our journeys, but my feeling is shaped by the knowledge of Park's return to this same place on the Niger.

In 1805, six years after his departure, Park came back and picked up his previous route where he had left it. He traveled for over a thousand miles beyond Sansanding in a boat he had constructed of two canoes or small pirogues, probably the size of ours. The boat is large enough to store provisions, including firearms. He wanted to move down the river, as it was much faster than walking and could help him avoid the Moors and the chiefs who had periodically tormented him on his earlier journey. But Park perished downriver on his second expedition, along with a few other men, in an attack led by a local chief. The chief ordered his people to bombard Park's boat with a hail of rocks in a canyon in Jebba, a riverside village now displaced by a dam in central Nigeria. This story was recounted by one of his African companions, who had left the expedition before the canyon, and was verified by subsequent explorers. Park's body and notes were never found.

We realize after two days that Mamadou prays each morning and afternoon and at sunset, the exact time varying more by our circumstances on the river than by the time of day. Although Mamadou stops our pirogue and steps away from us twice a day and at sunset, we begin to understand that we may not be accommodating his wishes to pray as well as we could. Salat worship prescribes prayers five times a day, a ritual that impresses us in its commitment. I have not seen or heard him worship at night but know that he quietly does. In the morning and during the day, we see him returning to the pirogue with sand on his forehead from bowing to the sandy riverbank on his knees. He never brushes the sand away. We have tea that he brews when we stop, after he prays, and share a pause from moving down the river. I adjust to the disruptive stop in our movement down the Niger, then accept it, and then, after several days, embrace it. When we stop for Mamadou, the river ceases for a short time as our obsession. Each time, however, our return to the river feels fresh and new. I want to communicate my respect for and appreciation of his religious commitment, but Mamadou is not

Fishing boats with our pirogue in the foreground in Djioro, Mali, 1991.

seeking that, and he does not thank us for stopping, either. I know from this that we are moving together, and that becomes everything for us.

I recall that Mike had brought a Koran with him. He had recently been a more religious man, he had explained, in the Christian faith. Mike was an explorer and learner; I now understood his curiosity and wish I had borrowed the book from him when he left. And I wish he was here to share what we were experiencing and could talk about it together.

Mamadou plans for us to halt for the night in a town where he has a friend. "Djioro," he says. The river grows wide before I can see the town. "Djioro," Mamadou says again and smiles. The Niger has filled with pirogues, none with motors, all with people who are fishing. Some use nets, others traps. Woven fish traps, all of slightly different sizes based on the size of the reeds they were constructed from, line the riverbank.

The Bozo have a proverb that no money on land equals the riches at the bottom of the river. That truth is obvious in Djioro, where emptied traps and boats brimming with fish line the bank with barely a space for our pirogue. The river's riches carry to the land, where two mosques rise above the small village of one-story homes. I escape through the people, who are busy to a person with the work of managing the fish catch, and walk alone to the closest mosque, only a hundred yards from the Niger's bank.

It is between prayer times, and the mosque is quiet. I am welcomed by a man at the front of the mosque and, after I remove my shoes, taken up a ladder to the roof. He allows me space and solitude, and a view of the town from its highest vantage point. The mud-packed spires of the mosque, just above my outstretched arm, have been worn by sun and wind to reveal straw, a few candy wrappers, and pieces of plastic that are barely visible packed into the mud. The mosque's spires are adorned with ostrich eggs, cradled in forged metal brackets with sharp ends to keep birds from landing on them.

From my perch, I count 116 pirogues on the river. From the water, I could not have guessed there were so many boats on the wide Niger. I count them again: 116. They move slowly on human power, sticking to their place on the river, making counting easy.

The wealth of Djioro comes from the river, though that wealth is most evident from above the town. Every dwelling is built with a roof surrounded by short walls. Food is dried and stored on the roofs—deep red hibiscus leaves on one roof, silvery dried fish flashing in the sunlight on another, and next to the mosque, green okra being cut and spread out to dry by a young woman.

"Aneekay," she says to me, a quick hello from an adjacent roof, before she turns back to her work. I hear the sound of the okra landing on a grass mat on her roof. Voices, the splashing of pirogues landing on the bank, men jumping into shallow water, the slapping of small fish in plastic buckets, a hum of insects I do not see. The sound of prayers will swallow the other sounds when afternoon salat starts. The men will enter the mosque, and the women and children will cease their work building the richness of Djioro, fish by fish.

The next major village happens to be a place known throughout Mali for an annual movement not of fish, like Djioro, but of cattle. A day's travel on the river that people call Djoliba, the Great River, down from Djioro, is Diafarbe, where Fulani pastoralists move their herds across the wide, shallow river at this time every year. We learn this because the river is filled with cattle.

Mamadou tries to explain. "Here," he says.

"Today?" I ask.

"Now," Mamadou says.

Now happens to be Thanksgiving Day, a day like any other for us on the Niger, except for the hundreds of cattle in the river. They are being herded through the water by boys who hang on to the tail of a lead animal with one hand and swing sticks against the water with the other. This annual movement of cattle happens in November, not on a specific day, but after the water recedes to present fresh green grazing grass on the northern side of the river. From the pirogue, I can see that Diafarbe has a mosque that rises, like Djioro's, above all other buildings. We pass the town in the short time it takes to move between cattle and locate a place to camp, where we eat a chicken with fresh okra for Thanksgiving dinner.

For the next few days we pass Bozo fishing camps of grass-mat tents circled with hanging nets. Mamadou does not fish, unlike all of the Bozo we pass, but he reads the river and maneuvers us. We move around islands from one side of the river to the other, a crossing that requires us to paddle in deeper water. He points out a pool of hippos we had skirted but not noticed. Mamadou knows where the hippos congregate, just as he understands the river's slight current. We stop when he chooses to stop and push hard against our bamboo poles for hours on end. Our pace is slow but it connects me more to the river. For one, I feel the bottom of the river with each pole stroke and know its depth always; second, we are moving by and at our own power and pace, just like every other pirogue on the river, which makes me feel, even as a foreigner, part of its community and commerce. At night, I ask Rick whether he feels the same, and he says, "Exactly."

We arrive in Mopti, another of Mali's small cities, thirteen days after leaving Segou. The Niger River has cut its course for 900 miles by the time it meets its major tributary in Mali, the Bani River, at Mopti. The Bani has traveled 680 miles though the south of Mali, gathering its water from a drainage area extending to the neighboring Ivory Coast, and is nearly a mirror of the wide and brown Niger when they merge. The converging of two great rivers is more an uncertain marriage, a slow and gentle comingling, than a combining of forces. The Niger is much larger now, lumbering without a purpose, more lake than river. We had seen on our maps that the river here begins to move in many channels, not just one main channel, as it begins to sprawl into the flat desert of central Mali.

The Niger needs all the water it can get, even with the combined force of the Bani. Two-thirds of it will evaporate beyond Mopti, into what our maps refer to as the Inland Delta, before it reaches Timbuktu. The massive evaporation of the Niger has almost killed it every year for centuries.

How a river can survive in the flattened desert gives heart to those who see the possible in the improbable. As tenuous as the river may be in this hot place of flat sponge-soil, it remains to all that sustain themselves from its water, fish, and foliage, Djoliba.

Near Mopti, up the Bani River, is the historic trading town of Djenne, whose mud mosque is the largest adobe building in the world. Travelers who see it say the structure is the most beautiful building on earth. But we did not. We had rarely left sight of the river. And when we did, we walked. We could have taken a taxi or bus, but we didn't.

We stick close to the river for practical reasons—our boat and food are there and we cannot risk losing them to theft. The Bozo people do the same, sleeping on their boats or camping next to them. The Fulani, too, sleep near their cattle for the same reason. Keep close to your assets, to your past—and future.

Our ranch friends near Laramie are the same. They rarely venture far from their land because, unlike those of us in town who aspire to roam, they need to be where they have their life's work and wealth. People might call it a lifestyle, but our friends on ranches would say it is just the way it is. There is always enough work on a ranch to keep the rancher undistracted. I had never understood their self-imposed isolation, but I began to when we were in Mopti, where I simply wanted to stay on our pirogue on the river. I did not need to go to Djenne, even though I knew I was missing something.

Next to where we land our pirogue, and where we will sleep, other boats are moored. We notice that the fishermen of Mopti also stay close to their boats. "We are river people, too," I say to Rick, in defense of our lack of exploration beyond the river.

"We should go to the Bandiagara Escarpment," Rick says, confirming my thoughts. The escarpment is a sandstone cliff south of Mopti where the Dogon people, defying conversion to Islam, relocated and hid over a thousand years ago. It is close to Mopti. The people live there to this day in much the same way they have for a millennium.

Like going to Paris and missing the Louvre, or to Cairo and skipping the pyramids, we were passing places at the center of Malian history and identity, not to mention UNESCO World Heritage sites. I began questioning whether we were drifting with an obsession rather than a perspective, whether we were missing the essence of Mali itself, which is what we were there to experience. I considered this while I was in the circular rhythm of poling our pirogue, poling, pushing against the mud of the Niger's bottom out of Mopti.

Out of Mopti, a day passes, and then another, in the quiet rhythm of moving our pirogue. The continual act of moving on the river keeps us alert to what is next, and less reflective than we might otherwise have been as travelers. Rick and I do not rethink, let alone rediscuss, our passing by the great places most people travel to Mali to see. I am fixed and focused on the rhythm of movement, and the regret of passing historic sites leaves my thoughts as if it had never begun to fester.

Then a mosque in the village of Kotaka rises over the horizon. Illuminated in late evening sun, it glows bronze as a god but is made of mud from the land on which it stands. It is as elegant as a cathedral in Prague or Paris, with every single structure around it oriented in subservience to the mud monarch. We stop to see the mosque, which is much larger than those we had seen thus far. Men had just completed a day's work layering new mud, by hand, onto the exterior walls, a continuous task given the building's material. The mud, of course, is not a choice but a practical necessity in this landscape of earth and river. Remudding the mosque is more privilege than chore for the men, who climb the scaffolding made of bundled sticks extending from the sides of the building. The annual work is done after the monsoon rains have worn the structure, but before the seasonal winds and sun sandblast and dry its walls. If the Djenne mosque bests all on scale, it is still hard to fathom it eclipsing the elegance of Kotaka's. Comparing Djenne's eminence in the nation with the many small village mosques ornamented with ostrich eggs, or to Kotaka's towering bronzed minarets, is like comparing the acacia trees around the town. The large old trees inspire reverence, but the upstart saplings pushing through the soil to survive in the sun encourage me equally.

Beyond Kotaka, the Niger meanders for two days past small hamlets and Bozo camps. The river slows, almost backing up, and is no longer a single route it creates with its strength. With little pull of current, the river starts spreading over its banks and loses its course in an ever-meandering weaving of multiple channels. The river bends around islands of grass, clumps of reeds like football fields, and thin passage-ways that are a path to nowhere. This, we realize, is the start of the Inland Delta.

The Inland Delta is where water meets heat and sand. The river spreads to fifty miles wide here during the rainy season. On the south-ern edge of the Inland Delta is the Sahel, a dry savanna landscape that stretches across the region. On the northern reach is the vast Sahara Desert, which dominates thousands of miles of North Africa, from where we are in Mali all the way to the Mediterranean Sea.

A river without direction is not a river I can understand. The mighty Djoliba becomes a creek, then a small bay leading to a swamp, then one narrow creek among a dozen creeks all at once. How do we travel by river when the water does not move?

We enter the geographic conundrum of the Inland Delta and face our own: we do not know where we are going in the stagnant waterway. We are following the directions of a man wearing pink glasses with no lenses, and a wristwatch without hands. Rick and I are quasi explorers, on our way down a great river, but are completely lost in a world gone green in the desert. I look at Rick. He shrugs. I look back to Mamadou. He smiles.

Mamadou reads the water and stays at the stern of our pirogue with his long pole, providing direction. Rick and I power the pirogue from the bow and follow Mamadou's choices, many of which I would never have made.

The Inland Delta is an enormous oasis, one that nearly kills the river but provides its habitat. Sand and breeze-bent grasses pull water this way and that, creating and re-creating paths that attract birds and some two hundred species of fish. The fish attract the Bozo, the fishing people of these waterways for as long as people have been here. From the bow of the pirogue, I see only a green world where tall reeds and grasses wave in the wind. When I refer to my compass, I discover that we are almost circling back and around, as directionless as the waterways. But we allow Mamadou to lead us without questioning him, and day after day he proves himself in these intricate waters by finding Bozo camps on small islands of soil, with fish for us to purchase.

These waterways would be better suited to our nimble kayaks, which are now luggage on the pirogue. The pirogue, however, is far better for navigation over the tall grasses and reeds that fill the shallows and hide hard ground. If we were in our kayaks, we would not be with Mamadou, and I suspect we'd be lost.

The Bozo people have lived in this Niger waterland of a stalled and sprawling river channel for centuries, for as long as historical accounts exist, living with the cycles of the delta, where fish flourish and water comes and goes. We had heard that some of the Bozo people, like the Fulani, shift to keeping animals during the dry season, and we see a couple of goats but no cattle or large stock.

One evening, Mamadou stops us and steps onto a small patch of hard ground, difficult to find in the green water-world, that houses yet another Bozo encampment. The mud walls of the huts are low and the roofs are made of reed thatch, woven and rolled out like tarps. The smell of fish and fire permeates the air. The speck of earth smells as wet as the mulch-water-grass smell of the Inland Delta.

Mamadou steps off the pirogue and takes time to observe fishing equipment before walking into the small camp ahead of us. In a moment, the adults, a few men and women, wave to us to come closer. We do not see children, which is unusual. Children always find us first. Lantern light comes from tin cans, probably filled with gas, though I cannot smell kerosene or gas. Wicks made of cloth burn bright against the low gray walls.

Along the riverbank next to our pirogue are two others, loaded with blue fishing nets, cage fish traps made of woven reeds, and several spears with metal barbs. It is getting dark. We are hungry.

I am grateful to be on hard ground with people who do not scramble at our arrival. Then a man cooking a large perch looks up at us and says, "Mungo Park."

I am again stunned, as I had been in Sansanding. Except that this place is not a place with a name, and it is beyond where Mungo Park had documented his travels. How did the name Mungo Park persevere here? Who was Mungo Park to them? And did his name mean that we were good or bad or just white?

If there was a hint, it came from the family, cooking fish over coals in a large wok-like pot filled with rice and root bulbs from wetland plants. They welcome us to their hearth. We eat with the family, using our hands in one large pot to eat hot rice, bulbs of water lilies, and fish. I do not know the day or where we are on a map, but our shared meal marks a time and place.

In a matter of only weeks, events and circumstances had gradually taken control of our clock and our calendar, and the definition of a day. The long morning escaping furious bees was a day, as was the day when we moved stroke after stroke on brown water to the sight of the riverbank home of hundreds of sunbirds nested in mud holes. Both days had twelve hours of light and twelve of dark. One became the day of the bees, the other the day of sunbirds. Tonight's dinner is the night eating perch with the Bozo.

Our days had been methodical, but we have no clock. I had my watch stolen off my wrist two months earlier in Guinea. At first, I missed the gauge of time, its definition of a day. But Guinea, then Mali, got me over the need of a watch. Near the equator, we had grown accustomed to twelve hours of daylight and twelve hours of night: 6:00 a.m. to 6:00 p.m. You come to orient around the sun and the light of the moon, under which, on its waxing to full, we could move into the night, but not on its waning.

But what of the time of day? What of the day itself—a Wednesday? It didn't matter. The value of clocks and calendars evaporates like sweat in the West African heat. What matters is that the river is high but receding. It is past sunset. The moon is large and waxing.

Yesterday fades away in a landscape that swallows you. Like yesterday, today arrives, and like yesterday, today has its patterns under the long sun until an event creates a contrast to the continuity of the day that is shaped by wind, the moon, and the river. Time elongates and repeats—not like a clock or calendar, but by longer and slower patterns, from the sky and land and water. When the sun's stare stops, the clock says nothing. It is the time when sweat stops rolling off everyone amid the cracked mud of building walls, path surfaces, and cooking hearths.

The rare patches of land that rise above the Niger, where the soil is hardened and cracked wide open from relentless sun, make a place for Bozo camps. Everyone knows that the day when rain will come is not near.

> They calculate years by the number of rainy seasons. They portion the year into moons and reckon the days by so many suns. The moon, by varying her form, has more attracted their attention.

I met a man in a place without a name on a day that was like all other days in the Inland Delta, where the bright heat takes time away. I met this man because I had moved to the shade of the one tree in sight. And there he was in the same shade, standing alone and looking at me, letting me arrive. When I met him, it was the time of the meeting, which meant the event itself was the time. Our meeting was the time from which sequences of events would be given color and context, should events follow. He made tea for me and then tea for a man with a basket full of fish. In the sun's heat you seek shade and tea made from hibiscus leaves, sugared heavily.

Then one day some days after I met the man with hibiscus tea, having gone day in and day out like the circling of a fan, a boy in a village died. The death was the time that marked the space between recycling heat and the moon, a point in time after which things were not the same. The boy had been writhing on the sand of the riverbank when we arrived. Mamadou motioned us to stay away. The village stayed away. I debated providing the boy something, a mefloquine pill for malaria, as I guessed what he needed. But it was too late. I could offer my sheet for him to rest in. Pointless, I decided. I saw he was pouring sweat in the cooling but still-hot evening. This day would forever be the day I watched a boy die and did nothing.

For the people in the small village, the event that shaped the day was not the boy left alone to die on the riverbank, but our arrival, because people die often in the desert, but white men arrive only rarely.

"Mungo Park, Mungo Park," two boys say in unison, as if they had practiced their words. They stand looking at us with wide eyes. Then they run away. We had just been getting out of our pirogue after a long day of poling, like every day on the river, half a day in sun on the river, the other half under the moon. This area of Mali is without electricity, without roads, without much except for fish and peacefulness. But this village also has stories. They know Mungo Park, a white man who had passed this place two centuries earlier.

10

Beyond Timbuktu

THE NIGER FINALLY FOUND its course in the Inland Delta after Lake Debo, a lake several miles wide that we crossed in a morning when Rick constructed a spinnaker sail from a blue tarp and tethered it to our bamboo poles, which served as a mast. We sailed for four hours across a lake that could have taken us two days to paddle. At the end of it, the river gained a gentle current again as we moved to Timbuktu, 150 miles away. We passed major towns, Diré and Niafunké, on both the river and the road to Timbuktu, where we heard warnings to avoid the roads because of the Tuareg.

Our last step off our pirogue into Timbuktu was just one step toward it. The city, once on the river's bank centuries ago when it was founded, is now ten miles north of the Niger, as the Saharan sands have pushed the river south of the city. We gave our pirogue to Mamadou with a handshake, because the pirogue was really his boat all along, not ours. He planned to sell it. We left our kayaks with a man who lived along the river—a bustling area of fishing boats, metal-roofed homes, and traders unloading and loading camels and trucks—and walked into the ancient city.

Just before we reached Timbuktu, police pulled us into their station, located on the city's edge, and made it clear that we would be leaving on the next flight out, whenever it would arrive. Flights into Timbuktu's outpost airport had gone from periodic to unpredictable and then to rare over recent weeks. They told us that the Tuareg were attacking the city at night. Two policemen also made it clear that they were in charge, and that we were subject to a curfew at sundown.

One pointed to 6:00 p.m. on his wristwatch. There was little mystery in mystical Timbuktu on this, the winter solstice, the shortest day of the year: the police controlled the day, and the Tuareg controlled the night. We were prepared for what greeted us, having tuned in to reports on the BBC's Africa Report on our shortwave radio over the previous week that detailed growing tensions between the Malian government and the Tuareg.

One of the policemen, who may have been a military man (it didn't matter; officials with guns all look alike, and their authority is not worth questioning), guided us to an unfinished concrete compound of forty-some rooms. It would be an accommodation of desperation for anyone but us. We were comfortable with the prospect of sleeping in an empty cement room and not in our tent. The toilet at one end of the hallway flushed and the lights flickered on periodically, but no one worked there or asked us for money.

If Timbuktu was subject to a curfew and Tuareg raids at night, the active city gave no hint of the alarming situation. Timbuktu was at work, with donkeys and camels tethered against mud walls on the main paved roads, while vendors sold goods in stalls and tables all over town. Shops had their doors open to the streets, the sign that they were open for business.

Central Timbuktu's roofed market overflowed with melons, canned goods, and dried okra. We eyed a caramelized sugar candy covered in sesame seeds at one stall, the owner's only offering. Another table had a peanut brittle that convinced Rick that we should stay for a few days. What convinced me were men at earthen bread ovens, several spread around the edges of the market, where men and boys sold hot bread cooked in the heat of smoking twigs.

A lone man dressed much as we were, in worn but clean Western-style clothing, approached us as we picked fruit to buy.

"Hi. Are you looking for something? Can I help you?"

"Are you traveling?" we asked, surprised to meet another American in a city devoid of travelers.

"Ken," he said, holding out his hand with a gentleman's formality. He was about our age, early thirties, bearded, and darkened by sun.

He did not question us about how we were in Timbuktu or why we were there. He explained in a measured manner that as a Baptist missionary, he had lived in Timbuktu most of his life. Unlike us, he had not been told by officials to leave.

"This is my home," he explained.

He discussed the situation in Timbuktu without discernible concern, as if he had seen it all before. The man maintained an undistracted calm that must be beneficial to a person in his line of work, living in an Islamic city. He warned, however, that this recent situation was more disruptive than others he had experienced. He detailed much more than the police had: all roads in and out of Timbuktu, if not closed, were dangerous for people. The Tuareg had been stealing vehicles but not harming foreigners—"yet," he emphasized. Twelve Malians had been killed in the city at night in the last week. "The bandits—or Tuareg, whoever it is that comes through at night—take their casualties with them." While eyeing vegetables on a table in the market, he added, "You will hear shooting most nights." He told us that without a Land Rover or other good vehicle, or gas, we would be of no value to the Tuareg. People robbed of their vehicles outside the city had been left to walk. "They take the gas from one vehicle to drive to the next before ditching it. This will pass, again. I am off to shop," he said. "Merry Christmas."

Between the boundaries of day and night, bureaucracy and banditry, our thoughts gravitated to how we would get past Timbuktu's officials to return to the Niger River. For us, it felt less like the end of our journey, and more like a place to begin. Our map put us at the edge of the desert, 1,100 miles down the river but with 1,500 miles to go, through the remainder of Mali, then Niger and Nigeria, to the ocean. That we were not halfway through our journey made us both crave to go deeper into the desert on the river. A New Year was upon us, as was a fresh start on the Niger.

Four days before Christmas, we began devising our way out of town. We decided to move during the afternoon to our kayaks on the river on Christmas Eve. Since the military and police officials had not seen us arrive, they did not know about our kayaks. If it took longer than we planned, a moon just beginning to wane would allow us to move in the dark. We decided for a rational reason that we would be back on the Niger by Christmas: we needed to be gone before things got more unpredictable and dangerous, and before we got stuck in Timbuktu.

Men in Timbuktu, Mali, 1991.

With a plan in place, a semblance of holiday ease—or at least the comfort and relative opulence of the city compared to camping on the river—embraced us in the desert city. The holiday was in our heads, and the food in the market and street stalls was in our eyes and our mouths. And with time during the days, we wandered to see the history of the city, a place without a museum.

We walked to the north edge of town, not far from the market, where we saw fences constructed of stripped-down pieces of scrap metal from vehicle doors, barriers with large gaps we could see though, but which were sufficient to protect fledgling seasonal gardens in sandy soil from wandering goats and untethered camels. Little was growing, but the remnants of dried gourds and their vines waved in wind as dry as parchment paper. Next to these gardens was a burial area for babies and the young, who had been left in dozens of clay urns. What might once have been an orderly cemetery had shifted in the drifting sand to eventually push and bury urns, many broken, in a dishevelment of remains and clay shards.

The burial site weighed on me because it seemed to have been constructed on the outskirts of the city to be taken by the desert, as if the wind and the sand owned this place and its souls. Down the road from the burial area was the Sankore Mosque, a shorter, stouter structure than those we had seen elsewhere in Mali. It had been built in 1324, as the beginning of an ancient university. The intellectual and cultural history of Timbuktu was shaped by Islam and still is today. It is, after all, home to forty thousand or so people who do not imagine themselves at the end of the world, but perhaps at its center.

Timbuktu, whose location had been chosen by scholars and traders, was once positioned like an oasis on the bank of the great Djoliba River, the precise place on the long arc of the river where it needed to be for its time, at the edge of the desert on a huge river. No one would choose to build a city where it sits today, with no soil to cultivate and sand in the doorways that must be scooped daily.

For centuries, this city situated in the deep interior of Africa—2,000 miles across the Sahara from Tripoli, 3,000 from Cairo, and another 600 from Bamako—has been a place that attracts, absorbs, and periodically rejects temporary residents. Foreign workers and the odd tourists, like Rick and me, who had managed to make it to Timbuktu over the past months, had been evacuated, but for the one American Baptist missionary. As a trading city, Timbuktu has always been a place where journeys culminate and long return journeys begin.

It will forever remain remote in a landscape of heat, wind, and shifting sand, though it has been seized and controlled by a series of empires since its inception before the twelfth century. And the Tuareg were trying to take control of the city today, as they had before. First, they fought against various kingdoms for centuries; then, they battled against the French starting in 1892, when the colonizers arrived to partition the vast savanna and desert into the nations of Mali and the French Sudan. Since 1960, the Tuareg have fought periodically against the independent state of Mali, after the French loosened their control. The Tuareg have had short periods of complete control, shared control, or at least a role in the trade of salt, gold, and slaves and have maintained a large part of Timbuktu's character and commerce for centuries.

The city's future may be constructed partly from the mythology, much generated now by the Tuareg, that attracts tourists and travelers like us, though it will remain important mostly for what has been quietly hidden there over seven centuries. Irreplaceable archives of medieval Islam, and other historic manuscripts on science and medicine, are placed away in the walls of Timbuktu. History has been saved and sealed over many centuries within the city's walls, protected from non-Islamic marauders, insurgents of any kind, and the ever-changing authorities. Timbuktu's scholars once hid them with the help of old families of the city and generations of friends. The hiding has worked. Anthropologists and scholars from around the world who have prodded and pawed through the tombs and walls of old structures for the last century have discovered some secrets. But other secrets have stayed in the mud walls for another generation to find. The rare documents found illuminate not only Timbuktu's history but also the evolution of religions and philosophies in West and North Africa.

Nobody knows who hid manuscripts or, as time slips by, where the remaining manuscripts are hidden in Timbuktu's maze of old mud walls, which are regularly repacked after being worn down by the wind. They are thought to be tucked into mosques, old university buildings, libraries, and possibly even the mud walls of homes we walked past.

The world knows about these treasures of history because many of the found manuscripts now reside in climate-controlled museums in Paris and elsewhere. But the history still buried in the walls keeps Timbuktu tethered to its past.

■ ■ ■

On Christmas Eve, we move on foot in late afternoon to the south end of the city, which is already silent and empty of people. We are surprised not to see police or military officials of any kind. Eventually we reach the stretch of road that leads to the Niger River. Once we are out of Timbuktu and nearing the river, it is as if the curfew in the city does not exist. At the river, lights are strung between a few food stalls surrounded by tables filled with men. Another group of men, with trucks idling, stand ready to move. In the face of danger, commerce continues. We continue.

We look for Mamadou and our pirogue in the moonlight, but both are gone, probably back up the river toward Mopti. We find our kayaks safe where we had left them, so we each thank the man who had watched them and pay him 1,000 CFA.

Not wanting to draw attention, we pack quickly and paddle in the moonlight reflecting brightly off the water and then camp on the southern bank, away from Timbuktu, after just an hour. We are away from view of anyone. I pull out two cans of Heineken beer I had found in Timbuktu to surprise Rick for a toast.

"Christmas beer?" I offer and hand him one.

I pop mine open, smell the honey of the Dutch pilsner, and drink half of it before I notice Rick's remains unopened.

He hands the can back to me. "Merry Christmas," he says. "You'll enjoy it more than me." I put it away for another night.

The following morning we pass a small village on the river's edge that is buried in sand to the rooflines of a few homes. We paddle closer to look for people, but there are none. Leafed trees next to the buildings extend over the roofs several feet, indicating that the sands took the village in a short period, maybe less than a year. The place is without footprints or any evidence of effort to clear the sand. If the river and desert are in battle, the desert here wins. Sand beats the sun, too, as the seasonal harmattan winds that descend off the Sahara begin to hit us like a constantly flogging whip, and the sky disappears in the dust. The wind doesn't hurt, but it penetrates like cold and makes us ache. It wears us down by the hour, by the day, and is inescapable.

We hug the southern bank of the Niger to keep from getting lost in the impenetrable dust; we can rarely catch a view of the northern bank. With little bearing but the river's edge, I see white egrets, stilts, plovers— all standing still in the river. I gain no comfort from seeing the grounded birds, as lost as we are and flightless in the sand winds, though the fact they are here indicates that an open sky will eventually come. I eye an ibis, a bird that migrates along waterways, and trust that the river will take us out of the wind.

I had not heard of the harmattan before being trapped in it, though it is famous. It is the world's greatest continuous wind. It changes the weather in South America after it blows south and west out of West Africa and circles the globe. Unlike the chinook winds of Canada that melt snow in hours, or the mistral of France that chills and dries the Mediterranean region, the harmattan stays for months every year. It is as much a season in the West African Sahel and Sahara as winter is in Wyoming. We had been given a clue in Timbuktu when we were told that, in Bambara, north is the sand's way.

In the sand cloud from the north, we are nowhere decipherable. Lost in the sand-dust fog, my mind goes everywhere. It spins away from the river, then back to the day in front of my face, blunted by boredom and fatigue. Then away again. In the deep desert sandstorms, the sky-land-water-nowhere is so brown and gray that I go to colorful places of comfort, like the bright green Guinean highlands. It seems like years ago that we were there, but it was only three months earlier. I close my eyes and paddle and let my mind drift. There is reprieve only within the blue walls of our tent at night, lit from our headlamps like the sky in Laramie at noon.

We wake to the same wind and dulled view and eat the same hot mixture of couscous, millet, and peanuts with powdered milk and sugar. We refer to it as fuel, and it is delicious. Then the next day, we wake again to the same sky and wind, eat, and proceed like soldiers against the river and wind for another twelve hours. This is what we do for days on end, for endless days, until endurance becomes not a day to get through but a way of life. The persistence of paddling is not yet desperate, because we have no choice but to move as we did the day before.

Then one afternoon, out of sky dust, a glimpse of donkeys on the riverbank comes, and goes. I see a few women wrapped in cloth the color of the harmattan sky. My sight of them appears and then disappears in pulsing gusts of wind. Closer, I see they are there, real people, getting water from the river in brown leather bags that they drape over the backs of a few donkeys. We stop paddling and the women see us. They stop working. We stare at each other ten yards apart. Tuareg. The women do not wear the blue robes of the men we have seen but wrap themselves against the wind in colors of the sky and land. I can see only women, but I scan for men and camels. No one speaks or moves. I see nothing beyond the women and their donkeys. I am immediately reminded, in the isolation of the river and the gray sky, that we are not alone. In thirty yards, we are past them as if they had not been there, gone into the harmattan.

The wind again becomes ceaseless, driving. Dust enters creases and corners of every single thing we have, and sand grit is in my mouth, nose, and eyes. Our heads ache and our lips are cracked, hands blistered, stiff fingers throbbing. The river moves against us. And then the nights are cold, almost too cold for our sleeping bags. My mind moves to escape to anywhere but here.

In our kayaks in the wind, Rick and I seldom talk, because we have little to talk about, and even if we did, we would have to yell over the wind to have a conversation. We paddle at our own paces, as we have generally done, but keep within sight of each other. Paddling is solitary, but here we cannot lose each other.

In our tent at night, our words have slimmed to practical matters. We have run short of subjects beyond hippos and the African fiction—Achebe, Okigbo, Armah—that we read and reread from our dry bag filled with books, now dwindled to dusty, dog-eared paper. We are far past the end of Mungo Park's journal and long ago tucked his book into the stern of my kayak in a dry bag with other unnecessary items, like our Ruger 9mm gun and a flare gun. Exhausted from recapping the day, or considering the physical monotony of tomorrow, our eyes focus on our last book, a heavy volume I am grateful to have, Birds of West Africa. We compare what birds we have seen.

After days of the brain-deadening view of the nose of our kayaks and a blurred sky of sand dust, when there is nowhere to go, our conversation finally goes home to Laramie.

Rick talks about his family. He tells me things I already know but like to hear again, such as how his father moved to Laramie as a math professor with his wife and raised Rick, his two brothers, and a sister in a house near mine. The family still owns the house, and his parents had kept the same jobs their entire careers.

"Same as me," I say. I too had grown up in the same house with the same parents, who had the same jobs their whole lives. We started listing friends who enjoyed the same stability, and the list was long. "It is the university," Rick surmised as the unifying force in Laramie.

Our experience differed only in that his family had come to Laramie just before he was born and mine had come to Wyoming four generations ago. Rick's father moved to Laramie from Wisconsin to teach. My father was a banker, the son of a banker father, and the grandson of a banker who started two stockgrower banks in another corner of Wyoming. They financed sheep ranchers mostly, not cattlemen. Sheep owners and cattlemen did not mix in Wyoming then, though they do now, after land battles and the differing cultures between cattle and sheep families finally eased. A battle between sheepherders and cattlemen once erupted into what is referred to as the Johnson County War. The university still offers a now overlooked history course on the war. University professors, their children, the subsequent generations of sheep and cattle ranchers, and associated land-related or railroad enterprises make up Laramie's demographics, except for the students who arrive in Laramie to study.

Young people come to Laramie from every corner of the state, and you know that because their vehicles have the number of their county on their license plates: 16, Johnson County, Buffalo; 2, Laramie County, Cheyenne; 22, Teton County, Jackson; 19, Uinta County, Evanston; and, of course, our home, 5, Albany County, Laramie. Everyone knows what county you come from in Wyoming, and because of the migration of students and their vehicles to the University of Wyoming, every kid in Laramie can name all the counties and county seats in the state. In Laramie, we thought of those people with other numbers on their license plates as outsiders.

Laramie's one middle and sole high school have boys dressed in argyle sweaters that smell of mothballs, like you need somewhere on the East Coast, from where their parents migrated for careers at the university. Other young men and their sisters come to school dressed in three wool shirts, an orange hunting jacket, or a lined denim jacket because they feed sheep at 5:00 a.m., long before the school day starts.

Albany County is Wyoming's poorest county, with mediocre soil for ranching and no minerals, gas, or oil. On the high plains, our county is too cold and windy for tourists, except for those who hunt or fish. But we have the state's only university. For that reason alone, I suggested to Rick that Laramie is the best place in Wyoming.

"I don't know," he challenged. "Maybe for you, maybe for me, but what if the university was in Casper? That's where it should be, in the middle of the state," he postulated.

Casper is the largest city in Wyoming. Oil money and influence flow from Casper to our capital, Cheyenne, the state's second-largest city, though the two swap the top spot for population and dominance depending on politics and the boom and bust of oil and gas. Laramie and the university get what funding the two major cities decide. I find nothing wrong with Casper except that, at the dead center of Wyoming, it is too far from the real mountains that ring the state. Casper has an embarrassment of a ski area, where you park at the top and ski down from what is more a butte than a mountain. Few kids from Casper can ski well, and their ski area is a legitimate excuse.

"We need another university," Rick argued, not because he believed it but because we needed to debate something. It was too early to sleep.

For most of Wyoming's high school graduates, the university is the stepping-stone out of the state. Some figure out a way to stay as doctors, teachers, bankers, geologists, and engineers, though the prospects are tough outside of the extraction industries—oil, gas, coal, and trona, a white sodium that is processed into baking soda. Wyoming is the world's largest source of it, and everyone in Wyoming knows that fact.

Resource extraction booms and calms but has never busted. The money from extraction keeps the university inexpensive for any high school graduate in the big square state. Every third person in Laramie is a university student, creating an energy that breathes fresh air into town every year, before students export themselves out of Wyoming as surely as our coal.

We were exports, too, we decided. We would not be here, in the middle of a long river, if we had not been formed in the remote landscape of Wyoming. It isn't romantic. Laramie gives everyone itchy feet and an urge to move.

■ ■ ■

We aim ourselves into the wind for the bend in the river, one we see on the map, the great arc in the Niger River. Our bows are pointed into the waves. I keep a bearing based on my compass, stuck between the coaming of my kayak, two feet from my nose. The southern bank recedes from view if we venture too far into the middle, where we are in real wind-whipped water. Paddling is a test of aiming our bow into waves with barely a sighting of land, our progression assumed but not evident. It is time to trust something, and I trust my compass and our map, which indicates that we are approaching the great bend of the river.

We reorient continually to the east along the right bank of the river. I check my compass to see if it has moved. It hasn't, so I test it by holding it in my hand and the arms aim correctly, but the river maintains its eastward course to which we adhere. The bend will be the place where one ancient river once met another river to make the great Niger River, and where it will move, at last, southeast to the sea after crossing the continent. And we hope the headwinds will turn into a tailwind. We have been moving east since October, and we are now into the New Year.

When we arrive at the bend, I know it only from my compass turning south. Sand dunes on the left, the east side of the riverbank now, are like avalanches of snow breaking free from thirty yards high and slipping into the river in fractured slabs hardened by wind, loosened by the eventual take-over of gravity. It is almost unbelievable to see sand in this desert look and act like snow on a slope in Wyoming, but everything in this desert is a blurring of unbelievable and believable.

From the great bend in the river, we start falling off the map. Just as when you arrive at the top of a high peak, the only direction now is down and down as far as you can go. After 1,300 miles, halfway down the river, we have finally turned toward the Niger Delta and the Atlantic Ocean.

We took a first breath without sand dust when the wind began to work with us at our backs. A town on the left bank, Bourem, to the east now, not north, appears regal on the high dunes in the evening sun. We choose not to stop because we fear encountering Tuareg. The river surface cooperates for the first time in weeks, moving as a river and not pushing backward with a head wind and waves. Waterbirds guide us—black-winged stilts, snowy egrets, sanderlings, whimbrels, and long-billed curlews. They guide us to Gao, the last city in Mali, then Ansongo, a town at the border with Niger, over four hundred miles from Timbuktu.

Near the border of Mali and Niger, several wood ibis and their smaller riverway companions, plovers, stints, and sandpipers, scatter and gather over and over when we pull ashore. A fish eagle in the morning fog circles above us in tight swirls before it dives into the river to catch a fish. Inside the border of Niger, the black-and-white sacred ibis we had seen in Mali no longer blend into the monochrome harmattan sky as the air clears and the advancing green plants along the riverbank consume the sand and soil, creating a thick edge of growth that lets us know that we are leaving the desert behind us.

Rick Smith approaching the riverbank in Lokaja, Nigeria, 1992.

The river in Niger is no longer referred to as Djoliba. It becomes the Niger, pronounced the French way, as is the name of the nation. The river runs along the far west thumb of the huge desert country that extends widely to the north for hundreds of miles to Chad and Libya, an area that is, like Mali, Tuareg territory, though we are told the Niger Tuareg are a different and competing band of the Tuareg than those who are challenging the government of Mali.

We decide to move the 350 miles through Niger quickly and with care. Officials had stopped us and tried to restrain, retain, or bribe us for having nearly extended our visa period in Ansongo, Mali. This awakened us to the potential of the same type of officials in Niger, where our visas had expired. The random policeman, military man, or some unidentifiable official could do almost anything to us, like confiscate our kayaks, fine or bribe us, expel us on an airplane, delay us for weeks, or all of them. The river was safer, and we camped on small islands to avoid these men.

Near Tillabéri, an area of the river filled with green islands, hippos are more plentiful but also more docile than they had been in Guinea and Mali. The pink legs of several black-winged stilts glow in the clear light in complete silence next to the hippos. We camp there to watch the animals and birds.

We get to Niamey, where we need to buy food and fuel for our stove. Peace Corps volunteers allow us to camp in their fenced compound, where we can shower and eat salads from the nearby street vendors, whom the volunteers had coached to rinse vegetables in bleached water. Those salads, and the company of curious Americans, energized us for the long haul of another 750 miles through the continent's most populated nation, Nigeria.

Below Niamey, we discover "W" National Park, where the river bends in the shape of the letter along the border of Niger with Benin. We spend two days paddling up the river's side channels hoping to find giraffes and elephants, once abundant here before long droughts decimated wild animals two decades earlier. We avoid police checkpoints by staying on the right bank in the nation of Benin, where our visa had also expired. But the river along the Benin border is rural, quiet, and free of police, military men, and bureaucratic officials.

We enter Nigeria, home to one in five Africans, on January 25, a month after leaving Timbuktu. On the southern side of the desert, in a more verdant landscape, we see birds impossible to imagine. A black-casqued hornbill has a beak with an extra formation on top, making it seem to come from another geologic epoch as it flies in undulating swoops in front of us. A crowned crane stands three feet tall, still and stalwart in a field on the edge of a mighty body of water backed up by Kainji Dam, a hydroelectric behemoth built in 1968. Villagers displaced by the reservoir had been moved to prefabricated huts surrounding it, but these are uninhabited, like an abandoned model of an African village. We paddle across the reservoir through the day, then the night and the following morning. We move fast now and with boundless energy as the miles fly by with the current, under the sun.

Two days below Kainji Dam is a much narrower reservoir, indicating that it had captured a canyon beneath its water. We had been waiting to get here since putting Mungo Park's journal away. I feel haunted because we know that beneath us is where Mungo Park died in a bombardment of rocks thrown by the people of Jebba, once a tribal village, now a small town with a paper mill. His body was buried on the riverbank in 1806. Today, Jebba remembers Park with a tall rock monument, indistinct in design and placed where few ever see it, with a plaque that reads "Died in Africa for Africa."

We drift through Lokaja, a city where a mighty tributary, the Benue, joins the Niger to double its width and accelerate its speed. The city howls with activity on both sides of the river. When we pull ashore, hundreds of people gather and cheer for us. Men watch our kayaks without us asking them, while we shop for food we will cook that night back on the riverbank, somewhere tucked away from the city.

We move in clear light on the river past the large city of Onitsha, into the heart of Nigeria. We have found camping places along the river, outside the cities, for sixteen nights. This is the easiest and fastest time we have had on the water in nineteen weeks, and we can almost envision the end, the ocean surf ahead of us through the Niger Delta.

11

The Niger River Delta

I HEAR NOTHING IN THE HOT, early morning until we are upon chaos. Fifty yards ahead of us, dozens upon dozens of men swarm the water, slapping long black mangrove limbs on the river's surface. The water foams with the thunder of sticks. Men attempt to climb aboard a tugboat with a glass cabin that towers like a bird's nest two stories over us. The tugboat pushes a barge, carrying bulky machinery and pipes, up the river. I have no idea what the machinery is for.

A glass bottle breaks against the side of the tugboat, and a bright flame spills down its side. Then a bombardment of Molotov cocktails starts. I make out Coca-Cola bottles—the thick, old bottles I knew as a boy—corked with rags, breaking and blasting against the hard metal of the tugboat. Bright fires fall down the fuselage of the tugboat's tower, now only forty yards away, with the current drawing us closer. I look up to the windowed helm of the tugboat and see a white man and a black man looking directly down at me. They do not move and do nothing to acknowledge me. I have no time to react to them, to seek direction from them, to receive an arm movement or any guidance. I quickly put on my life jacket for the first time in the last two months on the Niger. We had been on the river for nearly five months, and now we could be swimming for our lives in seconds.

I look for Rick, who is dead still in the water, just to the left of me, not paddling, focused on the scene ahead. After the ease of travel we had enjoyed thus far on the fast-paced smooth river in Nigeria, we had cruised into the mind-numbing meandering mangrove swamp extending to the river's end at the sea. The Atlantic Ocean is close, and we are timing our movement with the fluctuating tides to finish our journey.

Now the Niger is on fire.

The current is pulling us downriver toward the violence. I look to the bank, but it is just what we have seen for days—a thicket of mangrove and nothing else, no land, no village, no escape. Where did these men come from? What is happening?

A cold sweat comes over me in the hot, humid Niger Delta. We are dead, I think. "We are dead," I say to Rick. He shakes his head and says nothing. The river pulls us closer.

Many of the men had managed, by climbing over each other, to get onto the tugboat. On the side of the tugboat, the name "Willbros" is painted in red and white.

Men wrapped in what appear to be dripping rags are all over the tugboat, while men in the river turn their attention toward us. We spin around and paddle hard upstream but cannot move against the river. Rick lets his kayak turn back around and drifts toward the turmoil. I follow without choice.

Another man in the spray yells to us and grabs at Rick's boat from the water but does not tip him over, which shocks me given how aggressively the man had swum to us. The other men in the water, just yards beyond us, scream in a cacophonous roar in the heat of their action. Dozens of them, maybe a hundred, continue to pound the water with mangrove branches. More faces emerge out of the water and out of the mangroves with more sticks, the explosive splashing of bodies and mangrove limbs growing louder as we approach. We are going down with the Niger, I think, like doomed sailors in a storm at sea, like Mungo Park. I imagine what it will be like to suffocate as water fills my lungs and mouth: in my imagination, I cough water and then swallow before falling into a deep darkness. My mind races but I have no words.

The man holds Rick's boat and says something to him. I cannot not hear, cannot bring myself to focus on listening as the current takes me directly into the middle of the men. Even then, with a man now reaching for my kayak, I cannot summon a word, let alone a strategy to avoid them, to save myself. I am in shock, without a choice and without a voice.

I wait, numb for whatever they have planned for us in their warm, brown water. In a state of complete, inactive incompetence, my heart stops pounding and I grow calm, and acquiescence occurs. I am alone and alert to the moment and nothing else. This is an execution, like having a gun at my head.

Rick raises his hands and holds his paddle high on the thumbs and palms of his open hands, just above his shoulders, and shouts "Hello!" And then louder: "HELLO."

We had learned this way of greeting people, with raised hands, in Mali months earlier. But we had always been quiet when raising our hands or our paddles and had never said "hello" or anything else. The gesture alone had always spoken for us. Others on the river for the last 2,500 miles had offered the same greeting, but also always silently. It signaled that we had no weapons and had arrived as friends. We had come to use the gesture daily with fishermen, border bureaucrats toting guns, women cleaning themselves, and children racing along the bank. And now Rick uses it with men wielding sticks and gas in glass bottles, enraged with a tugboat and the damage to their fishing, to their home.

Rick blurts out, "We go to the sea . . . many months on Niger."

I echo Rick, raising my paddle and collecting my breath. With gathering lung power and desperation, I call out, "Hello, hello, hello!"

The man lets go of Rick's kayak, drops his stick to the river, and claps his hands.

"Welcome," the man next to Rick's kayak says to him in English. Then he turns to the other men in the river and calls something out to them.

The men immediately part in the water and shout "Welcome" and "Hello."

In a narrow path provided to us between bodies and mangrove sticks, we race forward. Beyond reason and beyond luck, something had happened. The men cheer for us as we move past them. With the identical intensity they had angrily displayed toward the tugboat in the middle of the river, they clap their hands and scream as if at a soccer match. The men who had climbed aboard the tugboat also turned to us. "Hello," they call out to us over and over as we pass.

I can no longer see the men at the helm in the tower of the tugboat, but I hear the engine power up and begin to move the barge against the current and past the men in the river.

"Hello. Good-bye," we scream back, dumbfounded.

Within the space of a held breath, we had been given notice of our death and then a ticket to live. I can say that for the rest of my life I will never feel more grateful and more baffled at the same moment. Terror and beauty together, because the men, the foaming brown water, and the mangroves were just that.

I look back to the tugboat for a split second and then turn away forever and pull hard on my paddle. Rick is abreast of me. The Niger takes us safely away.

We did not understand the anger we had just witnessed, but we needed to, and wanted to. A bend in the river came and went, followed by another. We were back instantly in the doldrums of the delta, surrounded by the monotony of the mangroves and the unchanging smell of sulfur. The scene implied a uniformity that was an illusion. The physical landscape disguised explosive human tension between the delta's people, who have somehow managed to live here for centuries, and, we would discover, the global oil companies working the big equipment on these otherwise isolated waters. The men in the river were rebelling with the only weapons they had against the oil companies and the tugboats, machines, and pipelines that had ruined their fishing livelihoods.

Nigeria's enormous oil reserves in the Niger Delta are the African continent's largest source of wealth. During the Carter administration's Arab embargo, Nigeria was the largest foreign provider of oil to the United States. But the country's wealth has been squandered by corrupt officials in a feeding frenzy on the Nigerian political food chain. In this uncontrollable place with little land and useless brackish water, I cannot imagine how oil could be extracted from the thickets of mangroves and the fluctuations of river and tides.

That this marginally habitable part of Nigeria is rich with oil is as incomprehensible as the oil they found under my great-grandfather's home, in a corner of rough rangeland in southwest Wyoming known as the Overthrust Belt. The overthrust is a fault line that shoved and breached impervious rock boundaries far under the dry soil. The geology brought unlikely wealth in the form of oil and gas to people living on what was otherwise high, cold ranchland. This was where my dirt-poor ancestors settled in windowless homes they built out of stacked slabs of range grass after moving West as far as their horses would carry them, but far short of their vision of the better place they had sought after leaving Missouri. They settled there to subsist. Below their dry soil was oil and gas. No one could have imagined the wealth it would bring, and no one did for another century. Who among the inhabitants of the Niger Delta could have imagined the wealth beneath the mangroves of their isolated home?

It is a testament to determination and adaptation that people have managed to carve lives out of the mangrove swamp, living on minuscule patches of soil or in a band of homes built into the mangroves, homes lashed together with reed grass, only inches above the water. It is a place where necessity creates ingenuity. Everywhere in the world, a child arrives to survive and construct a life where it is born—in the dangerous Niger Delta or in Wyoming's austere Overthrust Belt.

■ ■ ■

Some three thousand miles of West Africa's creeks and rivers converge in the Niger Delta to finally find the sea. The long flow of thousands of creeks and rivers joins at the river's end, a hundred-square-mile sulfurous snare of saltwater blending with the soil-filled brown water that has flowed for nearly three thousand miles. This no-man's space is barely habitable, a place between marginal land and marginal water. The Niger's dwindling main stem itself, which we have no idea whether we are actually on, divides into twelve named rivers—the Nun and the Forcados, among others, in this waterscape of mangrove mirrors. Indistinguishable creeks multiply in apparent anarchy through channels as we attempt to navigate to the sea. We know the end of the river, the end of our journey, is so close that we can imagine seeing the ocean around the next bend, then the next, as we wind our way through the mangrove passageways praying to see the scene open to the Atlantic Ocean.

We see a bird in stacked branches of a nest built four feet high among the roots of a mangrove, above the water. The bird, a hammerkop, does not move from us in fright and seems fixed to its nest, a fixture of vulnerability in the shifting senselessness of the river and tides of the delta—yet maybe not.

The bird's nest is a round sculpture the size of a dinner table and is crafted above the high-water mark of the spaghetti of mangrove roots. The stack of branches, cemented in places with mud, is built precisely for this place.

"Now that is architectural design," Rick says.

The bird itself is two feet tall and is two colors of brown—the same drab colors of the delta—but those same colors appear bolder and more beautiful in the shine of its feathers. It has a thick, square crest on the back of its head, like an anvil, and a long, sturdy beak made for probing in the mud. People rarely see the hammerkop unless they are in a place where people do not go, like the Niger Delta.

"The bird is our bird," a woman who lives in a home on mangrove stilts downriver later told us. "This is her home." The woman's home looked as impermanent as a hammerkop's nest and must have taken great effort to construct entirely of mangrove limbs, with the roof made of grasses, reeds, and leaf fronds.

The moving tidal mixing zone of the river and saltwater appears to be biologically challenged, a poor habitat for everything, including the few people we find. But we discover that the place is also home to enormous pythons that swim the brackish water of the delta like flexing black logs, making this landless land even rougher for its human inhabitants. We see one of the snakes, thinking it is a floating log until it bends and accelerates in the water.

"What do the big snakes eat?" I ask people in the next village encampment.

"Everything, anything," a man tells me. "Bird, fish, pigs, people. Anything they want." Later, we would hear that a worker spreading sand to make a road was eaten whole by a python. His coworkers found the python with only the man's boots hanging out of its mouth. They chopped the engorged and docile snake to pieces to free the body for burial.

The few people we find in the quiet areas of the mangrove swamp are a comfort to meet. They move by small boats. We sleep with them on the open wooden floors of their stilt homes. They offer us fish and share their water.

They speak of "our people," not of Nigeria. They identify themselves with the water and mangroves, not the nation. They speak of Shell Oil, a company they hate for a different reason in each village. "They ruin our fishing." "They don't bring us lights." "They don't share fuel." "They did not build a school." "They sleep with our sisters."

The next day, we round another bend, and like that we are upon a compound comprising what appears to be white shipping containers nestled on bare land several feet above us, like an island out of nowhere, and a dock. A high chain-link fence encircles the area, and we hear the dull rumble of engines and generators at the back of the compound.

I see a sign hanging from the fence with the name "Willbros," the same name we had seen on the tugboat in the river two days earlier.

"Come here," a man calls to us from the dock. He waves us in and is smiling. "Come here," he says again.

We oblige and climb out of our kayaks onto the dock. A large barge, with the machinery we had seen upriver, is moored on the far side of the dock. On its side is the name "Kitty Bean."

"What is that?" I ask the man.

"Dredger," he says. "It's from Louisiana. Like me. What in the hell are you men doing?" he asks us.

Rick answers with essentially the same words we had used upriver in Mali, Niger, and Nigeria with marine police, village chiefs, and periodic Peace Corps volunteers: "Many months on Niger River. Two of us. We are going to the Atlantic Ocean."

The man swivels on his heels toward the compound up a long ramp. I see a gun strapped to his hip.

"Fine," he says and then pulls out a radio from his vest and calls someone.

"You are in," he tells us. "Meet the man at the gate and get yourself some AC."

The camp's structures are obviously fabricated for easy transport and quick assembly as a town for workers, all white men, we notice, once we are inside.

The containers are housing. We see them lined as if along a suburban street. The compacted grounds, as austere as a hospital room constructed for surgery, have been cleaned of all plants, built on dried and hardened "dredge soils, mostly sand," a man inside the gate says.

"How did you build this place?" Rick asks him.

"That Kitty Bean down there pumps eighty-five percent water and fifteen percent in situ sand," the man explains. "It usually works around the clock but is getting work done on her today to adjust pumps and pressure valves. We are burning time and money with that girl sitting there. But pressure kills. Blows pipe parts and men from here to hell."

The camp is for a company based in Tulsa, Oklahoma. The W of the Willbros logo looks to me like the W of the Warner Brothers logo. But this is no cartoon.

We are taken to a central building, which is much larger than the shipping containers. The building houses a kitchen area, mess hall, and recreation center with pool tables, televisions, and video games. The entirety of this unnatural compound was shipped into the Niger Delta from Louisiana.

"We have some Okies, a few Texans, but we mostly all coon asses," one man tells me as he hands me a beer once we are inside. "Louisiana men need Cajun. You boys want barbecue brisket or chicken? Or both?" he adds. We ask for both.

Another guy, who appears to be in his early twenties, with a young gun swagger, comes over to us from a pool table after Rick starts asking questions about their work.

"We dredge," he says. "Our job is to pull sand and sediment from the river to build roads and berms for a pipeline path. We got seventeen kilometers built, going from nine meters to seventeen meters deep. That is good road," he says with a sweep of his hand toward the end of the compound away from the river, where we see the road out of the remote area.

We are told this is the largest civil engineering project in Nigeria. The biggest oil reserve in Nigeria is under us, larger than anything in the Gulf of Mexico.

"Shell pays us six dollars a cubic meter, and we pump ten thousand cubic meters a day, twenty-four hours. We've pumped over two million cubic meters so far, and we're just getting started. Do the math," he tells us with a quick howl. "This place is money."

"How about for you, how long are you here?" Rick asks him as we are brought plates loaded with barbecue brisket and chicken.

The man sits down with us at a long dining hall table, empty but for us. "Here is the good part," he begins. "I am on my second tour. Willbros has been here nine months. The Dutch own us now, but no matter, they don't come around much. They know the dredging business, so all's okay. I work four months, twelve hours a day, no days off, get my double time and go home for two weeks with forty thousand dollars in my pocket after taxes. Plus we get a twenty percent finishing bonus. I buy my wife her things back home and come back for more. Do the goddamned math."

"That's good money, sir," I say before I do the math in my head and realize this guy makes more in four days than we brought to Africa to travel for five months, and more than I made in a year at my bank job.

"Where you men from?" he asks us.

"Wyoming," we answer simultaneously.

"Wyoming. You kidding me?"

"Oil country, too," Rick explains. "But no dredging."

"I never seen two skinny boys eat like you two," a cook coming out of a kitchen tells us. "You men starving, stupid, or both?" he asks, shaking our hands.

"Both," I say.

The man swings another beer in front of me. "We'll take care of you fellas," he tells us with a laugh. "You are just our kind. Crazy sons-a-bitches."

The most alluring surprise in the camp is the air conditioning. I might have described it as cool, but after being hot for months without a break, I find the sensation less a relief than I might have imagined. I consider that my ability to feel sensation has narrowed from the dull steady heat. I like the cool air but I don't feel that I need it or will be disappointed to leave it. I can almost think clearly, I realize, without my body slowed by sun and pulsing constant sweat. We had not been out of the African heat for months, day or night.

It had been hot, hot for months. We had dodged something danger-ous and are now sitting in real chairs in a clean room in a compound with nice men offering us food and sharing stories of the place they have found themselves working, and reflections on what they were missing back home. We hear of wives, children, newly purchased fishing boats, and plans to buy trucks and even houses.

"It's not hot in here," I say to Rick, hoping for some perspective and wisdom from him.

"It feels strange and wonderful," he responds.

Now that we are fed, the questions follow: Why are you here? How are you here? Are you some official expedition?

These were the same questions Nigerian officials had asked us for the past month. We provide the same answers: "We want to travel the Niger from source to sea. We have come by river from Guinea, two of us. We are alone and not official anything."

The cook offers us pie, three kinds—cherry, apple, and chocolate cream. We continue to stuff ourselves with whatever they put in front of us.

"How did you avoid the men who bombed our tugboat and dredger?"

"We were lucky," I tell them. "We didn't know what the machinery, the dredger, was."

"How much did you pay them?" asks one of the men from what is now a becoming a crowd of a dozen.

I tell him I have $380 in a pouch in my kayak and didn't even consider offering it.

"Three hundred and eighty dollars? Three hundred and eighty dollars!" The men laugh.

"Where do you think you're going with that much money?" one man asks us with a serious look. "You pay people here to be safe and that money won't do you shit."

"We are going to the ocean, then home," Rick says.

"You men are crazy," one of the men says. "But you are getting close."

"How close?" I ask.

"A day. Maybe two in those boats of yours."

An older man named Buck, who seems to be a boss, offers us each a spare container, or "housing unit," in which to sleep, and we decide to stay. Inside, the containers are clean and put together just like a hotel room, with folded sheets on a real bed, soap, white towels, and a shower. We each take one. I enter mine, shower, and lie down on the bed and fall asleep.

I wake to a knock on the door. It is dusk and growing dark. "You want to come with a few of us to the Bush Bar?"

"What's the Bush Bar?" I ask.

"Women," he says. "Just down the road."

"What women?" I ask him.

"Let's go. I'll explain," he says. We waken Rick, who joins us outside his container.

The man explains that the bar is down a road, walking distance, and constructed on the same dredged sand as the compound and the road. A local man had built it out of bamboo, mangrove lumber, and spare wood taken from the Willbros compound.

"It's clean and out of camp. He charges too much for beer but the women are nice and cost fifty to a hundred Naira, the Nigerian currency—five or ten dollars. You pick and pay, simple as that. Two rooms in back with mats on the floor."

"Not interested," Rick says.

"Legal age is thirteen here," he says, "but they got college-age girls, too."

"Thirteen?" I ask, disgusted with him.

"Just enjoy. Nothing illegal going on. This is the way it is here, guys."

"I'm not going with you, either," I tell the man. But I ask him a question, since he had shared earlier in the day that he had a wife and baby back home in Louisiana.

"You are young, and you showed us a picture of your family. Does your wife know about this?"

"No, no. We tell them back home that it is dangerous to leave camp—and that's partly true—and that we don't, but hell, you don't need to leave camp. They come to the gate," the man tells us.

Rick and I say nothing, but I look at the young man. I glance at Rick, who has a blank look on his face before shaking his head in complete disbelief, or maybe belief, I am not sure.

"The local guys who work for us do it, too," the young man explains after an uncomfortable silence. "But they pay half what the girls charge us. It's just a job, man, like our jobs. Just a job," he says. "Help the woman. Help yourself. We are all here together."

"Thanks, but we'll pass," I tell him.

The man walks to the gate and leaves down the sandy road, the same one that will carry trucks and the pipe for oil.

"We've got to get out of here," I say.

"Yes, tomorrow morning," Rick says.

We walk to the compound's main hall, where we had eaten earlier in the day. A new man, the senior manager there, we surmise, based on his crafted words, offers information without asking us who we are. He seems to already know our situation without us having to explain it.

"They are upset about the fishing," he starts. "The dredger effluent disrupts their fishing areas." The man is dressed in a collared shirt and is not from the South, based on his accent and choice of words, but is American and is much older than the others we had met. He doesn't volunteer information about himself as the others had.

"That confirms what we thought," Rick says. The difficulty of extracting oil in the mangroves, I consider quietly to myself, puts the needs of local people at the low end of Willbros's list of priorities.

The man picks up his glass and takes a drink of what appears to be whiskey. He doesn't offer us any, a detour from our convivial engagement with the other men earlier in the day. He explains that the villagers blame Willbros, and they blame Shell. They blame everyone but their chiefs, "the big men."

"Shell pays the area chiefs for access to their fishing areas. But the chiefs, and there are many of them down here, use the money in many ways, mostly personal. They take it somewhere. Who knows? Who cares? Actually, some of this is mitigated when we give men in the villages a job," he explains.

"We pay the local men about two hundred dollars a month and they work damn hard, I'll tell you that. Good jobs, but . . . it is unfortunate here," he says. "We have another camp, on a barge, down the River Nun. You can stay there tomorrow. I will let them know you are coming," he says and drinks the last of his whiskey, its ice having melted during our conversation. He sets the empty glass down. "Good night to you, men," he says and shakes our hands. "You won't see me in the morning."

We get up before dawn and leave to the good-bye of the only guard, a tall and strong Nigerian, one of only a few at the camp, who bears a remarkable resemblance to Michael Jordan. I think of mentioning this to him but don't. He's heard it before, I reason. And we want out of here.

In minutes we are away from the compound and back in the delta, weaving our kayaks through the mangroves. Did I hear all that? See that? I kept wondering. I move on, paddling hard without talking with Rick about Willbros. We need to move on.

I feel our closeness to the Atlantic, to the Bight of Benin, the Gulf of Guinea—the various names on our map for the ocean off the West

African coast at the mouth of the Niger. The tide level, between low and high on the mangroves, is now four to five feet, indicating that we are getting into the tidal pulse and close to the sea. The air smells of salt, not the rotting sulfur of the mangroves upstream. But there is no land, no stilt encampments. We will be sleeping in our kayaks, which we have done before, but I think this barge camp may be worth locating.

We see it just before dark on the left bank of the river, a three-story white building on a barge. It looks like a frosted ice cube from a distance. A man posted on the railing around the perimeter has clearly been waiting for us and waves us in. An American, he talks fast but does not have the curiosity of the men at the Willbros compound.

The floating facility is more rudimentary than the Willbros compound, but just as clean. We put our kayaks on a narrow deck that surrounds the floating building. All the workers we see are Africans. We are taken inside and given space to sleep on the second floor.

"Come for a cold Coke," he says to us.

We gladly oblige. The American meets us in the boat's dining room and already knows our situation ahead of our explaining it. He tells us about the camp.

"I am an engineer, the only American, only white man here," he says. "These Nigerians work hard, mostly spreading dredge spoils. Some work heavy equipment, motor-packers and shovels. Others work security. We move this barge camp as we are directed. But we lose people, LTIs. It's dangerous."

"What's an LTI?" Rick asks.

"Lost Time Incident. Accidents—work or play," he explains. "The other night, one of the men took a canoe to a trail that leads to a village. The village boys run canoe shuttles at night. The canoe capsized, our guy couldn't swim, and he disappeared. The current can be unpredictable here."

He tells us that the boy with the canoe was eight years old, and he swam to the bank. The boy's father had drowned in the same place a few years earlier. "The kids are durable here," he says.

"We ask the men about swimming skills," the engineer says, "but the documents get forged because many just don't swim. And they don't wear life vests either, though it's a requirement."

"I let them come and go at night. They go to the village to find prostitutes. Most of these men come here from other places in the area," he explains. "I can't keep up with their names. The guy that drowned, though, we couldn't locate him for two days, until I brought in a man from the village, a spirit leader, to help. He told me the man sank because the money in his pocket weighed him down," the engineer said. "Sure enough, two days later, up came the body. We found him bloated with a wad of bills in his pocket. I had some of my men tie him to the roots along the bank until Shell came in to do an autopsy. They require it with any LTI death."

Haines, left, and Rick Smith at the Niger River's end in Brass, Nigeria, February 20, 1992.

A cook offers us rice with chicken, which was left over from what the work crew had eaten, and we sleep on a floor that is dry and safe, and as comfortable for us as any bed.

We push off early again. The American had warned us about the collision of tides with current. We ride the end of a flowing tide hoping to avoid an ebb tide that will push us back into the mangroves. A slack time between the flowing and ebb tide should arrive by midday to allow us to get toward Brass, the closest port city on the Niger Delta. We manage to move easily to the end of the River Nun, one of the river channels of the Niger we did not know we were on until meeting the men at Willbros. Where it meets the main stem of the Niger, the river is beyond huge, hundreds of yards wide, maybe a mile or two. Distance at the river's mouth is difficult to judge. Rick and I stick close together as we eye the far side of the river.

This is it, and it is more than I could have imagined. Crossing the river with the enormity of the ocean to our right is overwhelming. But we cannot be conquered now, cannot in fact do anything but move across the river. I look to Rick. He is not indecisive and has dropped his rudder to guide him across the expanse of the Niger toward the city in the distance, Brass. I look to the ocean, cresting in the distance to the west with rolling waves. The current of the river pulls me into its undulating flow. I drop my rudder, following Rick's lead, and attempt to keep a tack across the mighty Niger meeting its end.

But the distance across the river is too far, and the current pulls us past the other side of the river, past Brass and into the ocean. We are beyond the shore, into the ocean swells, riding waves from peak to trough, up and down, over and over. I lose sight of Rick periodically in the rising and falling swells, whitecapping in the wind at their crest.

"Where are we going?" Rick yells.

"With the water," I call back.

We are pushed south of the mouth and along the coastline, unable to guide our kayaks against the competing forces of tides and the river's converging current. After an hour, the tides push us into Brass as if we had planned it that way. When we get to shore, we are in a port compound with many tugboats lined up along a concrete harbor. We see signs for an Italian oil company named Agip. I get out, with weak knees from hours in the kayak, and realize I had forgotten to put on my life jacket.

After nineteen weeks and 2,600 miles, we completed our descent of the Niger River, from the source in Guinea to the Atlantic Ocean off the Nigerian coast, on February 20, 1992. Some years later, I discovered that two Frenchmen had also completed a continuous descent of the Niger in the 1940s, a confirmation that our trip was not as historic as Mark had hoped. Nevertheless, Mark did eventually write a book about the early stages of our trip, *To Timbuktu*.

In 1995, Mike died on an expedition in the frigid water off Baffin Island with his brother Dan and two other travel companions from Laramie, their boat capsized by a bowhead whale. Their bodies have never been found. Mike left a wife and twins.

12

What the River Says

In rivers, the water that you touch is the last of what has passed
and the first of that which comes. —Leonardo da Vinci

IF YOU ASK ME TODAY, years after kayaking the length of the Niger River, why I did it, I'd shrug the same way I did the day we were on the airplane out of Lagos, unshaven, dirty, and having already been given two meals. The Belgian flight attendant on Sabena Airlines asked us that question as she generously brought us our third meal. I remember the beautiful food as if it was the finest meal ever—sliced beef, potatoes, and bright green peas. I thought for a moment to consider providing her with an answer. But my only answer was that the next day for us on the Niger had been the best day, an explanation that may not mean much to anyone but us. I smiled, thanked her, and shrugged. Rick shrugged, too.

Old climbers famously repeat what has become a refrain: "Because it is there." We could not say that. We did not see it that way. A river is not "there" the way a mountain is. A river is there and then it is gone. To know it is to stay on it for its length. A day less on either the beginning or the end of the river would have been a hole in our experience. "The next day" became our answer for why we had traveled the length of the Niger by our own physical effort. The short answer, however, became a shrug.

When I unpacked my filthy Feathercraft kayak from its backpack in Portland, I immediately put it back together—its internal aluminum frame inside a durable rubber and water-resistant skin—and hosed it off in the springtime sun. The Niger River journey was over, but I wasn't done with it. I looked at my kayak next to the old bicycle that I had taken to Tibet and sighed. I loved them as trusted and durable friends, but my kayak was more mobile and could be put into its backpack and taken anywhere anytime. The Niger had put me on a river for life. Move, experience everything, but do not be captured by any one place or thing. It fit an earlier time in Japan and Tibet, when moving made sense.

I quit my job even though the bank had given me a generous nine-month leave of absence. Little frightened me then, including being unemployed. I kayaked by myself all around the lower Columbia River basin. I climbed Mount Hood alone and backpacked solo into the wilderness of the Wind River Range in Wyoming. Simplicity and self-reliance seemed luxurious for weeks and months to a year. I lived lean, baking bread, eating rice and noodles in the attic of a 1911 duplex I owned, renting the two apartments below me to pay my mortgage and giving me about $400 extra every month, supplemented now and then by writing pieces for travel and kayaking magazines. I lived as I wished, as I had on the Niger—moving, exploring, watching birds, and reading. I did not think of it as a good example or bad. Nor was it any form of rebellion or a spiritual pursuit. I simply craved wilderness and seeing other places I had dreamed of seeing. I couldn't face being defined or trapped by a job or place.

The Niger River has no eddies, those places along the bank where a river circles and stalls, except for one dangerous area below Bamako. Otherwise, the Niger does not have the hydraulic dynamics to create a single eddy in thousands of miles on the largely desert, low-elevation landscape of West Africa. I had not realized that fact, or thought about it, until I put my kayak onto rivers around Portland and Laramie—the Willamette and Columbia in Oregon, and the Laramie and North Platte in Wyoming.

The bends in rivers, especially in the mountainous American West, create eddies every few miles. The strong currents of creeks race into rivers that build larger and larger eddies. Bushes, broken branches, and every now and then whole trees are caught in the circling turmoil, tossed together in the swirling water for hours or days to months and years. Time in an eddy adds up. The trapped wood churns, banged up and bleached by the water, sun, and ice, logs dulled into similar-looking rounded pieces from lodgepole pine, ponderosa pine, blue spruce, cottonwood, and quaking aspen. Come winter, the trees in eddies emerge stripped of their natural beauty to become a new form of themselves, a mass in transition but lodged in ice, poised to move downstream.

> Some time when the river is ice ask me
> mistakes I have made. Ask me whether
> what I have done is my life.
> —from "Ask Me," William Stafford

A year after the Niger trip, I started moving from wild areas to new cities, living in three places in four years. A thread of finance-related jobs kept my mobile life on the semblance of a career track, and each place I landed was going through a transition: Trenton, New Jersey's capital, was changing to provide better paths for low-income entrepreneurs to succeed in a city where streets separated old Italian neighborhoods from new immigrants from Liberia and the black community. I started a nonprofit loan fund there. After two years, I moved to the Czech Republic, which was at the center of building a post-Communist environmental finance infrastructure after decades of enduring unimaginable air, water, and soil pollution. I worked in Prague as a financial adviser to the Czech National Environmental Fund for a US company, Chemonics International. Then I moved back to Portland, which was a ripe place to start a new type of bank, ShoreBank Pacific, to capture the opportunities of conservation and sustainable development. All places were hard to leave, and I felt each time that I was leaving something meaningful behind. But a fresh start in a new place was exhilarating and necessary for me, like running a river and moving from eddy to eddy.

I was not on this river alone. In fact, I was on her river. A woman, Milena, who moved swiftly for aspiration and academic advancement, had me alongside, adjusting to each place. Milena, who was ten years younger than I, went first to Princeton when she entered graduate school. We lived in the same type of student housing that I had lived in with Jennifer in Eugene eight years earlier. I never imagined then that I was trying to re-create what I had long lost with Jennifer, but I realized later that I was. Life had both of us moving, learning, and living together for four years. And having experienced the long, slow flow of the eddy-free Niger, I had a commitment to movement but also to each place and to one woman after previous years without such a commitment.

We shared many journeys. She used my friend Rick's kayak, which he had loaned to me after the Niger trip. The first time I saw her paddling in my closest friend's blue kayak, only days after we met, it looked right and felt perfect.

And everything flowed well for years as our lives moved from Portland to Princeton to Prague and back. Our kayaks went with us to rivers, coasts, and lakes: the docile tea-colored rivers of the Pine Barrens and the bird-filled shore in New Jersey; the Labe and Elbe Rivers in the Czech Republic and former East Germany while I worked in Prague; the islands of coastal Croatia after supervising elections in Bosnia. We shared vacation excursions to Maine, Florida, Washington, and Alaska. Over the years, my aging companion—a folding kayak—had become more and more faded by sun, patched and repatched from being dragged ashore, bent but never broken. After five years, I calculated that I had paddled as many miles in my kayak as Rick and I had on the Niger.

Our last trip together in the kayaks was our honeymoon. We were on the Shuyak Islands, a group of small wilderness islands near Kodiak Island in Alaska, where we had been dropped off by a small floatplane out of Homer. The islands are remote, loaded with spawning salmon, huge brown bears, breaching humpback whales, sea otters, and eagles. The afternoons grew dark and cold early, pushing us from our kayaks to our cozy one-room cabin. This adventurous time was no honeymoon, however, with secrets and uncertainty having accumulated between us. This last journey together served no purpose in shared experience compared to the multitude of other trips. But then, it served the hardest truth of our shared life: we were done being together. Love may have lingered but commitment did not. Our personal directions deviated from one shared with each other; or hers did, or mine did. It didn't matter. When caring for each other evaporated, the end loomed. We divorced less than a year later.

> Others
> have come in their slow way into
> my thought, and some have tried to help
> or to hurt: ask me what difference
> their strongest love or hate has made.

I always found a way to circle through Laramie when I needed to be there, no matter what it took me to get home. I had come to say I had many homes, with a place in my heart and head for each one. But returning to Laramie and heading always to our family cabin on Libby Creek reinvigorated me simply from the calm and comfort I gained knowing the sounds, smell of one creek.

Early autumn in the Snowy Range above Laramie is usually perfect, with a clear sky, cool air, and calm winds. The aspen trees turn bright yellow, lighting up the dominating lodgepole pine forest for about three weeks. It is also a quiet time, made more so with the resuming of university classes, hunting season yet to start, and summer tourists having evaporated from the campgrounds. It is the best time to be alone in our mountains. And I was alone, abandoned by a person I loved and yet acknowledging that I had abandoned her at the same time. I was in a turbulent state of mind, but the creek helped.

> I will listen to what you say.
> You and I can turn and look
> at the silent river and wait. . . .

From our cabin on Libby Creek, I'd go into Laramie to another comfortable place, Jeffrey's Bistro, where I had learned to bake bread and desserts years earlier from people who had moved on but whose presence remained on the chalkboard menu on the wall. The bread for sandwiches, daily rolls for soup, and tortes and cheesecakes were the same as they had been for years, a comforting aggregation of many people's recipes.

I learned to bake from three people at Jeffrey's. One was Sara, who had once cooked for timber-cutting crews in the woods of British Columbia, where she fired her shotgun over the heads of bears approaching her camp and its wood stove. I learned how to knead bread, shape a pie crust, and whisk with a wooden spoon from watching her move her arms, hands, and wrists, all specialized tools as much as a spoon or knife. I trusted her periodic tutorials, points of wisdom doled out only every so often. Then Zita, who had cooked and baked as a guide for Martin Litton, a legendary dory oarsman on the Grand Canyon. She was beautiful and shy and provided her detailed guidance only over time and after I had earned her trust. I took notes. If she was timid in public, she was anything but that in the kitchen or rowing a boat, which I witnessed when she invited me on her private trip on the Colorado River during a year when the river ran consistently and unusually high after a record snowfall in the Rockies. And then there was Jeff, my subsequent travel companion variously in Nepal, China, and Tibet. Jeff talked and talked when he baked. His ideas mixed with techniques, recipe variations, and travel stories. There was little way to keep up with him or capture all that he shared, so I gave up, listened, and tried to remember what I could.

Learning to bake from these three was a perfect blend, much like what I later gained from bird-watching with a man named Howie who was color-blind. He would call out details, like most people, but focused on the less obvious observations such as tufts on a bird's head, the length of a tail, the shape of a beak, or its call. Often, he closed his eyes to think as I fumbled through my book to identify a bird. Little tricks in timing, such as a pause during a deep breath, usually helped me when bird-watching or baking.

■ ■ ■

To know Libby Creek is to know its eddies. I had observed its fast-paced water and circling eddies since I was a boy. The eddy on Libby Creek below our cabin was changing but the creek was calm, unlike during high water in spring and summer, when eddies can be dangerous even on creeks. I once saw an animal, maybe a deer, in a big eddy, banged and torn apart to bones and hide over the course of a year.

Libby Creek had moved over many years to carve a path around a huge green quartz boulder, dispersing the creek around its sides as if the old eddy below the boulder had never been there. The freezing and thawing of soil on the bank, the pounding of logs and sticks circling in an eddy on the boulder's downriver side had broken a path for the creek at high water to encircle the rock in the creek. The enormous boulder on which I had always sat to watch the creek was now part of the creek. The old eddy gone.

In the days I spent outside Laramie on Libby Creek, remembering how I had learned to bake, I realized that I had been in a series of eddies since the Niger journey, just like the eddy that had broken loose on the creek. I needed to break loose again, if I could, and move more as a river flows through turbulence and calm.

The best bread I ever baked, after learning the basics, deviated from what I was taught at Jeffrey's in Laramie. Sometimes out of necessity or when willing to risk a bag of flour, I replaced yeast with yogurt, used beer in place of water, or honey and agave for sugar. I learned the slow reality of a fermented sourdough starter. That starter was a like a river, split and shared downstream. You can move the starter in its jar anywhere, but it comes from one place, its source, even if no one recognizes that fact.

> We know
> the current is there, hidden; and there
> are comings and goings from miles away
> that hold the stillness exactly before us.
>
> What the river says, that is what I say.

13

What the Silence Meant

You will never be alone, you hear so deep
a sound when autumn comes. Yellow
pulls across the hills and thrums,
or the silence after lightening before it says
its names—and then the clouds' wide-mouthed
apologies. You were aimed from birth:
you will never be alone. Rain
will come, a gutter filled, an Amazon,
long aisles—you never heard so deep a sound,
moss on rock, and years. You turn your head—
that's what the silence meant: you're not alone.
The whole wide world pours down.
    —"Assurance," William Stafford

IT WAS 3:00 A.M. AND I WAS AWAKE and feeling absolutely everything at once, like my bones could break without moving, like I could cry for every reason there might be to cry. In the hair-trigger of a warm and wet night, I saw clouds moving in the night sky outside the window.

The night was warm but cooling with a soft rain. I was on alert and alone. My wife, Milena, was sleeping next to me on a bed barely wedged into the small room. Between her and the door were ballots, sealed in boxes from the first of two days of elections in Pale, a small town in the Republika Srpska (the Bosnian Republic of Serbia), which is one of two entities of the former Bosnia and Herzegovina along with the Federation of Bosnia and Herzegovina. The town is part of a newly constructed

Bosnia, created after five years of war that left the former Yugoslavia fractured. We were election supervisors, holed up in a small hotel, and had been instructed not to leave the sealed boxes of ballots unattended for any reason. We had held each other and talked with soft words for what would be the last time a few hours earlier. Words between us thereafter would be taut or nonexistent. After four years together, one as a married couple, our time together was over. The long night with her in this place left me feeling more alone than if she had walked from the room.

On my side of the bed, the window was open to the late-night rain, the kind of rain that no one hears in the silence of night, but which makes everything glisten in the morning. If I moved, I would wake her, so I rolled slowly toward the window, against which the bed was pinched tightly. There was no space in this room for anything but the bed and the boxes of ballots. The window was level with the bed, and I hung my arm out into the soft rain. I turned it side to side as the rain flowed gently over it. The silence of the rain in the glow of the moon behind the clouds was as beautiful as anything I could imagine, the weight of the sky flowing over me until I fell asleep.

■ ■ ■

One year later, in 1998, I was working elections again in Bosnia, but this time alone. I had to go back. A year of reading history and contemplating the region's repeating patterns of conflict had better prepared me, I hoped, to observe and listen, and maybe understand the complex history there. How had an entire nation, its villages and families, turned on each other overnight? How had its people done so repeatedly for centuries, including during World War I, after a single shot in Sarajevo instigated war throughout Europe? How had the Croatians aligned with the Nazis in World War II? And I had my own lingering wounds, inflicted a year earlier in this place, that required a fresh view. I needed to understand how my wife's infidelities a year earlier could end a marriage but not provide me the peace to move on.

Why do some battles repeat, and misunderstandings never cease, as they do in the Balkans, where every person has known exactly where they come from by name and by neighborhood for centuries? Milena was now my ex-wife. Her recurrent unfaithfulness and lies over the year preceding our trip to Bosnia had left me disgusted and condemned to recycling thoughts: How did this happen? Why was I so blind to it?

■ ■ ■

En route to Srebrenica, on the road from Zvornik, my driver swerved as if our van were a boat meandering on the Drina River next to us. The road led to the site of one of the world's worst atrocities, in which Bosnian Serb soldiers murdered over eight thousand men and boys, Muslim Bosnians, referred to as Bosniaks, in a few days in July 1995. My mind, too, meandered between the road's sharp curves and memories of a year ago, with Milena, when I felt devastated.

Along the road, bombed and burned houses, one after another after another, were lifeless whitewashed ghosts—with few spared, and even those still empty. Heavy red-clay roof tiles lay shattered and spread in the fields around the homes, shards of war scattered to the soil. In one house, I saw a cow standing alone in an empty, windowless living room. The angle of the morning sun lit the cow through a blown-apart front door. A hole in the roof indicated that a bomb had blasted the contents of the house out through its doors and windows. The remnants were difficult to make out in the grown-over grass and yellow weeds in the yard. I had been thinking how perfect this landscape in early autumn appeared, like our beautiful wedding two years earlier during trailing days of summer entering the harvest season outside Portland, Oregon.

The glowing green hills in Bosnia had turned to sun-bronzed henna on their ridges. Plum trees, stirred by birds but not a breath of wind, were bursting with ripe, purple fruit. Many of the plums—the source for homemade sauce and family brandy—had fallen to the ground to be eaten by birds, uninterrupted as they gorged on their prize.

To the residents of Zvornik and the smaller hamlet, Bratunac, upriver where my driver lived, the Drina River was what connected them to Belgrade, but it was also the border between the newly established Republika Srpska and the nation of Serbia. On this second trip to the region, deeper into the Serbian area of Bosnia, I had come to supervise municipal elections—the second election after the Balkan War. I was again working for the Organization for Security and Co-operation in Europe (OSCE), an international group out of Vienna leading the election process.

▪ ▪ ▪

The previous year, Milena and I had slept with the ballots to ensure that no one tampered with them during two days of voting. We had supervised the first elections in Bosnia since the end of the five-year war. It was a several-day commitment we had rationalized as a working vacation. But it was no vacation. We were at the end of our marriage and should have questioned the wisdom of going into a war zone. Bosnia had been annihilated in a war that had rekindled the former Yugoslavia's complicated collision of culture and religion. It was clearly a place that, once fractured, could disintegrate precipitously. But we went anyway. It was days after our first anniversary.

"We have to go," Milena had said repeatedly. "Bosnia has the world's attention," she said, waving a New York Times in front of my face. "I . . ." She corrected herself. "We need to be there."

I agreed with her, but for different reasons. While she sought to add the experience and credentials of working in this election to her list of academic accomplishments, I wanted to put my hand close to the fire of the war and try to understand its history. We were both curious and predisposed to exploration, whether by book or by foot. This was how we had woven our lives together for five years, meandering between her books and university libraries, and my binoculars and backpack.

We were placed outside Sarajevo in the hills of Pale, the site of the 1984 Winter Olympic downhill race. It was here that the American bad boy Bill Johnson had won the gold medal after an out-of-control race down the mountain. For weeks afterward, Johnson was on the front page of every newspaper and magazine in the world. Seventeen years later, he was, like Pale itself, long forgotten.

The former ski town no longer had the feel or appearance of Olympic grandeur. It was a worn village that had become known as the hideout for Ratko Mladić and Radovan Karadžić, the notorious Bosnian Serbs whom authorities were seeking to capture for war crimes. Most of the world's media believed the men were still hiding in these Bosnian hills, protected by the silence of its citizens, the same people we had come to assist in their first democratic election.

We had been posted with about seventy other election supervisors from around the world at the same hotel where the Olympic downhill skiers had once stayed. Midway up the mountain, the hotel had degenerated into a desolate fortress, dusty with warped handrailings and rotting decks that had seen little foot traffic since Yugoslavia's Olympic moment in 1984. After hearing lectures during the day about how to avoid land mines, we slept under a heavy blanket with the Olympic rings hand stitched onto it.

The mountain smelled of mulch, the accumulation of deteriorating dried grass, leaves, and spent flowers. We wanted to walk along the ski trails but were told not to leave the hotel grounds or its parking lot. We were not to open the doors of other buildings and were prohibited from walking in the fields or forests, or along any riverbanks.

A former soldier, a Serbian, gave us a lecture on land mine safety. "Riverbanks?" I asked.

"Especially the rivers," he said. "Land mines are waiting for you."

How, I thought, could the entirety of the rivers in Bosnia be off limits? But to reinforce his point, the young soldier told us how the land mines could be made bigger by stacking two of them—a military tactic that, I sensed from the precision of his explanation, he had performed many times. Such stacked mines were placed strategically to blow up tanks and other large vehicles.

He told us that his commander had once explained to his troops that stacked mines were too large to be detonated by the weight of men marching over them. He had been telling them this, the soldier explained, to push his troops forward through a minefield. He yelled to his men, insisting that the land mines were stacked for vehicles and could not be engaged by the weight of a man. None of the soldiers moved.

His commander's face grew red with rage as he implored his men to march with him through the field ahead. Still, no one did. So, he picked up a land mine and positioned it on top of a buried land mine. He then climbed a rock wall above the mines he had stacked and jumped from the wall onto the mines to make his point. The mines detonated.

The young soldier stood before us with no emotion, eyes cast down upon us. The land mines, he told us, blasted the commander's body parts and blood onto his men. Two soldiers standing close to the explosion were also killed.

"Do not let anyone tell you that it is safe here. Not on riverbanks, or in fields, forests, and this ski area. It may never be safe in Republika Srpska."

He wiped his mouth on his sleeve and sat down. He had been given the job of advising us because he spoke excellent English. But his authority came from surviving hell.

▪ ▪ ▪

A year later, the physical and human landscape of Serbian Bosnia was filled with denial and damage. Yet the people—perpetrators and victims alike—were creating new lives for themselves on land-mined but fertile soil. And that was why I was there.

I didn't choose to go to Srebrenica. The posting was assigned to me. Yet after a year of reading about the region, I wanted to understand the Serbian myths that induced them to act heroically when threatened, but also to commit murder in places like Srebrenica. The place would be haunting, I was sure. The bombed and burned homes along the Drina River were only the beginning.

Srebrenica was not the place of calm I needed to contemplate Milena's deceptions and narcissism, which still infuriated me. Yet on the road into town I considered that the context of Srebrenica, relative to my pain, might be exactly what I needed to find perspective and a route past my recurring memories of a disintegrated marriage.

At a stop to fill the overheated radiator of the van with Drina River water, I referred to the country of Serbia on the other side of the river. My driver poked me in the chest with his forefinger to correct me.

"Ne," he stated. "Nema granice. Ti si u Srbiji." (No. Not a border. You are in Serbia.)

He then picked up a bottle of his homemade plum brandy and took a drink. He swung the bottle by its neck in front of my face in a testing gesture more than a friendly offer.

I chose not to argue about the border. Instead, I accepted the bottle from him and took a long drink of brandy. It smelled of sweet plums but hit my tongue like fire. I pretended that it did not surprise me, but it was like nothing I'd ever tasted. I told him I liked it and I meant it.

"Dobry, moc dobry," I said. (Good, very good.)

As he unloaded plastic jugs to fill with Drina River water, I imagined myself to be in Germany in the early 1940s. The historical parallel between the Holocaust and this part of Bosnia, particularly Srebrenica after the genocide in July 1995, had shocked the world. The atrocity had become an addendum to the place name itself. "Srebrenica: the site of the worst genocide in Europe since World War II."

My driver reached the riverbank with two yellow jugs that held twenty liters each, about forty-five pounds per jug. Built like the stacked rock walls that surrounded the fields in the region, the Bosnian Serb had likely lived through more than I could even imagine. He was not a man to argue with or, I suspected, to joke with. He was maybe fifty years old, but maybe only thirty, probably a former soldier but maybe not. I decided not to ask him his age or background, at least not until I got to know him better. He had walked down the steep slope to the Drina's edge, surely through land mines I had been warned to avoid. I kept silent and heard music echoing from the hills. Music and art can revive people, I thought. I was sure he knew that land mines lined the river. Maybe his defiance of danger kept him moving onward, as music and art can unify and inspire people to reconstruct their lives.

I was traveling with a book of Serbian poetry, an obscure book I was inspired to find after reading the writer Rebecca West's brilliant brick of a book, *Black Lamb and Grey Falcon*, written from her travels starting in 1937 in Yugoslavia, before World War II. One recurring theme in her mosaic of people—Serbs, Croatians, Bosnians, and Slovenes—is the prevailing perception of threat. On the expanse of land and sea between Turkey and Europe, war between Islam and Christianity, both Catholic and Orthodox, has always been just over the horizon. One epic Serbian poem about the lost battle of Kosovo, written in the fourteenth century and then rewritten over and over in story and song, exposes the roots of Serbian pride, but also the depth of their paranoia and their perpetual provincialism.

> Whoever is a Serb, of Serbian blood,
> Whoever shares with me this heritage,
> And he comes not to fight at Kosovo,
> May he never have the progeny
> His heart desires, neither son nor daughter;
> Beneath his hand let nothing decent grow—
> Neither purple grapes nor wholesome wheat;

Let him rust away like dripping iron
Until his name shall be extinguished!
Thus I cannot, sister, be unfaithful
To the master of this noble castle.
Then Vaistina goes up and wakes his master
Saying this: "The time is now upon us."
And Musich Stefan rises on strong legs
And washes slowly, puts on lordly garments.
He belts around his waist a well-forged saber,
Pours himself a glass of dark red wine
And toasts his holy patron saint,
And then a quick and providential journey,
And last of all the saving cross of Jesus.

The region around and including the former Yugoslavia has been in sequences of wars for centuries. The most recent ones have been between three primary quasi nations and kingdoms, each formed around religion and region: Catholic Croatia, Orthodox Serbia, and Muslim Bosnia. This place where I was traveling, the center of the former Yugoslavia, had been carved into an amalgam of the three historic rivals. A world convention in Dayton, Ohio, in late 1995, led by the forceful US diplomat Richard Holbrook (whose book, *To End a War*, I was reading), ended this most recent Balkan war, but it did so by creating a blurred-border area in what had been an ethnically blended state, Yugoslavia, since World War II. Now this part of the former Yugoslavia, sandwiched between the two dominant Yugoslav nations, Serbia and Croatia, had become two autonomous entities, the Federation of Bosnia and Herzegovina and the Republika Srpska.

The former Yugoslavians in Bosnia, whether Muslim or Christian, and especially those in rural hamlets, had been spurred by their manipulative and power-grabbing leaders in 1991 to protect themselves against their neighbors, nearby villages, people from the city, and people from the country. Fear overtook their lives. Almost overnight, people began looking over their shoulders, questioning their old friends, locking their doors, and loading their guns.

With centuries of distrust easily renewed, people turned on each other because of their last names. In a frenzy of paranoia, leaders had proven the power of nationalism once again. They resurrected stories of the Balkan Wars in 1912 and the First and Second World Wars, stories people knew well of Serbian Chetniks, the Nazi-aligned Croatian Ustashe, and even the threat that had simmered for centuries from the Ottoman Turks since the defeat of the Serbs in Kosovo in 1389. Time after time, the illusion of approaching threat has been followed by the reality of war in this region.

Some of those manipulated during the most recent war were Serbs whom I admired—like my fearless and capable driver—but whom I also feared for exactly the same reasons: I sensed that he, for example, could snap into anger at the smallest infraction or gesture of disrespect from me.

The young Serbs I met defined themselves by their ambitions, as the young do anywhere. But here, ambitions—be they in art or auto mechanics—are irrepressibly linked to national pride. People live large and loudly, bolstered by their shared food and drink grown from the land they love. They maintain a visceral connection to soil and song that is like a magnet, a beautiful fantasy into which it was easy to be swept. I needed to understand such passion, and how it grows blind to reality.

▪ ▪ ▪

I thought back to nights in Prague, where I had lived with Milena. She would come home late after studying and go directly into the bathroom before coming up the stairs to our bed, where I waited for her, usually reading. I would hear the water run, then her shoeless steps up the wooden stairs. She would angle into bed, wrapping her long legs around mine, and whisper warm words.

"I love you so much," she said as she kissed me good-night and turned off our light. "I don't want to talk," she said. "Hold me tight." How could life possibly be anything but peaceful and perfect? That she had slept with another man less than an hour before was inconceivable.

Months later I discovered that she had been in a relationship with another graduate student, with whom she had traveled to Turkey when she told me she was doing research in Poland. I had seen her off to Warsaw from the train station in Prague. She waved from the window as the train rounded a curve out of sight. I wanted to be with her, was pained at the sight of her leaving, but knew she needed time alone to work and think.

She somehow doubled back to Prague, met the man, and left for a week in Turkey. I never knew the details and didn't need to. The story I constructed from her confessions became facts I could not shake and did not question. Our marriage imploded from the damage of infidelity and the punishing quagmire created by deceit. I considered my role as the patterns of our life together circled in my head: my focus on work, our sexual complacency, our comforting acquiescence to wedding vows and the subsequent autopilot of marriage.

"He means nothing," she said, pleading for us to stay together. I decided I would, because I believed we were ultimately committed to each other.

Then another land mine detonated. Milena revealed to me the voracity of her desires, and that she had been with yet another man. She told me this while we were in bed together in Pale, during the 1997 elections. This time, I did not want details and skipped the obvious questions: Who? When? Why? They were irrelevant this time, the details pointless and the truth elusive. In my state of disbelief but not shock, her words turned into a warm wind. Images of the myth of what was possible in our marriage, which I had believed only months earlier, were all that lingered for me—an investment in a house, her wide and beautiful smile, the prospects of children, her sleeping breath on my neck in the morning. I searched for and then clung to new myths of my durability and to what I could trust—being alone in my dreams.

Letting go of love was painful but possible. I had stopped caring about her, and my admiration for her had disappeared. It was more difficult, however, to let go of my vision of a durable marriage with children, having abandoned that possibility with Jennifer years earlier. I struggled to relinquish our time invested in a dream, solidified in shared stories over our five years together, and, for me, that magnet of possibility, like a long river in front of us. Many of our best times together had been on water—rafting the Grand Canyon, sea kayaking on the Maine coastline, Florida's Everglades, Alaska's Shuyak Islands, and Croatian islands near Split and Zadar. Those shared experiences had united us, I thought, or united me. In either case, it was not enough.

■ ■ ■

The Drina River leads to the beauty of Srebrenica. Though that beauty
is diminished in the wake of the murder that took over the valley only
three years earlier, its magnificence is still evident and enduring, even in
the town's bombed and bullet-strewn state. Srebrenica sits at the end
of a green valley leading into higher hills, a hamlet perfectly placed,
protected from storms, and contained by verdant hills for grazing. The
place is endowed with free-flowing water in rivers and bubbling hot
water from aquifers. In the morning sun, the surrounding slopes cast a
cooling dark-green shadow over the eastern half of town, while the sun
brightens the western hills, illuminating sweeping contours of soft de-
ciduous color creeping upward with the coming gold of the season, and
interweaving with rich evergreen at the base of the hills. The hills also
hold mineral waters that were the Srebrenica's sustenance for centuries
as a spa destination. People once traveled from the western parts of the
former Soviet Union and Central Europe to reclaim their health and
calm their bodies here. Today, the famous hillside spas are abandoned,
isolated by land mines.

Despite the beauty above Srebrenica, the town itself is in much worse
shape than the area around Sarajevo and Pale I had seen a year earlier.
Little had been repaired in the three years since the town was the bull's-
eye of the war. The people living in Srebrenica are displaced Serbs from
elsewhere in the region, victims themselves of the conflict. Clear plastic
tarps and adhesive tape with "UNHCR" (United Nations High Com-
missioner for Refugees) printed in blue across it still take the place of
windows in many buildings. The walls of all the buildings I can see from
the road have been strafed front and side, and I suspect behind, by bullets and mortar shrapnel. The angles and trajectory of the bullet spray
indicate that shooting had come from all directions—from the main road
into the buildings, from the high surrounding hills downward, from windows straight toward adjacent homes. Flower boxes on a number of
apartment buildings hang splintered but half intact, with soil holding on
to a handful of surviving strands of green growth at one end, remnants
left to be repaired and replenished another summer, someday.

I can imagine seasonal sequences happening in Srebrenica—crops
being harvested, soccer matches, family weddings—all of which had

ceased in the windless air and had not resumed for three full growing seasons. The war crimes that had taken place in Srebrenica in July 1995 remain unresolved, and the city unrepaired, the instigators unaccountable, and thousands of victims yet to be located. The mothers, wives, sisters, and daughters of Srebrenica's eight thousand dead men now live elsewhere in Bosnia, dispersed and uncompensated. And yet—I had to force myself to remember—I am here to initiate positive change: a free and fair democratic election for those who live in Srebrenica now. I tuck my book of Serbian poetry into my bag, uncomfortable having Serbian Orthodox literature in this town of Muslim ghosts.

I take a deep breath before leaving the van and my driver and step onto the pavement in front of Srebrenica's half-blown-apart City Hall and its undealt-with pile of rock, bricks, bent metal, and indecipherable rubble that appeared to have been furniture. The other side of City Hall is lit through glass windows, which is a relief because it is to be my base from which to supervise two days of elections. Even with only part of the building standing, there is no better place in Srebrenica to assemble people for election preparations.

I walk toward the building and take another deep breath, having tucked away the book of Serbian poetry and my persistent disgust with Milena. Srebrenica is a broken place, and I had to admit that I remained broken myself. I had spent a year without Milena, erasing her gradually from my life, but I remained stubborn in my adherence to the myth of what our marriage could have been.

It is 7:00 a.m. and a dozen men in City Hall are drinking hard liquor as if it were morning coffee. But they had no coffee brewing. I notice that the mayor is already sipping rakija, the same plum brandy my driver had shared with me. A few other city officials and an assorted group of disheveled men who had apparently gathered to assist with the election are also drinking and smoking. The alcohol surely took the edge off the displaced, suspended, and otherwise bored lives of these men whose homes were elsewhere.

An interpreter assigned to me comes up and introduces himself as Dado. He is a shaggy and dark-haired young man, who had grown up in Sarajevo but had been moved out of the city during the war. He is on break from a university in Belgrade and had arrived in Srebrenica on his own.

"Do you want rakija?" Dado asks me at the instigation of the mayor, who had pulled him aside to talk. He is alert to my response to the situation. His training with other translators, who were spread around the region, had spelled out the same rules and regulations that I had been given, which included prohibiting drinking and smoking at all election sites.

"Yes," I say and am poured half a tumbler full of rakija, just as they all had. I take a big gulp, set the glass down, and smile at them. "Moc dobry," I say loudly and add, "Perfectni." And then, "Jekui." (Very good. Perfect. Thank you.) I speak in Czech, also a Slavic language like Serbo-Croatian, and they understand. Dado looks relieved. He'd had to translate nothing for me. He, too, takes a glass of rakija.

Keeping cigarettes and rakija out of anyone's mouth here would be like silencing their right to speak. Or vote. I sit down and collect my notes and thoughts. There are rules, I keep saying to myself, but this room is not a polling place where people vote. I scan the group and take a moment to gauge each man's demeanor. Their eyes take notice of me, too. I sense that they see me with the skepticism of the war-hardened toward a novice to life's pain. I understand that I could be easily dismissed and lose control of what is supposed to be a well-ordered process of organizing voting sites.

The recent history in Srebrenica makes me feel as though I am from somewhere so far from the truth and history of the place that, in fact, I shouldn't be there at all. The sensation approaches what I imagine it would be like to be at your own funeral, listening to eulogies that need to be corrected or that miss the essence of what you felt you had been. The truths in a war are elusive. And wanting the truth made me uncomfortable looking into the eyes of these men. Who here, I consider for a moment, had been a murderer, a pacifist and dissident, an opportunistic thief or a rapist?

What I can see in these men clearly at one moment becomes blurred the next. I am never sure. Eyes tell a truth and then they tell nothing. In Srebrenica, I discover that people do not often look into each other's eyes. These men most often look down at their shoes, stalled by indecision, with nothing to do this day at City Hall or at home. They walk in turn to the window to eye the beautiful and dangerous hills, scanning the pinched sun and shadows for something that is simply not there. The

The mass graves of Srebrenica from 1995, identified and honored in 2003.

energy in the room would feel explosive if not for the dull eyes of the men, fidgeting for the possibility of change.

One thing you cannot miss in Srebrenica is the sun's shadows, which move so precisely that each hour has its own look, its own glowing angle defining a moment of the day. Here, you can know the time of day by shadows on the hills. But those slopes encircling Srebrenica are littered with land mines, the landscape empty but for unseen bodies lost and unaccounted for after the war.

The election is methodical and meticulous, supervised by me along with international observers who are there to ensure that the procedures of election are followed. I put up the signs prohibiting smoking and drinking and then pray that I will not need to enforce those rules. The key to the elections, we had been told, is that the process be consistent and transparent to everyone who votes. And everyone in town seems to be voting, based on the lines at the eight stations I supervise. We mark the hands of those who have been checked off on the voter registration list before they vote. The mark is visible only under a special light at the door next to the entrance of the polling station. The hands of everyone who comes through the door are scanned under the light to confirm that they have not already voted. Each person votes alone in a cardboard voting booth and then folds the ballot before placing it through a slot in a ballot box at the end of the four voting booths. The process is just like at home in a library or school where I had voted. The line outside circles one by one into the voting booths, and then each person deposits a ballot into a box. The only difference between Laramie and Srebrenica is the special light and the marking of hands, and the fact that everything is made of cardboard, almost an indication that the election is a one-time effort, as if the voting process might not repeat another time.

The one periodic source of conflict I encounter involves men who attempt to enter the voting booths with women, usually their wives, to vote with them or for them. Sometimes they simply take the ballots from their wives or come asking for their wives' ballots without their wives being present. In all cases, the men can vote only once, casting their vote alone, and are not allowed to accompany their wives into the voting booths. Women go into the booths alone or they do not vote. But each one does vote alone, despite objections from her husband, and aided by the occasional encouragement from me or another supervisor. One man, who tried to get his wife's ballot, walked home and brought her back for presentation as if in a display of ownership or honor. When I keep him from joining her in the booth, he acquiesces after a voiceless face-off. It isn't personal between us and I am relieved he doesn't think it is, either. The scars on his face alone frighten me more than his hands, which are blackened by something that looks permanent. The cuticles on his right hand are bloody. The election rules are a small matter to him, a minor battle he does not care to fight. While his wife votes, he sits down and has a glass of brandy, pulled from his pocket. I look away.

The ballot boxes are sealed with tape and then signed across the tape by each polling station's local leader, then by the international election supervisor. One man tells me that the unchecked names on the voter registration list are those of people who have died. But we have a second day at the polling stations, a day when we will see very few people. I sleep with the ballot boxes that night in an old school dormitory, as do the other election supervisors. I lock the door of my room. Since I am alone, I cannot leave it.

The year before, in Pale, I had also slept with the ballots in a sealed box in my room with Milena, who slept next to me. I thought then, and again a year later, of the poem I had read at our wedding. I could not shake my original interpretation of it, though now I could imagine another way of understanding what the poem revealed. I loved the poem as much as I always had, but it was trapped in my head:

> You turn your head—
> that's what the silence meant; you're not alone.
> The whole wide world pours down.

The voter turnout in Srebrenica was 98 percent, with only a few stragglers coming in to vote the second day. That night, the election supervisors convened to count and tally the votes with international monitors observing us. Then other supervisors checked our original count and their tallies were subsequently retallied under the eyes also of local people, the mayor included, to ensure accuracy. The count stretched far past midnight. At the end of the night, we realized that nearly everyone had voted and they had all voted for the same people, sometimes the only person on the ballot for a particular post, for several national and local positions. There were no unmarked ballots, indicating little confusion and no indecision.

Back in my room, finally, after a day that had stretched through the night and into the next morning, I had trouble falling asleep as I considered the election process. I wondered about its merit and cost. I questioned my own effort to shuffle my work schedule and travel several thousand miles to supervise an election that secured roles in local and national government for candidates who might eventually be tried as war criminals.

On the road back to Zvornik after the elections, we passed a man who had scrambled down to the road to wave our van down. He was wearing an old JNA (Yugoslav National Army) uniform.

"Jesi li vidio mog konja?" the man asked us. (Have you seen my horse?)

"Nisam," my driver said and then asked, "Kad si ga zadnji put video?" (No, when did you last see it?)

"Prije dvije godine," the man said. (Two years ago.)

"Mi ce mo ga potrazti," my driver said. (We will watch for it.)

We drove farther down the valley on gravity more than gas, accelerating past hills that gave way to the widening swath of the Drina River's gathering of side streams. The van's radiator had overheated on the way up to Srebrenica but was now running cool, and we had no need to stop. We moved from the shadows of the high hills into steady sunlight, illuminating the long Drina River ahead of us, running low but strong on the water of springs alone. We careered around corners, moving along with the Drina as it spread itself into a more predictable course ahead. I could now see miles in front of us. My driver looked away from the road for a moment and smiled. The journey ahead, following the river, looked like one we might make before it became dark.

14

Moving as Water

BOSNIAN SERBS SOLIDIFIED a perspective for me of the necessity and the inevitability of movement, adjustment, and hope. As a people, they were judged as perpetrators, villains trapped in history with that label. Yet the Serbian people I had worked with were also victims of the war. They needed a future, but not the one that was in Srebrenica, where they had landed because the war had displaced them from their homes. Meanwhile, the Bosnian Muslims, the Bosniaks, had left their home in Srebrenica. Exactly to where? No one spoke, no one knew. "They are gone," I heard.

"Where?"

"Away. Gone."

I left Bosnia with a clear image that despite damage beyond resolution, a transition starting with hope and durability seemed possible. I knew that the people I had met would rebuild their lives from their families outward, not from a new nation downward. After fighting, moving, hiding, and grieving, people wanted to grow a garden, milk a cow, gather plums, and raise their children. I was inspired by the damaged but persistent spirit of the displaced Serbs in Srebrenica. At the same time, the Bosnians displaced from places such as Srebrenica were not there. It would take another three years to verify for the world what I suspected many of my Serbian friends already knew: some eight thousand men and boys were dead and buried in mass graves south of Srebrenica, their wives and children scattered to the winds of the war throughout Bosnia. Secret smaller mass graves around Srebrenica would be found for many years afterward.

■ ■ ■

Not three weeks after I returned to Portland from Srebrenica, another act of shocking violence hit even closer to home. Matthew Shepard, a young man from Casper, Wyoming, and a student at the University of Wyoming, was murdered in Laramie. Matthew was tied to a fence and beaten to death on a cold October night on a dirt road up Pilot Hill, once known as Pole Mountain, just east of town. Many of us had cycled past that place many times over many years. For me, Matthew was a person I had never met but knew in friends from Laramie, Cheyenne, and Casper, a gay boy in a man's-man land. These friends—boys turning into men back then—were, I realized after moving from Laramie, bold and brave beyond our measures of a person.

I had just been in Bosnia, and it hit me hard that Laramie and Srebrenica were linked in a way. In both places, unimaginable violence had occurred, and both places were associated with that violence. Two little-known, isolated hamlets had become infamous.

My home was in a national media turmoil and I was not there, though I wanted to be, felt I should be. I looked to friends and family in Laramie for an answer, a response, anything. Meanwhile, university students catalyzed marches to draw everyone through the parade route otherwise used for the same annual, predictable rodeo and homecoming parades. Laramie moved forward, a small town in the world's eye. People young and old in Laramie stood in solidarity with Matthew toward a cold cloud of judgment against him and our home from the wide outside. Among the most visual and inspirational leaders in Laramie were women dressed as angels with giant white wings. They blocked from view the screaming antigay protestors from a Baptist church out of Topeka, Kansas. People in Laramie came together in shock and sorrow to protest in their own way without screaming, even if they wanted to scream.

At the same time, I remained concerned about Bosnian Serbia's transitions. I wrote an op-ed to the *New York Times* in which I attempted to make a case for the redemption of the Bosnian Serbs and their evolution from being perpetrators of war to being in a place to join, if not initiate, reconciliation.

Life's experiences had been colliding in my head and heart for a year—a broken marriage, work in the Balkans shattered by war, then Laramie exposed to the violence of a hate crime. I decided to go back to Central Europe and Prague in November 1999 because I wanted to see Berlin, a place of transition and resolution, ten years after the Berlin Wall had been breached and eliminated and fourteen years after I had last been there.

I then fell from a train into a dreamscape of imagination and reality, recirculating images of running in fear and searching endlessly for safety. I was in the northern Czech Republic, where my life should have ended but did not.

Suspended in a coma for three weeks, I lived through dreams that remain as real to me as lived experiences. They were influenced by real experiences I had in Bosnia and other stark places in Central Europe, witnessing people's dominating impulse to adjust and survive. Now, so was I.

■ ■ ■

Move without panic and without pause. I am in a gray-black nightmare, a place I do not recognize but a constellation of places I have been—the back streets of Bucharest during an interminable power outage; Ostrava's smoldering steel plants; the disintegrating coal plants, acidic leather-tanning factories, and putrid sewage plants in Most and Ostrava in the Czech Republic—places now distilled from memory into one dripping, drip, drip of water falling off the roofs above me, concentrated into this one bleak place on this dark night.

Move.

The light is stiff with scattered beams illuminating metal flakes falling from the sky through shadows that hint at an industrial land from another time. I pause. The shards are beautiful in a small way, glittering metal falling from the sky. I cannot give up an inch to uncertainty, because something better or different is ahead of me. Maybe a calm place. A safe place.

And yet, I do not know what is unsafe about where I am except that in its hard surfaces, rain, and deep darkness, I imagine people become trapped forever—like Srebrenica or a coal mine in Teplice.

Keep moving.

Ahead, I hear the breathing of unseen machines and smell something that makes my nose constrict, but I cannot identify any one decipherable thing. Sharp metal needles on the back of my neck, first chilling me as an ice rain does before snow arrives, and then burning me like a desert sun. In a dreamscape, I act on instincts alone, like a rabbit or rat, alert to smell and sound in a world gone colorless.

Out of the passageway and into a main thoroughfare, moving in and out of deep dark into light dark, I run to get through the industrial city. It emerges again in glimpses as every worn and weary Eastern European place I have been, an impossible colliding horror of hard-surfaced Communist architecture and pollution. The place is hell, should I stop to think of it that way. But my urgency and uncertainty are familiar. I keep moving on instinct because, short of hiding in a dark corner, there is no other way but to move forward. I had been in such situations before.

Once in Tibet, I bicycled for weeks from Lhasa to Kathmandu with five friends from Laramie, a journey I had dreamed of making until it became drudgery. I was pedaling alone, as we all were, on a dirt road, pushing in pain against the cold at over eighteen thousand feet. Too far away from any place to retreat, I buried my head into the wind, stomached the dry air, and pushed onward. After I coughed up blood, my pain clarified into awareness of where I was. I saw the beauty in the clear sky at night, the unfathomable and thankfully calming wind, the waning ache in my lungs when I finally slept, all slivers of beauty during inescapable pain.

So, I moved.

There was another time. I was on the Niger River, kayaking its length for weeks that stretched into months. I was subject, by choice, to its long route. But once on the water, options dwindled, because the river—the only world between banks of solid soil—became everything. Hippos on the Niger came to the surface without warning, unseen and unanticipated like land mines, maybe not for days or weeks but then like a detonation from the mud bottom of the river. One hippo, then three, and then too many to count. If one hippo was on the surface of the water, there were always more below, moving to protect but never to flee their territory. I moved forward as predictably as possible without weaving, my sole strategy to avoid alarming them. The beasts' pink skin around their eyes and nostrils flashed against murky water as they surfaced and then sank. There is nothing as pink and as perfect as a hippo disappearing below brown river water. I have rarely been more surprised and grateful than to see that beautiful singular color of pink slip away.

These memories are indelible because of the clarity that arrives in the calm after fear. The calendar and clock stop. When everything ceases, the experience is about the kiss of life. Not the time or the place, the danger or the pain. Even in mud and blood, the beauty intensifies. And that awareness never fades.

"Did you learn anything?" the doctor at Ivinson Memorial in Laramie asked me. My friend Ron had rolled his truck, with me in the passenger seat, on our way from Laramie to Denver to see a Broncos football game.

I said, "Yes."

"Good," he said.

In my hospital bed that night, I thought about what I had learned. I acknowledged that I should have put on a seat belt, which was probably what the doctor was referring to, but if there was a message waiting for me to understand about safety, it was lost on me that night. Instead, I could not shake the beauty I had seen after the accident: the crystal ice and mud covered by the crimson of my own blood is what stuck in my mind. It could have been frightening, and should have been. But the feeling of calm while crawling on icy mud after the chaos of rolling in a pickup truck was beautiful. I had never seen any snapshot of color and texture as perfect as that ice, mud, and blood until years later, when I saw the pure pink hippo plunge into the brown Niger.

These experiences were not wake-up calls, though they served to keep me more alert to that far edge of danger that damages people. I knew I could not have revised the path that led me to each of those places, and I didn't want to. Each time, the experience kindled a fire in me, rather than doused it. Every single experience in my life that followed became more important, something to pay special attention to.

■ ■ ■

I wake up in water, embraced by a woman's strong, winter-white arms slowly swinging me back and forth. I see my legs in the water in front of me. I feel warm water on my face and neck, but nothing else, as I watch my torso and legs below me sway side to side. I cannot speak and can barely breathe but am floating on my back, with my head against the

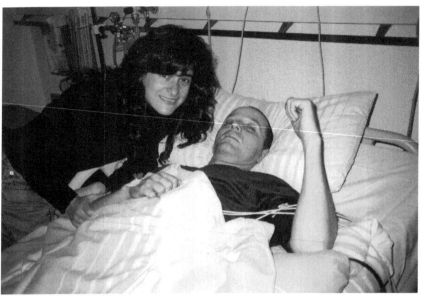

Jill Ory with Haines at Bergmannstrost Hospital, Halle, Germany, December 1999.

woman's chest, and her long arms under my shoulders, as she moves me in the water.

"I am Claudia," she says, with a German accent.

I try to speak, but only a whisper arrives. "Claudia?"

She puts her mouth to my ear. "Claudia," she whispers.

She loosens her hold and swings me around and pulls me to her face. She pokes me gently in the chest but I feel nothing.

"I am boss," she says and swings me back around, as she had before, gentle and strong.

I have no idea where I am, but I know I am safe. I try to move but I can't. After my industrial dark nightmare, I am now in a beautiful world with light coming in the windows and warm steam-fog rising from the water.

I look around and see my father standing on the side of where I am in warm water—in a swimming pool?

I try to talk. "Where am I?" I ask. "Why am I here?" My voice does not work beyond a difficult whisper.

Claudia hears nothing. She continues to move me in the water like a willow branch in a stream, subject to the current bending it back and forth.

Am I dead? I consider.

I see my dad talk to my brother Doug, who seems concerned and fidgets.

"He looks good," my father says a few times and nods his head up and down.

I hear people speaking German. Steam from warm water and bright sunlight is all I see when I am swung one direction. In the other direction, I see my father and brother through the sunlight. To their side, in the shine of the wake's reflection, I see my mother and sister-in-law, Lisa. I feel relieved at the sight of my family. I feel comfortable moving with the water. I call out to them but only a whisper comes from my lungs.

Claudia hears me and leans toward me.

"Morgen," she says. "Guten morgen."

This is the time: morning. I am in warm water, a day like any day except I am here with Claudia. I am here, now. I still feel the press of the dark industrial city where I had been moving just moments ago in my dreams.

I see Jill, my girlfriend, standing with my family. They are all smiling, pointing at me and talking with each other as if sharing secrets. I see them in the fog of the pool and feel as if I am in a dream where people, places, and times weave together without reason. My hands tingle and are cold but do not move. I feel a pulse in the tips of my left fingers and I feel my heart pound, but not like I had been kayaking or bicycling. It just pounds. I sense with some assurance that I am not dreaming. A breath comes but is small and short. My lungs seem to barely work. I hear my heart in my ears and imagine that everyone around me must hear how loud my heart is.

"Gut, gut," Claudia says.

Is it Claudia's breath, or is it steam from the water that I feel on my face? She speaks slowly but I do not understand much. "Wasser, gut?" she asks.

I close my eyes and fall into dreams that recirculate rapidly. I am back on the dark industrial street. Then I tumble out of a closet in a train onto a train platform and land at the foot of a doctor who introduces himself to me. "I am Doctor Becker," the man says. "Your brother Doug said you would be coming."

Later, I discovered that it was late November 1999, and that I had been dreaming in a coma since the early morning of November 10, when I leapt from a train at a stop to get a cup of coffee. The stop was in Ústí nad Labem, a polluted, worn-out, post-Communist city in the northern Czech Republic. I was going to Berlin with Jill for the anniversary of the fall of the Berlin Wall.

"Familie. Familie," she says as she swings my body to the side of the pool.

"Here," I yell, but no word leaves my lips. The effort to push air from my lungs to my mouth exhausts me. "I am here," I try again. I can almost see air trapped in me, like balloons ready to burst. The effort to communicate is the most difficult thing I have ever attempted. Nobody hears a sound from me and my work to communicate gains no attention. It makes me cough, but even that makes no sound. I find it almost impossible to get air and I convulse, vomiting nothing but air.

Nothing yet makes exact sense in the warm water, falling into dreams and waking. Claudia continues to guide me in the water and speaks softly in my ear. Still in Claudia's arms, I fall asleep.

I wake up as I am being put onto a sling and lifted from the water. My family comes near me.

"You did great, John," Jill says.

"Where am I?" I ask.

"What?" Jill asks, putting her ear to my mouth.

"Where am I?" I repeat.

"I hear you, John," Jill says. "You are in Halle, in Eastern Germany. Do you know who I am?" she asks.

"Jill, Jill," I whisper. She turns away and starts crying. My brother hugs her and my father steps up to me as women dressed in white and speaking German lift me onto a bed on wheels and cover me in white sheets and blankets.

"Son, that was good to see you in the pool," my father tells me. "You have been sleeping for two weeks," he says.

My family is around me next to a swimming pool. Why am I in a swimming pool?

I am taken through long hallways with medical equipment and I realize that I am in a hospital. I recognize Expressionist artwork on the walls of long corridors. Beckmann, Kokoschka, Kandinsky. I see a sign on one wall: Bergmannstrost, Halle.

We come to a room and I am picked up to be placed into a bed that raises and lowers in all directions. My brother tries to help but two nurses politely push him back. They take charge and I am quickly in a white bed with bars around its sides.

I whisper to Doug about the paintings. "Kandinsky," I say.

"What, what?" he asks.

"German art," I say.

"How in the world?" he says. "You know the artists?"

"Max Beckmann," I whisper.

My brother turns away to the others—his wife, Lisa, our parents, and my girlfriend, Jill.

"He's okay," Doug says.

15

The Black Triangle

THE PHONE RANG AT 5:00 A.M. I struggled to pull my legs and then my body across the bed, awake in an instant and alert for the bad news that comes at odd hours by phone. It was just beginning to get light outside.

"Hello," I answered after a dozen rings, my legs unmoving in a tangle of sheets after wrestling myself to the phone on the bedside table.

"Hello," I repeated.

"Hello, John Haines?"

"Yes."

"This is Dr. Ebert of Leipzig. I cared of you when you grew critical."

I had never been in Leipzig. What was this about?

"Yes?" I answered.

"I am finding you for payment of bill."

"What bill?"

I had been in a hospital not far from Leipzig in Halle, three years earlier after the rough accident with a train that left me a quadriplegic. I had been injured in Ústí nad Labem and was moved three days later, in a drug-induced coma, to the Dresden Airport for medical air transport to London. I was later told that the medical airplane could not land in Dresden because of weather and telecommunications problems, and that I was raced to the nearby town of Halle, where the Germans had recently built a neurology hospital, added to a trauma hospital built originally in 1894 for injured miners, to promote economic development in the former East Germany. At 1:00 a.m. on a Sunday morning, I had arrived in Halle to be cared for by doctors who worked without concern for my name, nationality, or insurance, and who saved my life by performing surgery on my broken neck. I was swollen, with black and blue legs, a broken femur in my right leg, my skull fractured in two places, and, as a result of my broken neck, spinal cord damage at the C7 vertebra. After surgery the medical team put me on life support in the Intensive Care Unit, where I woke up two weeks later.

"Your bill for my services to you," Ebert said.

"Sir," I said, "I do not recall your name."

My German doctor had been Dr. Stephan Becker, not a Dr. Ebert. Dr. Becker had explained to me, as I woke from the fog of drugs and the coma, that I had been struck by a train in the Czech Republic, an accident of which I had no memory. For Jill and me, the trip to Berlin was a whim during our vacation in Prague. We planned to spend a night or two in the transformed city to see the new architecture around where the Wall had stood. I had evidently been running to reboard our train in Ústí nad Labem when I tripped or fell on the train platform and onto the tracks. Ústí is a polluted second-world town north of Prague in what was known as the Black Triangle, a coal-producing region of the former Czechoslovakia, East Germany, and Poland. The area had vast forests dead from acid rain. I had worked in the region two years earlier, and despite its physical austerity, I was fond of its slowly rebounding environment and its people, whom I admired for their stubborn endurance amid the dead trees, strip-mine pits, and polluted water. I had kayaked the Labe River from Ústí to Dresden, on flowing pollution sprinkled with migrating geese.

On that trip, I had been near Berlin, though short of the city I had dreamed of going back to since 1985, when I had first arrived there by train from Warsaw after my trans-Siberian trip. I knew I would return to Berlin eventually. Finally, on that cold November morning in 1999, I was on my way.

The German train had stopped in Ústí, and I raced off it for a quick look around and a cup of coffee. My brother later visited the train station and tried to reconstruct what might have happened to me there. The train between Prague and Berlin stops for one minute, and in that minute I had somehow gone from sitting on the train to being sprawled and near death on the tracks, while the train moved ahead on schedule toward Berlin with Jill onboard, wondering where I had gone. I was pulled from the tracks, Ústí train and hospital officials later told my brother, by Czech travelers waiting for the next train.

My last memory was of putting on my Adidas running shoes before leaving the train. My next memory was of waking up completely paralyzed and hooked to a machine. It was past Thanksgiving by then, and I was confused but felt no pain, felt nothing at all, as I moved only the fingers on my right hand and whispered questions and answers over the sound of the ventilator pulsing air into a hole they had cut in my throat as a route to my lungs.

"Leipzig?" I questioned this Dr. Ebert. "I have never been in Leipzig," I told him.

Ebert continued: "Yes, you were taken from Dresden by helicopter to Leipzig to meet medical airplane, a turboprop. I am military doctor based at Leipzig. You were loaded on turboprop for London."

I remained silent on the other end of the phone, confused and unable to think of what to say or ask this man. None of what he told me was part of the history I had been told of my accident.

"I am doctor," he repeated. "I check your condition and remove you from turboprop. You had grown critical."

"Please fax me the bill," I responded, not about to argue.

The invoice was waiting for me in my fax machine when I arrived at work. On one page, with small type, in German, it identified my caller as "Dr. med Klaus Peter Ebert." The bill totaled 835.55 deutsche marks or 427.21 euros, about $350. It detailed my deteriorating condition, with the words mit trauma interspersed several times in the descriptions. A German-speaking friend explained to me that the bill was stamped, signed, and itemized in a fashion that only a former Communist bureaucrat could have produced. It was unquestionably authentic, despite initial assertions from my family that it could not be real, because I had never been in Leipzig, and because Dr. Ebert was a new name in a string of doctors they had come to know well over the course of the months I had spent in various hospitals. But the bill filled in a puzzle I did not know was missing a piece.

The story I had been told was that I was first handled by Czech ambulance drivers. They were taking me from a substandard Czech hospital in Ústí, where I had been attended to by a dedicated but underequipped doctor (a Dr. Radek Šplechtna, who did not leave the hospital for seventy-two hours while caring for me), to Dresden. Dresden is thirty minutes from Ústí, probably faster by ambulance, and that's where I was to have been placed on the medical airplane for transport to London, where my family, who had come to Europe after learning of my accident, was waiting for me to arrive.

It had taken three years and this persistent Dr. Ebert for my family and me to learn of the string of events and mistakes that took place that night—mistakes that, it turned out, saved my life. The first trip-up hinged on communication problems resulting from construction work in Dresden that caused power outages, which were compounded by storms and which prohibited airplanes, including the medical transport plane, from landing in Dresden on just that one night. The medical plane landed instead in Leipzig, not far away. The Czech ambulance got this news at Dresden's airport, where it was paid to deliver me. Then, because the ambulance had left and Dresden had a helicopter for medical emergencies, I was loaded for a short flight by helicopter from the Dresden tarmac to the nearby Leipzig Airport, where the medical transport plane was ready, waiting, and being paid to take me (regardless of my condition) to London. I was taken from the helicopter to the airplane and readied for takeoff. One lung had collapsed, I later found out, but I remained on full life support and was set for the flight to London.

Then, just before takeoff and past midnight, Dr. Ebert, who was neither authorized nor paid to care for me, intervened. Taking action as the airport doctor, he ordered that they remove me from the plane and put me in an ambulance for transport to the specialized neurology hospital in nearby Halle. The Halle hospital, the Bergmannstrost, had been recently expanded as a teaching hospital to help that region's struggling economy. The hospital employed the city's underemployed while the doctors came from around Europe. Halle is the historic home of the earliest German studies in neurology, an asset and a history that were lost during the stagnation of the Communist years, but resurrected in the form of this new hospital staffed by Europe's finest neurosurgeons working side by side with nurses, technicians, and therapists from the former East Germany.

Dr. Ebert had not been hired to do what he did that night, but he took on the task, I suspect, because he had long been the boss at the Leipzig Airport. Vestiges of East Germany have endured in this region, which also produced Handel and Bach before Communism but now produced men such as Ebert, authoritative despite having been stripped of their prestige and credentials. He was the product of a system and a bureaucracy that persists to befuddle foreigners, as it did me when I had worked in Prague two years earlier.

Though I had never met Dr. Ebert, I pictured him as the same intransigent bureaucrat I enjoyed drinking with but detested in working relationships. These people—both men and women—living in the wide post-Communist swath of Central Europe from the Balkans to the Baltic Sea are, in my experience, resourceful, hardheaded, and heavy drinkers, much like my friends in Wyoming. They are large in appearance and physical in action and are generally not to be argued with, because debates with them can go on and on in circles and ultimately navigate nowhere near new territory. A large number of middle-aged men and women in the post-Communist region of East Germany, the Czech Republic, and Poland barely subsist on the margins of large and changing institutions such as schools, government ministries, hospitals, and airports.

Had I flown on the medical air transport plane to London as planned, my doctors told my family, I would have died before leaving German air. I discovered later from other German doctors that I had flatlined twice while in the ambulance from Leipzig to Halle. But I had responded with a heartbeat each time to their efforts to resuscitate me. The airplane would not have had the systems to save me in that condition.

The international medical air transport company sent by my family to save me from poor hospitals and underequipped doctors never paid Dr. Ebert for his intervention that saved me. Nor, evidently, did the hospital where Dr. Ebert directed the ambulance to take me. The Leipzig Airport, where he had access to assist me in the turboprop plane, would not pay him for his work either. Yet the medical air transport company charged my insurance company $35,000 for flying an empty airplane round trip from London to Leipzig, a charge my family and insurance company never disputed. I paid Dr. Ebert's $350 bill myself immediately. I have since framed the bill, which hangs on a wall in my house.

Dr. Ebert never asked me how I was doing, a detail that bewildered my family. But I understood. The man wanted to be paid for his work. After the hundreds of thousands of dollars in medical bills I had accumulated, ultimately it was Dr. Ebert whose quick decisions had kept me alive so that I had the chance to drag my paralyzed body across my bed in the coming light of morning to answer his call.

16

The View from Here

The river is famous to the fish.

The loud voice is famous to silence,
which knew it would inherit the earth
before anybody said so.
—from "Famous," Naomi Shihab Nye

THE WIDE PASSAGEWAY BETWEEN the domestic and international concourses at San Francisco International was quiet and empty, though it had been constructed to accommodate several airplanes unloading at once. It was a riverbed—dry down to hard soil and stone—ready for floodwater. Floor-to-ceiling windows lit the space in the shadowless light of the city's interminable fog.

I was racing, a little lost and a lot late for my flight to Beijing. After traveling throughout the United States in a wheelchair for five years, I was used to the airline industry system putting me onto airplanes first and taking me off last. This meant that connecting flights were usually a push, and I had missed many. I headed to the gate for my first international flight in a wheelchair, after connecting from Denver, where I had attended a family gathering.

It had been five years since I had been on an international flight: the last one, in 1999, was the medical flight from Leipzig to Denver and Craig Hospital, two hours from Laramie.

I was concerned about traveling alone overseas. But I wanted to go to China on my own, as I had before. It was a modest effort, as I would be in Beijing for a conference with colleagues from around the world. There I would be housed and fed. I told myself that this trip would be nothing compared to what I had managed since breaking my neck, or to my journeys through dangerous places before that. I was vigilant, nevertheless, and concerned about my ability to access bathrooms, navigate steps and curbs, and find vehicles. I worried about how my body would respond to the long trip. These concerns tested my perspective of myself as a world traveler.

A man was walking toward me, fifty or so yards away. He was the only other person in the terminal passageway, an indication that I might have missed my flight. I lowered my head and pumped hard on my hand rims, pushing as fast as I could but still going slower than I needed to be. I looked up and saw him moving to the middle of the passageway, as I had. I slowed as we approached each other and looked up briefly to say hello. His words came first.

"Hello. You carry on, sir," the man said.

"Hi," I responded.

He smiled and slowed, veering closer to me.

After a few years in a wheelchair, I was used to people making brief eye contact with me. I often catch looks down into my eyes and a smile, gestures I take as a quick form of sympathy or respect. I had occasionally done the same to people in wheelchairs before I was in one myself. More often, I am nearly invisible—except to almost all children at my eye level, and the homeless. "Hey, brother," I have heard hundreds of times from men on the streets.

But this man was different. He was like those children who look curiously and then look away, except he kept looking directly into my eyes.

"Hello," the man said again and nodded firmly up and down with a wide smile. It was Bob Dole.

We held eye contact. I smiled back. The moment, a quick but sincere exchange, passed as swiftly as fishermen in boats on the Niger River whom I kayaked past with a raised paddle to say hello.

In his early eighties, Bob Dole had gentle eyes and a smile that reminded me of my grandmother. She died at age ninety-three, soon after I left Laramie for Switzerland to ski and work for a winter after college. I visited her the day I left Laramie, knowing I might not see her again. When she kissed me on the forehead and told me to "see the world," I knew she saw herself in me, even though she had never left the country and rarely left Wyoming. She had long ago given me energy to continue alone. So did that short exchange with Senator Dole.

I took my seat at a window of the airplane out of San Francisco, the last person allowed onto the flight. I reflected on the timing that had put me in a position to meet, however briefly, the longtime senator from Kansas, 1976 vice presidential candidate, and 1996 Republican nominee for president. Jimmy Carter, then Bill Clinton, had thwarted Bob Dole from ascending to the top rank of the nation. On this day in November 2004, the former senator was free to walk alone without security. A lucky man, I thought.

A World War II vet with a damaged arm and—it turned out—a month away from hip-replacement surgery, Bob Dole made the effort to greet another man whom he did not know, did not need to meet, and had no reason to acknowledge. I wondered later whether he thought I was a veteran. Or maybe his gesture was one of understanding and care for another person who managed his life, as he had since the war, with the limitations of common body functions.

Or maybe Senator Dole did the one thing in a quiet place with another person that he simply wanted, and was predisposed, to do. It was a modest gesture, and an easy one. From my experience, most people don't make the effort to connect with another person for no reason in a public place. His gesture was a reflection of the man, and it was more than I had offered him.

I wish I had said "Hello, Senator," or something thoughtful, because his connection mattered to me, whether he was a man of historical significance or not. I doubt it mattered to the senator that I may not have recognized him, though I instantly had.

> The cat sleeping on the fence is famous to the birds
> watching him from the birdhouse.

I would flash through the Beijing airport's security with a virgin passport, unstamped but for my Chinese visa. I would negotiate a taxi late at night and would find a hotel in a huge Chinese complex on the edge of the city, though not the hotel I was trying to find. I would get a room with a bed but without a bathroom I could access. I would construct a

214 ■ CHAPTER 16

toilet out of two hotel chairs, a garbage can, rope, duct tape, and a toilet seat I traveled with. I was exhausted but exhilarated to be in China again.

I could no longer hide myself in China as I had before, when I traveled alone, dressed from government stores in the long green jacket, hat, and blue pants that fit me into the crowds. To move unnoticed among strangers had been my way to travel in China. But I had changed. And China had changed. In preparation for the Olympics, Beijing's airport was now better than London's Heathrow, though most airports are. Beijing's was now as good as any airport in the world, including the one in Portland, Oregon, where I lived. And people now wore colors and Nike shoes (or counterfeit versions). China's Great Leap Forward, though not Mao's version, was finally happening a half century later.

I had been in China three times before. The last time was a quick trip in 1993 when I had traveled as a courier. The job, if you could call it that, because it involved no work whatsoever, was a good deal: a free round-trip airline ticket from LA to Hong Kong. The courier job involved me taking bundles of late air express packages from companies—DHL, FedEx, Flying Tigers, and others—as my baggage. It was a perfect way to get to Hong Kong for free and travel on the $300 they paid me. I took the seven days before my return flight to see the Yangtze River at Wuhan and visit Macau, the tiny old Portugese gambling haven near Hong Kong that would transfer to Chinese control in 1999. I had done such trips to Taiwan, too. My passport reflected that activity, along with stamps and visas from a decade of traveling around Asia and Africa and working in Europe.

The passport had become my timeline of travel, fat with extra sets of pages, and a once-blue cover nearly black from the touch of a thousand hands. I had friends from Laramie with similar worn-out passports, all of which listed our place of birth: Wyoming, USA. I was always curious why US passports listed the state where the holder was born, but I loved mine for that small reference to home.

All was as it had always been on that courier trip, traveling between borders with a busy passport, until I returned to LAX in 1993.

"Where have you been traveling?" the woman who took my passport at Customs and Immigration asked me. It was a question she asked as a matter of procedure, hundreds of times a shift, a question I had been asked coming and going from forty or so countries over the years.

"Hong Kong, Wuhan in China, then Macau."

"How long?"

"Seven days," I said.

She looked up at me. "What do you do?"

"I was a courier. Mail," I said.

"Wuhan and Macau?"

"I went to Wuhan to see the Yangtze River and I went to Macau to see it before nineteen ninety-nine."

"Nineteen ninety-nine?"

"When it becomes part of China," I said.

"Stand aside," she said.

A man came up to us. "Follow me," he said.

A voice behind me said loudly, "Right behind him. And walk straight."

I did, following the man and trailed by another down a long hallway into a concrete-floored room with white walls, a stainless steel bench, and nothing else.

"Strip," one of them told me.

I stripped to my underwear. One of the men took my shoes, removed the insoles, and turned them around in his hands.

"Everything," the other one demanded.

I did, immediately, without question.

I felt relief over humiliation, fascination over self-righteousness. What a blessing to be innocent and free, I thought. I had a day to kill in Los Angeles anyway, and this disruption was a perfect experience to have—once. Thank God, I thought, standing naked before two men in uniform, that I was not in Nepal, carrying something I should not be bringing into the country.

The larger of the two men held my arms out to the sides of my body from behind while the other pressed on my abdomen, then stomach, and both sides of my waist.

"On the bench," one of the men said. "I want you to jump off."

I got on the metal bench, as shiny as the bumper on a new truck, and jumped to the ground.

"Do it again, and then do it again, immediately," the man said.

I did exactly as I was told. Twice.

"Where have you been?" one of the men asked.

I repeated my answers exactly as I had to the woman at the Customs and Immigration counter and then realized she still had my passport, which instantly angered me as a violation greater than being naked and interrogated.

"What do you do?"

I took a deep breath and repeated, "I was working as a mail courier."

"That is your job?" he questioned.

"No, that is what I was doing."

"What is your job?" he asked.

'I don't have a job, exactly, but I write."

"Write what?"

I told him I had written recently about bees, wind, and kayaking for the outdoor magazines Backpacker and Sea Kayaker.

"Where have you been? What do you do?" the man repeated.

I answered without additions, without deviation. I was fascinated.

"Where in China did you travel? Why did you go? What is your job?"

I answered again, as I had before, calmly—no longer angry.

These men were less judgmental than methodical. I didn't judge them either, because they were professional, unfriendly but not unkind. I began to feel sorry for them after the third round of repeated questions, which were delivered to assess any change in my response.

They had been trained well, rewording their questions slightly and then gauging my responses precisely. They wanted to do their job well as much as they wanted to catch a fish. One was young, the other middle aged. I knew that these same men on a border at night along a mountain pass anywhere from Asia to Moscow would pick a bottle of Johnnie Walker Red out of my backpack and let me go. LAX was not one of those places. They got nothing from me but straight answers and found only a coat, book, and binoculars in my backpack.

After about two hours, I was escorted back to the woman at the Customs and Immigration desk. My passport sat in front of her. She handed me a piece of paper that had been photocopied so many times it had creases and marks as if from an archive. It announced: "Are we sorry we stopped you?" Below that: "You fit the profile." A list followed of the drugs and other illegal contraband—animals, plants, and food—the authorities look for and often find, and below that were statistics on the problems such illegally smuggled items create.

"Welcome home," she said and handed me back my passport.

▪ ▪ ▪

I wondered what profile I fit now, with a new passport and traveling to Beijing in a wheelchair. I would be meeting colleagues from around the world who worked in difficult and dangerous places—Pakistan, Afghanistan, Iraq, Somalia, Bosnia, and Indonesia, among some forty countries. We were in Beijing at a "global leadership gathering" for the international nonprofit Mercy Corps, which works in places of conflict, crisis, and economic collapse.

I, on the other hand, had directed a program in Oregon and Washington for two years as the domestic representation of Mercy Corps' international work. In Portland, where Mercy Corps is headquartered and where I worked, the program I managed seemed from the outset to be a nominal, if not nearly irrelevant, experiment in the context of Mercy Corps' work internationally. For me, it was like being in a wheelchair at a dance. I wondered about my role and my relevance in Beijing.

The gathering was the one time every two years when all the country directors and other senior people in the organization meet face to face somewhere in the world. On the flight I had reviewed the lengthy agenda for the week. It listed a series of meetings and outings all designed to reflect on our work and align our efforts for the future of the organization over the next two years and beyond.

I was prepared to be intimidated by men and women who worked in insecure countries. Unlike workers in areas of conflict or disaster, the five-person staff I inherited made a handful of microloans to small businesses, distributed matching savings grants to entrepreneurs who did not qualify for a loan, and offered business training for refugees in Oregon. I had been hired to turn around a fledgling group that the agency might have instead put out of its misery. I had the urge to do more with what was then called Oregon Programs. The first thing I did was change our name to Mercy Corps Northwest to widen our footprint beyond one state. The international Mercy Corps platform for action was mine to shape in the Pacific Northwest. Constraints were low and expectations high. In an organization where ideas were embraced and bureaucracy abhorred, I had to sell our work to government agencies and foundation funders in Oregon and Washington who were much less risk tolerant than anyone I would meet at this gathering in Beijing.

Mercy Corps was a place I had imagined working when I had functioning legs and some sense of the endurance required for such work. Now in a wheelchair, I did work there. Ironically, it was my wheelchair that guided me to Mercy Corps.

The tear is famous, briefly, to the cheek.

The idea you carry close to your bosom
is famous to your bosom.

I had quit my previous job after exactly five years. I left without another job, which is unwise for anyone and possibly idiotic for a quadriplegic. I was not naive about my prospects for work, but it was time for me to change things, even though none of my colleagues, family, or friends agreed with my decision. I wasn't giving up; I was simply fed up and bored with my job.

When I broke my neck, I had been working for two years as a vice president and lender for a start-up bank in Portland. ShoreBank Pacific aspired to lend to businesses that cared about not only their profit but their community and the environment as well. That mission—to be an environmental bank—sounded like an oxymoron in 1997, when we started. But we plowed forward, guided by a loose hand from our parent bank in Chicago, ShoreBank, and a supportive intelligence from our partner in Portland, Ecotrust. Ecotrust's CEO, a visionary named Spencer Beebe with forever tousled hair, called our work an effort to build "a conservation-based economy," which soon after became more widely known as "sustainable development." We focused on the interaction of enterprises, people, and the landscape of forests, farms, and fisheries in the bioregion from Northern California into British Columbia.

The collaboration of the two groups from Chicago and Portland was inspiring. We started by financing projects other banks dismissed. Many of the businesses became mainstream, capturing the market transformation in organic products, car sharing, stormwater treatment, and green building.

We moved fast in a small, dispersed, and marginally managed group, sustaining ourselves on the energy of a start-up and the successes of the businesses we had financed. We had several million dollars in philanthropic equity and deposits raised nationwide, and we were making loans to companies poised to flourish.

After two years of this fun, and with the bank an inch from profitability, I took a vacation and broke my neck. Doctors advised my family that I'd likely never work again and should go on permanent disability. Three months after my accident I started to argue with that assessment, though I struggled to hold a spoon without a strap around my hand and could barely get onto a toilet without the assistance of two nurses at the hospital. It took me seven months to gain the ability to return to work half-time.

By that time, my Social Security disability funds—about $940 a month—had already started arriving. The bank's long-term disability insurance policy would pay a portion of my salary to assist in the transition. It seemed great for all: I could work again, and the bank had my services for free. The CEO, a man who was hired during my absence, told me this was exactly the way it should work.

Working four hours a day exhausted me. I slept twelve hours every night, and needed to. It took three to four hours each day to get out of bed, sit on a toilet, shower, and dress before taking a bus to work. I worked four hours, took the bus home, ate, read or watched sports, and fell asleep. Three days a week, I went to a warm swimming pool to do hydrotherapy with a man named Doug Kinnaird who, more than anyone, helped me to gradually gain mobility, endurance, and strength. Another person, Anita, an instructor at a chiropractic college in Portland and a former girlfriend of my friend from kindergaten in Laramie, Mark Cupps, worked with me every single Thursday afternoon exactly at 2:00 p.m. "You'll kayak and you will walk," she said over and over until I believed her. After a year, I had learned to swim for the first time in my life, dragging my body through the water with my arms and shoulders. I finally got back into my kayak one celebratory summer weekend with friends. My days were long and full and had become, thankfully, a routine. I started working full-time a year after my accident, with the bank paying half my salary and the insurance company the other half.

One day a caseworker for the company that provided the bank's long-term disability insurance came to my house to assess my situation. It was a reckoning that, in retrospect, I should have anticipated. The man presented me with a list of bank job openings in Portland that involved call centers or data entry. He was, on one hand, a pleasant social worker aiming to help me, but he was also an employee tasked to get me off his company's expense list. He had low-level and, frankly, insulting aspirations for me.

I listened patiently before explaining that I knew finance and was a lender, a vice president of a bank.

"But these are jobs you are qualifed for now," he explained, handing me the list.

"I can do any bank lending job now," I explained.

"I am talking about today, not before," he said.

"I have a job now, the same job I had before. I have been working full-time for over a year," I told him. He asked for, and I shared, my bank account statements and pay stubs.

"Your bank pays half and we have been paying half," he stated and then paused. "You do not require disability payments," he said.

"Yes," I agreed.

A month later, I received a bill from the insurance company for the amount it had paid me after I returned to work full-time. I learned that I should not have been working at all if I was on disability support. I owed the insurance company for an overpayment of more than $40,000. I felt stupid. Of course, I thought, the bank now owes the insurance company the money. I realized I should have questioned this earlier, and there was no excuse for me, or the bank, not to have done so.

When I presented this situation to my boss, the CEO, he said: "That's not the way I see it. The money was to get you back on track."

I thought about the circumstances: I had made 87 percent of the bank's loans before my accident. The bank had stalled since, and I felt responsible for that, though I was not there. I had chipped in with ideas and energy to help fix the situation, along with our new lenders and new support staff, but the thrust of loan activity had abated and management was under the gun to build our balance sheet and grow.

This small, visionary bank had, in its five years, gone from boldly capturing new opportunties to scrambling in hope of grasping them. Our mission had become more a slogan than a practice of innovation. But I still adhered to the founding vision of the bank, and especially that of our partner, Ecotrust, to build a conservation-based economy in the bioregion. And I maintained great respect for ShoreBank in Chicago, which remained a legendary innovator in inner cities but was over its head in the economy and emerging market sectors of the Pacific Northwest.

I again made my case to the CEO—a backslapping banker from a family in an oyster-farming town where the bank maintained a commitment—that the bank pay back the insurance company.

He told me that it was my problem. I was offered a commission-based incentive and a half-time salary.

I consulted an attorney. His words: "I would not want to defend the bank in a jury trial." The option to fight was mine to take.

But I didn't want a lawsuit. I only wanted the bank to pay back the insurance company.

My situation was unfair and it was illegal, but I was in a bind. Everyone would be hurt if I sued, especially my friends at Ecotrust, who had no role in the management decisions of ShoreBank Pacific.

My dad wanted to intervene. He was a retired Wyoming banker and felt he could talk sense to people to "square things up." But we weren't in Wyoming, and it was not 1985, and if he had any gravitas beyond the square borders of Wyoming, it was limited to old-fashioned, horse-sense thinking. He wanted to do that man-to-man thing he knew and had done throughout his life in business and banking. He even drafted a letter, a good letter that did not threaten anyone. It appealed to common sense and to common good. It may have worked. But I was impatient and ready to move on.

After a few difficult months spent deliberating a range of imperfect options, I chose not to fight, not to sue, and to keep my mouth shut. My family and close friends disagreed with my choice. But it was not in my character to burn bridges, and I knew that a suit would be damaging to me personally in the short term, consuming my time and energy, and possibly damaging in the long term if my name was associated more with a disability suit than with the good work I was proud to have contributed in building the bank.

I started repaying the insurance company on a three-year plan. I repaid the Social Security disability income I had received, too, after nearly a year of writing letters to try to stop the payments, stating that I was working and not permanently disabled. The checks from the US Treasury had continued to arrive anyway. I paid the debt in one lump sum from a line of credit I obtained on the equity in my home.

"Goddamn it, you are stubborn. I would not do what you are doing," my father said.

He wanted me to reconsider my decision not to take action against the bank, both to satisfy his desire to correct a wrong and to redirect my resolve. Dad stopped short of taking control, and I could feel how tough it was for him.

"I am proud of you," he finally and firmly said.

I wanted his approval, not so much as his son—because my life decisions had long varied from his—but because he had offered two years earlier, and I had taken him up on it, to match half of my payments to Craig Hospital for medical bills that had exceeded my insurance coverage. The expenses had wiped out my investments and retirement accounts.

"It's what we do, son," he had said then. "We pay what's due."

I would live with the decision and move on. I had a decent house. I had a good dog. I cashed out of my diligently accumulated investments. I quit my job.

Two months and four days later, Mercy Corps hired me.

The boot is famous to the earth,
more famous than the dress shoe,
which is famous only to floors.

In the morning at the Beijing Hotel, I washed up using a thermos of hot water meant for tea. I found my Mercy Corps colleagues after an hour of rolling around a series of roads in a complex that included hotels, a mall, a camp for youth with archery ranges and bowling alleys, and conference facilities. Acres of buildings built decades earlier, once on the far edge of the enormous city, had been refurbished somewhat here and there. On a smoggy November morning, the location had the feeling of an aging suburban development with leafless trees and winter-weary planters. The complex could accommodate any convention imaginable, and surely had. Its scale reminded me that I was back in China, where everything is big. A Mercy Corps sign in front of one of the hotels helped me find where I needed to be. Our presence in the hotel was no greater than that of the school group in the adjacent building.

I entered a meeting hall where some 120 colleagues were beginning their second day of meetings. A few who knew me from Portland came up immediately, expressing their concerns.

"I'm late. I'm fine," I offered, instead of explaining that I had landed at night and slept at the wrong hotel somewhere in the complex.

"How was the flight? Your room?" Mignon, my boss, asked. She was clearly worried about me, having hired me, and knowing I was traveling alone from Denver, not Portland, where she and many others had flown from. Mignon is a woman of enviable insight and a provider of explicit guidance. I was always as direct with her as she was with me, but as I eyed the crowd I calmed my response.

"It will work," I answered, not wanting to discuss the inaccessibility of the hotel in a room filled with aid workers—men, women, all ages, all colors—who lived and worked every day in places without the comforts of Beijing, not to mention Portland.

I found a table at the rear of the room and sank deeper into my chair. It is the back or the front of a room for a wheelchair, because the center of any room of tables and chairs is a confining place that is hard to get to, and nearly impossible to get out of once people are seated. Plus, I wanted to observe from the rear of the room and consider my potential contribution. I looked around, wondering who was there. I recognized many people from Portland, all executives, like Mignon, regional leaders, and board members. I wondered most about the others: What made them do this work?

> The bent photograph is famous to the one who carries it
> and not at all famous to the one who is pictured.

I felt the urge to tell people that I had been in China before, mostly alone and for months, and that I had worked in Central Europe and Bosnia, and had moved in dangerous places for months in West Africa.

But I didn't share any of that history. I decided I didn't need a credential to be there but I needed to listen and learn.

At my table were two Americans: Keith, an agriculture and livelihood expert from Illinois who based himself in Italy but was on call to travel everywhere; and Sarah, who worked from Beirut and traveled throughout the Middle East. I was welcomed instantly with curiosity and questions about our work in Portland. It was not a distraction to them that Mercy Corps worked in the United States. Sarah asked whether I had thoughts about her region's interest in accessibility for people in countries after conflict, which had created a disproportionate percentage of disabled people, many of them children. Keith offered to visit our start-up farming program for newly arrived refugees in Portland, most of whom were Somalis who had come via refugee camps in Kenya, and Meskhetian Turks from Kyrgyzstan. He had worked in both regions and had ideas to help us.

Another man, whom everyone referred to by his last name, Holdridge, stood up and spoke to the crowd. He worked outside the Green Zone, the fortified and protected area, in Baghdad. He explained that he left the Mercy Corps office the same time every day of the week and walked a circuit around the neighborhood, talking with the same people, checking in with those who had come to know him and expect his visit. He told us that the walk, which takes most of his day, was his job. The effort, he explained calmly, was a way to ensure the security of the small staff in his office. I was amazed by this man, a Vietnam veteran I later discovered, whose work in Iraq involved primarily a long walk each day. I understood how essential and visionary that daily walk might be for our long-term work in Iraq.

Mercy Corps was preparing for greater efforts in Iraq: meeting the needs of internally displaced people, reconstructing schools, and assisting with the development of health systems. But that work remained on the horizon until circumstances in the country calmed. Holdridge talked of establishing trust and said that the relationships he earned on his daily walks were the basis from which meaningful engagement would occur.

> I want to be famous to shuffling men
> who smile while crossing streets,

sticky children in grocery lines,
famous as the one who smiled back.

I left our meeting during a break to go to Tiananmen Square by myself. A large clock over the square ticked down the days, hours, and minutes to the Olympics set for August 2008: 1,188 days, 9 hours, 24 minutes, and counting. I sat in the middle of the square and spinned to see the cranes erected for new buildings. In the smog, I lost count and started over. I got to at least fifty buildings, but my view of the explosion of new buildings in Beijing was impaired by air pollution.

A few people walked up and asked to be photographed with me. This was something I had experienced in China during the winter of 1985. It surprised me that it was happening again almost twenty years later.

I rolled along the avenue to a place where a single man had stood on June 5, 1989, in front of a line of tanks, stopping their advance against student protestors who had, for seven weeks, taken over the square in a democracy movement. The place is not marked but the image remains for me, as it has for the world outside China, an indelible image of bravery. The man's resolve proved ephemeral in the face of the crackdown by the army against the students' "counter-revolutionary" effort.

I thought of Holdridge, standing firm and staying determined to walk his daily route through Baghdad, in a world of experts providing different advice on whether, rather than how, to help Iraq. His approach would become a source of motivation for my work with Mercy Corps in the Pacific Northwest: get out of the contained environment of thinking about economic development and talk with people; look for a way to guide people when others grow frustrated or give up on them.

New routes would open for us in Oregon, then Washington, to work in women's prisons, then with all people leaving incarceration. I believed from my time in New Jersey that these people should be considered potential assets to their neighborhoods, not liabilities to society. We hired ex-offenders to lead this work, and they became unusually committed and influential professionals. We would build asset development models in real estate to provide access to investment options people with low incomes would otherwise not have.

Like Holdridge, we would work with people where they were, depending on where we could listen, and where people could be heard. Our work would be to build a place to move from, not to give a prescription to follow. I knew it would require patience, mistakes, and restarts to get there.

> I want to be famous in the way a pulley is famous,
> or a buttonhole, not because it did anything spectacular,
> but because it never forgot what it could do.

To do this work, I summoned my experience with how and when to move. And when to stay put. I once moved slowly through a dense fog that had descended on Lincoln Summit outside Laramie while I was cross-country skiing. Seasons were on the edge of each other, with a late spring storm depositing just enough snow for a last-gasp ski.

I could retrace my ski path in the snow back to where I had started but was otherwise blinded by the fog that drifted past in a wind that pushed through it, giving teasing glimpses of a longer view. During one view, I saw a pronghorn antelope only a few yards away. Then I saw several, all aimed to the east, away from the wind, their heads and dark eyes forward, their lean, muscled bodies unmoving.

I stopped to realize that I was impossibly in the center of a herd of pronghorn, a skittish and swift breed that, while more numerous than people in Wyoming, are impossible to get close to. I had skied on a thin line of snow out of the trees and onto an exposed ridge, barren but for the snow I had passed over earlier. The only other sound was the drizzle of water on the edge of the melting snow, rivulets gathering to find creeks that would descend to the Laramie River.

I listened and observed the shades of white fog in front of me. I knew I should stand firm. In another pulse of sunlight through a break in the fog, a greater view opened and the animals leaped together, undulating onward like waves.

It was then time for me to move.